Foundations of Psychological Profiling

Terrorism, Espionage, and Deception

Foundations of Psychological Profiling

Terrorism, Espionage, and Deception

RICHARD BLOOM

CRC Press
Taylor & Francis Group
Boca Raton London New York

CRC Press is an imprint of the
Taylor & Francis Group, an **informa** business

CRC Press
Taylor & Francis Group
6000 Broken Sound Parkway NW, Suite 300
Boca Raton, FL 33487-2742

First issued in paperback 2019

ISBN-13: 978-0-4665-7029-0 (hbk)
ISBN-13: 978-0-367-86777-5 (pbk)

Library of Congress Cataloging-in-Publication Data

Bloom, Richard.
    Foundations of psychological profiling : terrorism, espionage, and deception / Richard Bloom.
      pages cm
      Includes bibliographical references and index.
      ISBN 978-1-4665-7029-0 (hbk. : alk. paper)
      1. Criminal behavior, Prediction of. 2. Terrorism. 3. Espionage. 4. Deception. I. Title.

HV8073.5.B586 2012
364.3--dc23
                                                           2012039602

Visit the Taylor & Francis Web site at
http://www.taylorandfrancis.com

and the CRC Press Web site at
http://www.crcpress.com

Contents

Preface

Profiling remains a hot topic—so hot that it shows up in films such as *My Name Is Khan*, in broadcast and cable television such as *Criminal Minds*, and in various online platforms and mobile devices. Now don't groan or shudder. I thought I'd begin this way only because other authors on profiling do and, thus, it serves to profile them as well as me for profiling them in this way. Also, by even suggesting that profiling is hot and so hot that it's featured in the world of make-believe, I'm also profiling the world in which we live that each of us makes to believe or believes and then makes. (This last sentence is a takeoff on the writing style used by the German philosopher Martin Heidegger, who has been alternately labeled as the most profound and insightful thinker of the 20th century and as an obscurantist charlatan. Can you guess which I hope you apply to me?)

Profiling often comes with the presumption of accessing different worlds whether real or make-believe, but when two worlds collide—as a title of a novel, songs, films, or the task of a profiler confronting what is to be profiled—all bets may be off. But the bets are still on profiling as a cultural product, a commodity, a current *big thing*, or its posture to become the next *big idea* as described by the Austrian author Robert Musil in his unfinished *The Man Without Qualities*. I wonder how one would profile a man without qualities.

I'll add that whether writing fiction or nonfiction or developing dance choreography, painting, sculpting, or creating performance art, creators of culture as cultural product necessarily engage in profiling. Although I will provide a detailed definition of profiling and some of its connotations in Chapter 1, now I'll just share that however it may be defined, it is used to bring order and meaning to what transpires in life with varying degrees of validity and utility. Here are three immediate profiling implications of what I've just written.

First, that popular entertainment and other cultural production involve profiling is a backhanded tribute to the French philosopher Baudrillard (2008), who popularized the concept of *hyperreality*. He described a contemporary world populated by initially empty and then vacuous humans consuming culture so as to be filled with something that takes the place of what is real—because representations of what is real seem fuller and *realer* than the real. Thus, he commented that the Persian Gulf War (Operation Desert Storm) never occurred because most of us experienced it only through mass media representations. Moreover, even military personnel who were deployed in the Mideast experienced the war through their imaginations and cultural production. Their seemingly direct experience was constructed and modulated through present and remembered contacts with the mass media on the war, past wars, and other events associated with ongoing experience. How might one profile a world or what is in it when reality is so elusive? When something that looks realer than real is like a sand castle, better yet like the latest multisensory entertainment experience that seems to first envelop us in some exraordinary and timeless *everything,* then at least in a time-out from our quotidian *something*, but soon enough in an approach to the *nothing* of forgotten reverie as the grains of sand of our worldly lives scatter to the winds.

Second, one way gangsters learn to be gangsters is to try on fashions, behaviors, and storylines from gangster films; similarly, so do profilers. Various psychological processes—*identification, internalization, introjection, social learning, vicarious conditioning, empathy, association*—may be the culprits. All of these terms variously encompass how people take from outside themselves and figuratively put them inside, leading to a psychological change. What was once something *not us* is now *us*. Given that one needs contact with people and things from the outside to place them or parts of them inside oneself until they are part of oneself, parents who are concerned about what their children access and view through online and other media and with whom their children associate may be onto something. As I'll note in Chapter 8, "Profiling Applications: Espionage," the same applies to personnel security authorities entrusted with selecting and managing people with security clearances and special access to sensitive information. By the way, in this book, *espionage* refers only to a betrayal of trust, a generic treason, or an exemplification of some internal threat, not espionage in the service of one's country, organization, or family. But as analogous to the gangsters, profilers learn to be profilers through fiction and nonfiction. What they read or view may focus largely on profiling's past and present, but they actually are profiles of profiling's future.

Third, as intimated already, depictions of profiling from popular culture communicate that the world is controllable, can be influenced, is predictable, and can be understood. This is relevant to a psychological research tradition: *terror management*. Based on the work of American cultural anthropologist Ernest Becker and popularized by three American social psychologists (Pyszczynski, Greenberg, & Solomon, 1999), terror management posits that human behavior is motivated largely by a fear of death and a foreboding sense of one's mortality. Maybe this helps explain why very reputable people become enmeshed in sexual scandal. Yes, they're self-destructing in terms of professional career, but how can this compare with—as American author Ernest Hemingway might explain—entering the ring, going a few rounds with death, keeping it at bay, and even getting in a few shots or having it on the ropes for a while until it launches an ineluctably victorious assault. Much like adhering to diets of seaweed and ginseng, excruciating exercise regimens, or belief systems featuring an immortal soul and eternal life through belief in some sacred or secular entity—even including beliefs in nothing—terrorism, espionage, and deception might be anticipated, deterred, or benignly managed via profiling focusing on a terror management angle. This might be why many law enforcement, security, and intelligence consumers continue to use, support, and fund profiling, even if the associated validity-related data are sparse. And this might also be why horror films are popular in that we can look through our fingers or not, walk out of the theater or not, turn it off our screens or not, and choose to be alive or not unless we read the 20th-century Irish author Samuel Beckett's take on life as waiting for death.

In any case, well over 40 nonfiction books of a professed scientific bent in the English language have been published on profiling since the late 1990s. The quality of these books varies. Some miscommunicate essential features of profiling and estimates of validity and utility. Some include insufficiently explained jargon—for example, jargon in the next-to-last sentence of the third paragraph of this book all bearing on bringing something outside oneself inside. Some focus on only one profiling approach or technique as in some late-at-night infomercial that also promises *but wait there's more!* Some politically pontificate more than scientifically enlighten, especially when racial profiling is at issue. (Of note here is a recent publication by Jody Feder [2012] of the Congressional Research Service emphasizing that, regardless of scientific validity and utility, racial profiling may qualify as unreasonable search and seizure under the Fourth Amendment to the U.S. Constitution and a denial of equal protection under the Fourteenth Amendment. Whether *racial* profiling encompasses any profiling with race as a component and whatever *race* might actually denote are left unclear). And the authors of some of these books seem to assume that people can be easily read, that is, that certain human characteristics or events invariably have the same predictive validity linked to behaviors or situations or some events of interest regardless of deceptive intent of an alleged perpetrator or of fate, chance, and natural law.

For reasons of due diligence bearing on litigation and, perhaps, unfortunate personal cowardice—the Greek philosopher Aristotle might term this *prudence*—I have chosen not to specifically cite which books share the qualities just listed except for the government document of which I correctly assume I funded through taxes and incorrectly assume I have some controlling authority. But nonfiction books on profiling vary not only in quality but also in combinations of authors' implied and inferred motives—scientific explanation, contribution to the common welfare, political agendas, material profit, fame, self-aggrandizement, and the acting out (being in the throes) of unconscious personality conflicts. I plead the Fifth on and also claim no special access to my own motives.

Very important to me, these books almost always are written in a manner that does not threaten those with significant political and social power. Thus, there seems to be an inordinate amount of attention devoted to very infrequent crimes like serial-cannibalistic rape-murder; to murder of the common folk and not the assassination of the uncommon and high and mighty; to street crimes involving murder, drugs, and assault; to prostitution on the streets and alleyways, in massage parlors and local brothels, and on Backpage.com with a few high-class madams and pimps thrown in for equity; and little if any attention to war crimes and gross incompetence by political leaders or gross malfeasance by financial titans and business and social leaders. Why is this important? As the American journalist Steve Coll (2012) points out in his excellent new book on ExxonMobil, there is a huge influence by those in power on the writing and use of science through their own combinations of rewards and punishment and the anticipatory behaviors including self-censorship and choice of topic and conceptual treatment by those claiming the scientific mantle.

Yet from an applied scientific perspective, I do have my favorites among nonfiction profiling books, including Alison and Rainbow (2011), Canter and Youngs (2009), Harcourt (2007), Hicks and Sales (2006), Petherick (2009), and Turvey (2011). I have provided some of the salient features of these in a brief review of the contemporary history of scientific profiling in Chapter 1, "What Is Profiling?" and in the following section "Research Studies" herein.

I even more greatly favor Plutarch's *Lives of the Noble Greeks and Romans* as well as intellectual biographies such as that of Richard Ellmann on James Joyce or Peter Gay on Sigmund Freud, even though they are not usually grouped under profiling. In fact, a tension that will be apparent in my take on profiling is its very modest stature when compared with the richness, depth, coherence, and seeming truth of biography as well as the *see it now* skills of great writers of history such as Herodotus, Thucydides, Livy, Machiavelli, Gibbon, and Toynbee. And yes, a student of crime may sincerely believe that nothing takes the place of great novelistic fiction like Dostoyevsky's *Crime and Punishment,* in which the character's name, Raskolnikov, connotes a soul in schism, or an ancient Greek tragedy like Euripides's *Medea,* the eponymous character placing us within the seething emotions in a manner that William Congreve's Zara in *The Mourning Bride* (1697) can only cognitively outline as "… Heaven has no rage like love to hatred turned, nor hell a fury like a woman scorned …."

But back to *profiling as hot*—this time because of public discourse on searching for terrorists through profiles and massive data mining underlying profiling to identify terrorist threats at airports and throughout the world. These, in turn, are fueled by memories of and public discourse on the 9/11 attacks and the quest to connect terrorist dots (Savage, 2011; Transportation Security Administration, 2012)—even if there may not be ways to link them and may not even be any dots to link.

There are also growing awareness of and controversy on data mining for commercial purposes (Duhigg, 2012) going far beyond what Don Draper and his *Mad Men* on AMC have at their disposal. I think of this every time images of wingtips and brogues pop up during my online searches—all because of one unfortunate purchase made in the throes of nostalgia and narcissism. Whether in terrorism or commercial terrorism, there is plenty of controversy on how to comparatively consider the validity, utility, politics, and ethics of profiling (cf. Bloom, 1999).

For less recent examples of profiling, one might go back to the film *Silence of the Lambs* (Ult & Demme, 1991) on the Federal Bureau of Investigation's (FBI) search for a serial killer. Isn't it ironic that who might be called a psychiatric profiler who's *also* a serial killer helps them? Just a year earlier, the FBI termed 1990 the *Year of the Spy* because of the U.S. citizen arrests for espionage-related betrayals of trust on U.S. soil (Federal Bureau of Investigation, 2012b). For even earlier examples, one might go back to 1921, when John Larson and then William Moulton Marston popularized a technology-based deception detector known in popular and criminological lore as the polygraph (Marston, 1938). As I will share in Chapter 1, the history of profiling under various names and guises goes back centuries. It is perhaps intrinsic to human nature and its history.

However, the main purpose of this book is not to comprehensively enumerate and describe the various theoretical perspectives, techniques, and standards for success or failure of profiling used now or at any time in the past—even as some of this turns out to be necessary. Instead, I intend to identify the five *foundations* of psychological profiling: (1) the definition of profiling and what it is not, along with its history and politics; (2) the validity and utility of profiling and the many challenges to them; (3) the two types of tasks—developing a *narrative* and developing a *matrix* upon which the narrative is based—that are crucial to profiling regardless of specific theoretical perspectives, techniques, and standards; (4) illustrations of the first three elements through a critical examination of profiling attempts bearing on terrorism, espionage, and deception; and (5) speculations on the future of profiling.

I also intend that this book have multiple, if partially overlapping, audiences. I have written for (1) local, state, and federal law enforcement officers; (2) intelligence and security officers, especially within the fields of counterterrorism, counterintelligence, and counterespionage; (3) lawyers confronted by or cooperating with profiling experts and data or more generally working with forensic psychological data; (4) researchers, professors, and their students studying forensic applications of the physical, life, social, and behavioral sciences; and (5) the general public seeking and attempting to develop informed opinions on profiling. Alas, for all audiences, I will not be able to demonstrate how a case can be wrapped up neatly, flawlessly, and quickly, like those films and shows interspersed with commercial messages and product placements of higher volume and contrast.

As well, I intend not only to use scientific theory and data but also to integrate interdisciplinary knowledge and practices rarely used in books on profiling. For example, *historiography* covers the principles of constructing history, what constitutes history, comparative analysis of source credibility, how to pick and choose from among infinite events to explain yet other events, and how one can or can't keep oneself and one's times (e.g., historical era, social and personal concerns, contemporary public discourse) out of what one is constructing (cf. Butterfield, 1981). This is relevant to what I refer to as profiling's history problems: for example, how the past affects the present and may affect the future, how the present affects our views of the past, and how views of the future affect the present. For any event of interest of the past, present, or future, such as terrorism, espionage, or deception, what events of the past, present, or future are meaningfully associated them? Recurring historical themes of this book include the following: (1) the good or bad may lead to the good or bad; (2) persons or things—*things* here denoting other animate as well as inanimate entities as well as abstract human constructions such as *society* or *human nature*—may lead to persons or things; and (3) profiling confronts infinite choice in levels of analysis from an individual's neurophysiological to some assumed universal life force. As another preview of the book's contents, profiling is constructing not only *his*tory and *her*story but also *story*.

Another example of interdisciplinary knowledge is *hermeneutics* defined as the study of interpretative strategies and tactics essential to constructing both linguistic and nonlinguistic meaning from text (Ricoeur, 1981). In profiling, various events are assumed to have meaning, but *what* meaning for a specific *who, what, where, when, why,* and *how* is the challenge. Concrete examples of the challenge include the text of a voice intercept—*tomorrow we begin*—or of a door flapping open and shut at night at a home at the end of a suburban cul-de-sac. The most important type of meaning in profiling is the one that suggests relationships among events and then between these events and some event of interest—terrorism, espionage, and deception for our purposes in this book.

Epistemology covers the nature of knowledge, criteria for knowing knowledge, and associated techniques for discovering or constructing knowledge—in essence, how one knows what one knows and that one knows (Goldman, 1999). In profiling, one assumes or attempts to assume some degree of knowledge in arriving at five desired endpoints: (1) predicting, (2) post-dicting (what occurred), (3) peri-dicting (what may be occurring now), (4) understanding, and (5) influencing events of interest and associated events. This knowledge is based largely on inferences about the association between and among events and these with the event of interest.

Narratology is the study of stories—their main structural features, their effect on how we perceive ourselves and others, their consequences for how we and others behave, even their impact on how we perceive the world through abstract concepts such as human nature and physical forces that may, in turn, affect yet other perceptions and behaviors. Profilers knowingly or otherwise create stories forming the context within which events occur, in essence weaving together events in a sea of yet other events. Sometimes these events are themselves stories or a story. From assumed mental phenomena (*she loves me*) to specific behaviors (someone or something knocking on the door or, for those with paranoid tendencies, someone playing a tape of knocking sounds as part of a counterdeception operation designed to render one paranoid) to historical epochs (a Victorian era in which no one had sex but people were still being born), events and their associations fall into place as stories. In fact, people can easily create stories by making *dramatis personae* out of a handful of nonsense syllables—both a threat and an opportunity for profilers whose collection of facts looks like nonsense. Profilers need to know the characteristics of stories, especially of a special kind—the plot—that will be described in Chapter 5, "The Profiling Narrative," because profilers are storytellers.

This book consists of a preface and 10 chapters written to support 30 learning outcomes (LOs). The LOs require that either something be constructed (e.g., a profiling narrative or matrix) or something be described, exemplified, and critiqued (e.g., *signal detection theory* applied to profiling; see "Statistical Issues"). Just a word about the latter requirement. One *describes* by providing the essence of *what* something is, *exemplifies* by providing an example of the *what*, *critiques* by proving strengths and weaknesses of the *what* as applied to profiling. I suggest a neologism for this requirement—to *dec* something.

You are reading the preface right now, and it relates to the first two LOs. P.1 is to *dec* at least three cultural phenomena affecting public interest in profiling. P.2 is to *dec* at least three areas of interdisciplinary knowledge relevant to profiling. I also hope readers are beginning to profile me by now and have engaged in an ongoing dialogue with the text and indirectly with me, for good or ill. I'd like to think we're on a journey together, and I hope to hear from you about the book and about profiling in some way, perhaps through texting or email. Like most people these days, I'm not that difficult to find.

Chapter 1, "What Is Profiling?" contains material on the definitions, histories, and the politics of profiling. Three LOs (1.1–1.3) *dec* at least three instances of each of these three aspects of profiling, respectively. I hope that readers will also begin to appreciate that definitions and histories may significantly affect expectations about what profiling is, should, and might be; the quest for information in the profiling process; likely consequences of profiling; and the validity and utility of desired profiling endpoints—again, predicting, post-dicting, peri-dicting, understanding, and influencing various events of interest.

Chapter 2, "Challenges of Profiling: Validity and Its Estimates," describes how valid and useful profiling seems to be when confronted with various challenges. These challenges apply not only to the five desired endpoints of profiling identified in Chapter 1 but also to contextual events within which profilers function. One such challenge comprises the common scientific methods employed by researchers of profiling, because there is controversy about whether these methods are more suitable for the physical and life sciences or for the behavioral, psychological, and social ones. Another challenge comprises social deviancy theories processes—that is, what events are deemed deviant and how this deeming occurs, explanations for the occurrence of deviancy, and how deviant events are valued. These processes affect what kinds of people and situations profilers end up working on or are asked to work on as well as how they construe these people and situations. A third challenge comprises four basic perspectives that profilers and researchers on profiling make in deriving meaning from information. These perspectives are best illustrated by examples from the fields of literary criticism and hermeneutics as already mentioned. So, there are three learning outcomes in Chapter 2 (2.1–2.3) to *dec* at least three instances of each of these three challenges.

Chapter 3, "Challenges of Profiling: What Is Being Profiled?" may strike readers as controversial. The basic assumption is that what profilers may view as reality are actually languages and schematics assumed to correspond to or represent what is real. By *schematics*, I mean theories depicted by diagrams on how some *whats* assumed to be real act on and relate to yet other such *whats*. Schematics allow profilers to best ask and answer the right questions when attempting to predict what might happen, identify what is or has already happened, and understand and influence any of the previously mentioned and related events. Readers might want to reread *what* I've just written several times and wonder if it has anything to do with reality. An implication of the basic assumption is that profilers are operating on conceptual quicksand or, better yet, attempting to arrive at any of the five desired endpoints by creating something that may sink without a trace. And even more controversially, some of the languages and process diagrams may be used by profilers unconsciously—even as profilers use them in thinking about their work and how they communicate this work to others. The five most significant languages are those based on psychodynamics, conditioning theories, traits, biological phenomena, and existential and humanistic concerns. Many of the significant process diagrams arise from classics in theoretical psychology. All represent implicit and explicit decisions about the relative roles of internal and external events stemming from people, the situations in which people function, and interactions between people and situations. Readers should note that *situations* denote some context in which people find themselves—anything from some emotional moment to a seedy or magnificent venue to some long-term historical trends spanning generations.

A significant challenge to the languages and process diagrams used by profilers is how long and how strong specific events may be associated with other events and with some event of interest and with what meaning—that is, the same event may affect some same *other* event in different ways at different times, including no way at all. This is often of special concern, as the following two examples will show. First, individuals being profiled may or may not believe that they are being profiled in specific situations, and they may or may not be right, so this may or may not change their behavior. Second, personal or cultural trends alternate on contributing to significant differences in the frequency and contingency of events believed to lead to some event of interest, as when terrorist chic turns a sign of some incipient terrorist operation into cultural sophistication and hipness. The American author Tom Wolfe described a swank New York City cocktail party held in 1970 by swells including the American maestro Leonard Bernstein with Black Panthers as guests of honor that suggests what I mean here, regardless of whether the Panthers or representatives of the U.S. government might be considered terrorists.

Another significant challenge to profilers is the evolving impact of the cyberworld—especially the ease of global communication and the growing sophistication of the virtual world—on human psychology. The questions are how, how much, and *if* well-validated associations of events to events of interest remain valid and what sorts of associations may be taking their place. The very truths deemed most true by profilers may be so, but for a world fast disappearing or already disappeared.

I apologize for waxing on about this chapter, but the contents have been of primary interest to me for many years. I'll leave readers with the chapter's three learning outcomes (3.1–3.3) to *dec* five significant languages of profiling, five profiling schematics, and four possible psychological changes courtesy of the cyberworld with relevance to profiling.

Chapter 4, "Challenges of Profiling: Who Is Doing the Profiling?" describes various psychological events within or exhibited by profilers impacting the five desired endpoints of profiling. One class of events comprises the use of basic *epistemological* tools used by profilers in attempting to know anything and to arrive at what they think is knowledge. A second comprises the use of concepts popularized by *formal argumentation* theories—the same ones long used by practitioners of influence from rhetoricians to lawyers to pitchers of commercial messages. A third class of events comprises examples of *logic* and *logical fallacies*—the upside and downside of what is often termed reason and popularized in the Western intellectual tradition by the Greek philosopher Aristotle. A fourth class has been termed *heuristics under uncertainty* (Kahneman, 2011), denoting explicit and implicit approaches to making important decisions with incomplete, ambiguous information, often with constraints of how much time is available. I'll provide an opinion on whether these heuristics help or hurt profiling accuracy and whether one's knowledge of these heuristics can increase or decrease their downside. A fifth class comprises quantitative thinking and the assumptions accompanying *statistical procedures and models* common in contemporary profiling. A basic point will be that profilers may not be sufficiently aware that the choice of any statistical approach necessarily makes specific conclusions about what humans are up to more or less likely—fitting a structure on reality as opposed to helping to identify reality's structure. (Of course, this will not be of any unusual concern to epistemological skeptics and nihilists who may believe there is no reality, there are multiple realities, or reality is just inaccessible or doesn't matter.) A sixth class comprises *deception analysis* and the ways profilers try to identify deception leading to or within some event of interest and the after-the-fact deception of perpetrators. A seventh class comprises *close reading through interdisciplinary sources*. The idea is some intensive immersion in information may lead to profilers coming up with they seek. As an example, of which I'm ambivalent, many years ago I asked *the* formal profiling expert of an intelligence organization how he came to conclusions about a person after going through the case files and other related information. His answer? "Read, read, read." My issue is what do we do when different people read, read, read but come up with different conclusions? Finally, profilers live and work in a political world, and *politics* affect how they think and feel and their work. Eight learning outcomes in Chapter 4 (4.1–4.8) *dec* four instances of each of the italicized psychological events just presented applied to profilers.

Chapter 5, "The Profiling Matrix," contains theories, constructs, and illustrations of one of the two tasks crucial to profiling regardless of the many profiling approaches and techniques used. This task is to create a representation of how events relate to each other and to events of interest. I recommend varieties of quantitative matrices for representation. For a specific profiling case, one matrix will seem most valid and useful based on the information collected and interpreted but will be thrown over for another matrix based on new information and new interpretations of information. There are two learning outcomes in this chapter. LO 5.1 is to *dec* the three constructs of the profiling matrix. LO 5.2 is to choose an event of interest—some example of terrorism, espionage, or deception—and construct a matrix.

Chapter 6, "The Profiling Narrative," contains theories, constructs, and illustrations of the second task crucial to profiling regardless of the profiling approaches and techniques used. This task is to create a narrative based on the matrix. A narrative has elements not of a story but of a plot (to be differentiated in the chapter), and it can be characterized by various constructs from narratology, historiography, and philosophy. The narrative changes as the matrix changes, and all elements of the narrative must be traced to aspects of the matrix. There will be two learning outcomes in this chapter. Readers will be required not only to *dec* five constructs of a profiling narrative (LO 6.1) but also to construct a narrative based on the matrix they have constructed in Chapter 5 (LO 6.2).

Chapters 7–9, "Profiling Applications," address terrorism, espionage, and deception, respectively. They illustrate how the materials in Chapters 1 through 6 can facilitate profile development, validity, and utility. This is done by focusing on what various experts have contributed to our understanding of these three areas. There are two learning outcomes each for all three chapters: to *dec* at least four definitional challenges of terrorism (7.1), espionage (8.1), and deception (9.1) based on close reading of interdisciplinary sources; and to *dec* at least four constructs that experts have used in profiles and that might constitute part of a matrix and a narrative on terrorism (7.2), espionage (8.2), and deception (9.2). I hope that through attempting to achieve the LOs of Chapters 7 through 9 (and secondarily of Chapters 5 and 6) readers also will better understand how difficult it is to aggregate different types of events as they relate to each other and then to some event of interest.

This is a very important point, because it so happens that there is a still festering controversy going back at least to the work of the late American psychologist Paul Meehl in 1954. The controversy is about whether socially sanctioned and self-styled *experts* can predict, post-dict, peri-dict, understand, and influence an individual person or situation with adequate validity and utility based on professional experience, judgment, intuition, gut feeling, and overall expertise when compared with just referring to very simple statistical models based on a very few variables. The controversy is several-fold. Although an overwhelming amount of research supports the proposition that experts come up very short compared with the statistical models, most experts deny this (cf. Dawes, 1994). So why not just use the statistical models? There are two problems. Experts seem to persist in adding their own wisdom to the models, thereby lowering overall validity and utility. Also, most often, the statistical models have not been developed even as they cry out to be developed. And they are not developed because they (1) threaten claims of privileged wisdom of many experts, (2) await increasingly hard-to-get funding, and (3) are often difficult to develop (to collect enough information across enough cases) for low-frequency and high-impact events of interest such as terrorism, espionage, and high-stakes deception. Moreover, even if enough information could be collected across enough cases, the majority of people who draw the attention of profilers will not likely engage, have engaged, or are engaging in the event of interest. Readers might then wonder, why not stop writing a book on profiling because there's not enough valid and useful information to write such a book. My response, and the response of researchers like Meehl (1954) and Dawes (1994), is that experts and experts-to-be should be collecting information, identifying potentially important events bearing on events of interest, and then developing and testing statistical models. So the present book, while reviewing pertinent scientific and multidisciplinary sources as the foundations of profiling, might be considered an attempt to provoke present and future researchers to strengthen those foundations and consumers of profiling to be more sophisticated about what they're being sold.

Chapter 10, "The Future of Profiling," contains my speculations on how projected developments in scientific method, statistical procedures, integration of close reading of interdisciplinary sources, politics, and the cyberworld may impact on the next several acts of profiling's history. LO 10.1 is to *dec* at least four such speculations in the context of what a book on profiling foundations might look like a generation or two from now. And both through this chapter and the book as a whole, readers will be able to develop critical thinking capabilities to evaluate such speculations.

Well, how might readers most likely achieve the 30 LOs in this book? They'll notice that throughout the text I have described and analyzed cultural products— viz., film, paintings, novels, poetry, and music—in a manner so that readers might better appreciate aspects of profiling. So here's what I have decided: For each LO I have chosen a fragment of film from one of the top 100 films of all time as promulgated by the American Film Institute. Readers are challenged to engage in their *dec*ing and other LO requirements in the context of each respective film fragment—that is, applying the book's contents to the people and situations on the big screen. This will help bring the abstract to an applied concrete level through confronting the real, maybe what Baudrillard termed the *hyperreal*. The URLs of all film fragments related to the LOs were available through YouTube at the time I wrote this book and are cited in the book's References section. (I strongly recommend that readers find the time to watch each film in its entirety through renting or purchasing a DVD or other legal means. I believe that the film medium uniquely captures human psychology through its finished product; the variety of people, including directors, producers, actors, and diverse technical experts involved in that product's creation; and even all of us who choose various means both legal and illegal to access the product. Film is a multipurpose and multimodal profiling product of human psychology.)

And I hope readers already notice that I'm writing to them, that they're very much in mind as opposed to some Muse or omnipotent Platonic ideal. I already have and will continue to intersperse tangential comments and asides within the text, just as if I was standing outside the text with readers and talking to them about it before together we plunge back in. In fact, here comes an aside right now! I had worried about whether the eventual publisher of this book would tolerate (allow) this method; how dogmatic I might become in insisting the asides be left in; whether readers would become distracted, look forward to the next aside, or view the asides as frivolous drivel; and whether I should try a safer and more traditional route. Well, I hope you get the picture. I believe that the knowledge quest is an ongoing discussion, and I want to do my part. Hopefully, readers will do theirs and engage.

I owe a great deal to many of my prior professors, professional colleagues, fellow students, and my own students for lessons both intended and unintended. I have greatly appreciated the technical support of Dr. Jana Whittington in developing diagrams, graphs, and tables. I also thank my wife, Nancy Cay, for making a life with me. Her profiling decisions leading to *this* decision continue to be a hot topic of discussion between us and less often among friends, family, and others from those practicing hagiography to those emulating gossiping harpies. So *dec* that.

Finally, let's return to this preface's two LOs. P.1 should be worked on through watching a charming fragment from the film *Silence of the Lambs* (Ult & Demme, 1991). The cagey, killer psychiatrist cages two of the security team within his own cage. What about the mixture of classical music, blood, cannibalism, politeness, dinnertime, routine, and ritual bears on at least three cultural phenomena affecting public interest in profiling—what are they, where are they in the film fragment, and how does one critique them in the film's context?

P.2 should be worked on through watching the ending of the film *The Apartment* (Wilder, 1960). Can the viewer of this film fragment identify at least three interdisciplinary areas of knowledge? Once they are identified, how can they be used to help understand who the people are and the meaning of what they're doing? How useful are these areas of knowledge to such understanding? In answering these questions, it may be helpful to consider that the fragment *is* the film's ending, that many events have occurred by then, and that somehow the ending has to *make sense* of what has so far happened. This pressure to make sense poses a quite difficult challenge for people who have thought they were making sense until receiving undesired or unexpected feedback after taking an exam, making a business pitch, or requesting a date. What to make of a woman (Shirley MacLaine playing an elevator operator, Fran Kubelik) dealing a deck of cards to play a game while taking off her coat in a man's apartment (Jack Lemmon playing a low-level business executive, C. C. Baxter) in 1960? How about if it's New Year's Eve, and she has just left a public party at a restaurant jammed with an inebriated, boisterous crowd and a Lothario with bad intentions (Fred MacMurray playing the boss, Jeff Sheldrake)?

About the Author

Richard Bloom, PhD, ABPP, is a fellow of the Society of Personality Assessment and a diplomate of the American Board of Professional Psychology in clinical psychology. He is past president of the Military Psychology Division of the American Psychological Association. He previously coedited *Evolutionary Psychology and Violence: A Primer for Policymakers and Public Policy Advocates* and has written book chapters and articles on applications of psychology to security and intelligence issues. Dr. Bloom is a contributing editor for the American Psychological Association's journal *PsycCRITIQUES*, reviewing books and films for their forensic and philosophical implications. He also founded the online *International Bulletin of Political Psychology*. He is chief academic officer at the Prescott Arizona Campus of Embry-Riddle Aeronautical University and teaches courses in deception detection, psychological profiling, counterintelligence, and philosophical psychology. Dr. Bloom is currently working on critiques of post-modernism and post-structuralism in the contexts of hermeneutics, historiography, psychological assessment, and biographical and autobiographical narrative.

1 What Is Profiling?

Can one know that someone else is *gay* just by looking at them? Do we all have different degrees of *gaydar*—the ability or skill to make this connection, to identify events leading to an event of interest like sexual orientation? What would the best definition of something called gaydar be? Is posing such questions only a marker for homophobia, just as gaydar may, for an astute observer, be a marker of certain access to knowledge? Tabak and Zayas (2012), who used this term, found that there may actually be a gaydar, that it may yield on average a 60% success rate (later the chapter provides different takes on what *success rate* may mean), that it can be based on very short visual exposures (less than a second) to faces of people, and that the spatial relationships between and among facial features may be significant in such determinations. After reading Chapter 1, readers might consider if gaydar is an example of profiling.

1.1 DEFINITIONS OF PROFILING

Profiling involves attempts to *predict* events of interest and what other events may be associated with the event of interest becoming more or less likely; to identify those events of interest that already have occurred and other events that were associated with their arising, that is, to *post-dict*; or to identify events of interest that may be occurring now and what other events may be associated with their ongoing presence, that is, to *peri-dict*. Profiling also involves understanding and influencing events of interest and associated events. So there are five profiling events in attempts to profile events and events of interest. Depending on the situation, even a profiling event may be an event or event of interest to profile—as in establishing that the post-diction of a profiler may be profiled as an event exemplifying an instance of a betrayal of trust by that profiler. (The profiler has been *turned* by enemies of the state.)

Before we go any further, I want to share the complexity of the term *event*. It's something that happens, but not just something for the moment. It may seem to have always been there and may seem always to be there. Or it might be there or have been there for only nanoseconds. It might be the color of one's skin, a religious belief, the existence of God, how one's parents drank themselves into oblivion, the color purple, a brief interlude of lust, the shape of the isle of Elba. I often use this term to underline the assumptions about *time* that characterize how people including profilers view the world. An *event* may be termed an *event of interest* when it is the main event—that about which profilers seek to know by knowing other events. Yet again, profilers attempt to know—itself an event—through the five events of prediction, post-diction, peri-diction, understanding, and influencing.

An example of prediction is to anticipate the who, what, where, when, why, and how of the next terrorist event of interest; post-diction is to consider the same six questions after the event occurs; and peri-diction is to try to answer the same questions as the event occurs. There appears to be the least amount of empirical profiling research on peri-diction and much more about prediction and post-diction—not just for terrorism but for most events of interest. I assume most readers have surer footing on *understanding* and *influencing*, even as epistemologists and philosophers of science may be less sure about what it means to have surer footing on them or anything else.

This classification approach with the five events constituting profiling—like classification approaches throughout history—is not intended to cover absolutely all possibilities. One might seek to add *explaining* as something beyond or different from understanding or to create an exciting academic career by positing that profiling is timeless in the sense that it is independent of time. If this latter were the case, then looking at the before, after, or during an event would be senseless. However, the five-event approach does present a structure to help readers see common possibilities based on how profilers and the general public discuss profiling. What ends up becoming an *event of interest* as opposed to merely an *event* and worthy of profiling is covered in detail in a discussion on social deviancy in Chapter 2.

Profiling's attempts to predict, post-dict, and peri-dict events of interest (and understanding and influencing them) are based on developing linkages between and among yet other events and between and among them and the event worthy of profiling. There are two main kinds of linkages. One assumes some degree of association between at least two events so that the existence, frequency, or intensity of one has some bearing on the existence, frequency, or intensity of the other. An example might be that severe family abuse is associated with a higher probability of homicidal intent in victims of this abuse when they become adults than in a random sample of adults. Another example might be that parental annual salaries over $1 million is associated with a lower probability that children in such families end up matriculating to an inferior community college than children in families with annual parental salaries under $20,000 (at least until certain universities with huge endowments began implementing variations of needs-blind admissions replete with grants and very low-interest loans).

The other kind of linkage assumes not just a degree of association but also actual causality. An example might be that Kim Philby charmed James Jesus Angleton over alcohol-fueled lunches into making decisions contrary to the best security interests of the United States. Another might be that a federal prosecutor was afraid to secure the indictment of the chief executive officer of a large bank for fraudulent manipulation of collateral debt obligations, because the latter was blackmailing the former over some tired indiscretion that could be sensationalized by the paparazzi.

There's also a reciprocal circularity among the five events of profiling. Influencing an event or event of interest may substantiate conclusions reached by prediction, peri-diction, and the rest. The influence may involve deterring or minimizing the probability of undesired events of interest, maximizing the probability of desired events of interest, or maintaining the frequency and intensity of desired and undesired events of interest. Understanding an event may be substantiated by influencing the event in a manner consonant with the latter's understanding. In its most generic sense, then, profiling takes one way beyond crime and the popular term *criminal profiling* to all events in all walks of life. Profiling is how we live.

Anyone or anything may be profiled. Anyone may profile. Again, the essence of profiling is that one attempts to predict, post-dict, peri-dict, understand, and influence some event of interest based on linkages between and among yet other events—and these to the event of interest. For people, some of the events associated with an event worthy of profiling may be psychological, internal to the person, not directly observable, and inferred. Examples of such events include thoughts, images, emotions, intentions, desires, and motives. Other internal events may be physical or biological in nature such as neuroanatomical structural dynamics, neurotransmitters, hormones, and various neurophysiological processes.

Yet other events are external to the person, observable, and behavioral in nature. Of course, one still makes inferences about these, and examples of such external events include the wearing of certain clothes, crashing an automobile, shorting a stock, or choosing to participate in a political organization. Inferences about these external examples may vary toward the infinite; thus, there often are disagreements between and among profilers and the general public about the meaning of the things people do.

Both events internal and external to the person may be carried out not only by an individual who has generated an event of interest—the former being a mark for the latter whether it occurs before, during, or after the latter—but also by other people whose events may affect this individual, the event of interest, and yet other events that may be associated with or may cause the event of interest. And other events of the individual and of other people may become events of interest and the latter just events through time. So profiling can get complicated really quickly.

In fact, internal and external events of an individual and other people who may somehow influence the individual are nearly inseparable. One may infer internal events when one attempts to construct a meaning for an external event. For example, the event of premeditated murder may include not only dropping poison into a glass of wine but also the emotion of rage and the image of a soon-to-be-dead *bon vivant*. And an accumulation of external events may be essential to positing something about a person's desires, as when mounting gambling debts may fuel the urge to do anything to repay them.

Situations also may be profiled. One may attempt to predict, post-dict, peri-dict, understand, and influence observable and physical events like the weather, an unlocked file cabinet, missing money, seismic activity, or the spatial relationships of facial and body components of what the East German intelligence director Markus Wolf termed *swallows* and *ravens* who would be sent to obtain and influence classified and other sensitive information from the psychologically vulnerable. American social psychologists like Stanley Milgram (1963) and Philip Zimbardo (Zimbardo et al., 1974) achieved extraordinary professional reputations—not always positive—for demonstrating the power of situational events to be associated with or cause events of interest linked to atrocities and the human dark side. American clinical psychologist Martin Seligman (Seligman et al., 2005) and Zimbardo (Drury et al., 2012) also have been doing this for more positive behaviors and inferred internal events of interest bearing on compassion, happiness, and heroism.

Situations are not just extraneous events that impact people. People may choose them knowingly or unknowingly. A great example of this is a recent book by Alice

Kaplan (2012), professor of French literature at Yale University, titled *Dreaming in French: The Paris Years of Jacqueline Bouvier Kennedy, Susan Sontag, and Angela Davis*. The Paris experience meant things quite different to a high-society future First Lady; to a nobody out of Tucson, Arizona, who takes the New York public intellectual world by storm; and to a black woman stigmatized in the South who grows up to experience revolutionary politics, political violence, and a tenured professorship. Dreams of Paris and a Paris experience might constitute events helping to shape the significant events in their lives, but they chose Paris as well.

For people and situations, events of interest—whether largely associated with or caused by internal or external events—also may serve as being associated with or causing yet other events of interest. For example, predicting the next earthquake may be an end in itself or merely a way station toward the desired outcome of understanding a volcanic eruption that already occurred. Living in a consumerist world— wherein the contemporary viewing of sexual and violent events per unit time via mass media technologies far surpasses the rate of viewing such events by any means in all of previous human history—may be associated with other events to help predict a specific rape by a specific individual (an event of interest) and other future rapes. Living in a capitalist, consumerist world may be the event of interest associated with an inevitable progression of history. It also may be associated with another event of interest like a take-no-prisoners profit motive operating at the sociocultural level elaborated upon by the German political philosopher and sociologist Karl Marx (1932). With only a hint of facetiousness, merging the last two examples together might yield linkages of *events of interest* becoming *events* leading to an accidental, autoerotic asphyxiation by a capitalist who saved, not sold, the rope with which to hang oneself. This takeoff of a quote by Vladimir Lenin—"The capitalists will sell us the rope with which we will hang them"—may illustrate a communist profiling fallacy.

What follows are more concrete examples of the interactions of people and situations, events, and events of interest. Explosive residue on a kitchen table, the number and depth of wounds on a corpse, the violent content on popular entertainment of the last week, a butterfly fluttering over a field of whatever it usually flutters over, an overheard conversation, a bag being placed over someone's head (Zimbardo did this in his research), and the level of radioactivity near the Hanford Reservation are but grains of sand in a desert or drops of water in an ocean within which profilers operate. This might be a point of departure for perspectives from classical philosophy and contemporary physics on seeking knowledge in an ever-changing world, on whether anything can slow down enough to be known, or on whether knowledge can but whistle in the dark with error-ridden probabilistic statements. I will pick this line of thought up in Chapters 2 and 4.

Now for some pabulum, in that pabulum is a processed cereal for infants and what immediately follows may be suitable for novices to profiling but not veterans. The latter may in all likelihood respond—sure, profilers have to do what you're describing, but how do you do it well? I'm not sure there's a great answer to the veterans, but the materials in Chapter 4 largely constitute my response.

To arrive at predicting, post-dicting, peri-dicting, understanding, and influencing events and events of interest constituting profiling, one must collect information, analyze it, produce it in a usable form, transmit it in a secure and responsive fashion, and then act on it. Something like this is often cited as the essence of the intelligence process by intelligence analysts.

One may collect information by interviewing people; by observing people and situations; by collecting physical substances within, on, or carried by people and from situations; and by consulting various sources of information—for example, research databases, archival data like school records or real estate documents, or tweets. Collection may be carried out by people and by technology with the caveat of collecting in a world of deception (see Chapter 4).

Then, this information is analyzed so that events seem to be associated together and with events of interest—from a sudden drop in a stock market to a seeming truth becoming a whopper of a lie. Chapter 4 describes some of the processes involved in analysis: so many processes, so little certainty, especially as most events of interest commonly worked on by profilers are statistically deviant so that the best analysis is that any individual will not engage, has not engaged, and is not engaging in some event of interest. But do we pay profilers for such this sort of accurate conclusion? Once the links are developed, the results are produced in a form that can be easily communicated to potential users. Chapters 5 and 6 describe in great detail the generic processes involved.

After production, information must be transmitted timely enough for appropriate use and secure enough so that bad actors and their enablers and supporters won't be forewarned. The latter seems difficult in a media world of competing talking heads shouting out their profiling conclusions far and wide through various communication media.

Then comes use of the profile. Important decisions may be made about the event of interest, who allegedly created it, or how to increase, decrease, or maintain the event of interest's frequency or intensity in the future. Scholarship and research described in the massive tome edited by the American psychologist David Faust (2012) suggest that the valid use of profiling may be tenuous at best—as I earlier intimated in referring to the work of Meehl (1954) and Dawes (1994). There are just so many impediments to valid and useful linkages between and among events and from these to some event of interest—leading to the findings on contemporary empirical research and logical analysis related to profiling described in Chapter 3. Just a few of the most significant impediments Faust and his associates found include inappropriate generalization from samples of subjects to a specific case, assumption of associations and causes as true even as the consensus among researchers and practitioners is questionable, and inadequate integration of the values of personal and situational variables for specific cases—even as these values may be unknown for both reference samples and for the specific case at hand.

Now, I'm not the first person to have offered a definition of profiling, but I believe that various other definitions of profiling from other textbooks or documents usually embrace at least some but usually not all of what I've described. For example, Hicks and Sales (2006) and Holmes and Holmes (2009) give most of their attention to events and events of interest stemming from an individual perpetrator, not situational data. Canter and Youngs (2009) provide a helpful table (pp. 38–39) listing some examples of profiling situations, such as crime scene assessment and geographic profiling (cf. Rossmo, 2000). The Federal Bureau of Investigation's (2012) Behavioral Sciences

Unit seems to have engaged in profiling as exemplified by mostly identifying behavioral sequences once the implementation of what will be a crime is ongoing, modus operandi of specific perpetrators and kinds of perpetrators, and demographic and psychological information on specific perpetrators and kinds of perpetrators. In this book, however, I'm advocating profiling to be about events from persons, situations, and their interactions—with the five components of predicting, post-dicting, peri-dicting, understanding, and influencing—bearing on not just crime but on anything that occurs in our world. And I'm advocating this in a way that is not necessarily bound just to something called the *mind* (or personality), as in a criminal mind, a mind of evil, or a one-track mind. In this, I believe I'm closer to Canter and Youngs (2009) and Turvey (2011), but I cast a net wider than just crime and believe I'm more inclusive of various social, cultural, political, economic, and macro-historical variables as well (see Chapters 3 and 5). To readers, this last paragraph, if not the entire book, shows my healthy respect for an anxiety of influence, wherein an author struggles to break free of those who come before (Bloom, 1973). Anyone cited in this book for agreement or disagreement is deserving of respect.

Finally, all definitions are plagued with the challenges of what Cronbach and Meehl (1955) called *nomological nets*. Whether with people or situations, profilers take leaps from observable data to concepts often enough having unknown relationships to observable data. Examples include ascribing an event of interest like espionage to believed-in anarchistic ideology or a need for money, terrorism to feelings of inferiority or beliefs in violence as purging and cleansing for all involved, deception against nonbelievers as living according to God's Word. The further one moves from observable data and the more events within a profile are not direct observations, the more one might be ensnared and enmeshed in smoke and mirrors with unknowable consequences. Interestingly, *nomological* is partially derived from the classical Greek *nomos* denoting a law, a truth, a word, as in the right word. Profilers are on the trail of the *nomos*.

As an example of how some of the previously mentioned abstractions might be in play, I refer the reader to a few minutes of the original film *Double Indemnity* (DeSilva & Wilder, 1944). (It's not so much that I'm a Billy Wilder fan than that he's cited for excellence in books on film and film history). An insurance salesman, Walter Neff (played by Fred MacMurray), first meets the wife of a sales prospect, Phyllis Dietrichson (played by Barbara Stanwyck). In viewing the meeting, one might conclude that Walter has substituted one event to be profiled (how to sell insurance to the husband of Phyllis) for another (how to have a tryst with Phyllis). Phyllis may have had no interest in profiling any event involving Walter at the first moment of their meeting (except for some general, free-floating being on the make), but this changes toward using sex, its promise, and her feminine wiles as a tool to have her husband murdered with Walter's help. During this first meeting they collect information on each other—both verbal and nonverbal. Walter focuses not only on the face and body of Phyllis but also on her slight lingering on an upstairs balcony where she has come, perhaps, from sunning herself; her buttoning up the last few buttons of her dress as she finishes coming down the stairs and enters the room; her sitting posture with her legs displayed; her ankle bracelet; a few framed photographs of her family; the room's ambient light and temperature; and her careful choice of words, including double entendre. Phyllis seems to need less information and less analysis to size up Walter and what certain events will increase the probability that what she desires will occur. By the end of their first meeting, both are already using the fruits of their profiling. I'll leave it to the reader to figure who is the better profiler. It turns out that even Billy Wilder was not sure, because he filmed an alternative ending. In the widely screened version, Phyllis shoots Walter, then Walter shoots and kills Phyllis, and, after confessing to his boss, Walter collapses from his wound with ambulance sirens in the background. In the alternative ending, Walter shoots and kills Phyllis and ends up being executed via the gas chamber. Either way, profiling can be a serious business.

I now ask readers to *dec* the five-component definition of profiling (LO 1.1) described in this section after viewing the initial meeting of Walter and Phyllis. How many components are there, which ones, what event in the film corresponds to each, and can you observe any difficulties with the definition helping us understand what's going on in the film?

1.2 HISTORIES OF PROFILING

I have already shared intimations in the preface and Chapter 1 that there are difficulties in demonstrating profiling's validity and utility. Yet given the definition of profiling I'm advocating, it turns out that profiling has been with us throughout human history. I'd like to provide three cross sections of this history—from classical multicultural cultural texts three to four millennia ago, from changes in usage of the English language term *profile* as a verb going back close to 350 years ago to the present, and from the contemporary scientific history of profiling beginning about 160 years ago.

As I do this, I'm quite aware of what profiler of historians German philosopher Friedrich Nietzsche (1980/1974) warned. Developing, studying, and acting on history weaken the personality of the historian through contrasting the inner self with the historical self, leading one to falsely believe in one's virtue and justness, impairing instincts and hinder one's maturation, suggesting that one's species is nearing an end, and inducing irony and cynicism in one's everyday stance toward life. Well, that's a profile of historians, but as much as profiling involves constructing histories, does it apply to profilers as well?

1.2.1 FROM CLASSICAL MULTICULTURAL TEXTS

An example of very early picture-writing shows a group of 19 horses represented by the animals' heads only (Breasted, 1944, p. 2). This is accomplished on a clay tablet discovered at Susa, the ancient capital of Elam, a civilization from about 5,000 years ago in what is now the far west and southwest of Iran. This is one of the earliest representations of domesticated horses, and some of the horses have upright manes while others do not. The relevance for profiling is that inferences are being made in assigning manes—viz., what events are more likely to differentiate domesticated versus wild status. This would be a case of peri-dictive profiling pertaining to the present status of the horses at the time of the representations. Later Egyptian wall reliefs depict interactions of animals and people (Breasted, p. 30), as do early Babylonian cylinder seals from about the 25th century BCE (Breasted, p. 149). Here the relevance for profiling is choosing what events—such as representations of movement and body posture—convey or even constitute yet other events such as how people have interacted or will interact with each other and with animals. These are cases of post-dictive and predictive profiling. (As I was writing this book, earlier examples of profiling through creating images were described going back as far as over 40,000 years ago, at least in Europe [Pike]).

In the *Mahabharata* (ca. 9th century BCE), Arjuna has the task of convincing the fearful Uttara not to flee from battle. He needs to understand what is causing Uttara to flee and what could change his behavior. Arjuna is partly successful by appealing to Uttara's identification with the Ksatriya who, Arjuna argues, would never flee. Arjuna also coerces him, because Uttara does not at that moment lose his fear, nor does he develop a desire to fight. Here post-diction, peri-diction, and influence are successful and prediction is not (Narasimhan, 1965). The pull of the situation may be so strong that internal and external events of the person may yield little variability. Chapter 3 describes in much more detail the tension between the person and the situation. I also wonder whether Arjuna is like profilers who try to force the truth of a profile through coercive self-fulfilling prophecy or just plain coercion.

In Homer's *Iliad* (ca. 8th century BCE), epithets are used to post-dictively, peri-dictively, and predictively profile various warriors. These epithets pose the essence of a person's nature including their internal and external acts. My favorite is the use of *breaker of horses* for Hector, the Trojan hero, many times throughout Homer's account, especially at the end of his funeral that closes out the *Iliad*. The epithet conveys that Hector has vanquished the most courageous and spirited of adversaries. But, as readers of the *Iliad* remember, he has broken and run *from* and then has been broken *by* Achilles. Achilles is *God-like*, yet he succumbs to an arrow shot by Paris, *Prince of Troy*. Some prince *he* is, because earlier, Paris has been berated by *lovely-haired* Helen for not being manly—which doesn't keep Helen from going to bed with him immediately after this, even as the battle with the Greeks rages outside the walls of Troy (Lattimore, 1951). There are no counterexamples of her lovely hair, but she certainly does not have a lovely spirit or soul. Just as with the contradictions and complexities of epithets, human traits used for profiling pose complications. This is because constructs of traits at any moment are events that also lead us to other events and often are acted on by these and yet other events and events of interest as well.

In the *Analects* of Confucius (5th century BCE), there is commentary about how events bearing on people lead to predictive, post-dictive, and peri-dictive assumptions (Ley, 1997). For example, a dutiful son may still make his parents worry when he is sick, even if he wishes not to worry them at all because he is dutiful (p. 7). (If only he never was sick or less than always dutiful.) Those who make virtue their profession are the ruin of virtue (p. 87)—something that still rings true to some viewers of televangelists today. Or some further trait ascriptions—"Zigao was stupid; Zeng Shen was slow; Zizhang was extreme; Zilu was wild" (p. 51). Leaving technology out of it, how different were the events leading to these ascriptions, then, compared with the same ones today?

1.2.2 FROM LEXICAL HISTORY: USAGES OF THE ENGLISH TERM *PROFILE* AS A VERB

With the support of the *Oxford English Dictionary* (OED) (2012), I offer the following. As far back as 1664, *profile* denotes outlining or drawing in cross section. This may connote constructing boundaries that capture at least the spatial essence of an object, not yet a person, even if in psychoanalytic theories *object* often refers to some perception and introjection (taken within oneself) of perceived features of a person. From 1715, *profiling* suggests that the boundaries of something not only characterize it but also highlight something else adjacent to it. From 1839, *profile* denotes defining an outline against a background for objects and people. Here there is more than a connotation of an interaction between an event and yet other events. From 1882, *profile* denotes composing or presenting a short biography of an individual. (Chapter 6 describes how structural features of narratives are crucial in this endeavor for profiling.) From 1925, *profile* denotes investigating, summarizing, and recording physical elements. This seems useful for what I've called situational profiling. From 1951, *profile* denotes recording and analyzing the psychological and behavioral characteristics (often these may be the same thing) of a person or to evaluate someone by these means. This captures something quite close to carrying out formal psychological assessments or studying the *mind* including the *criminal mind*. From 1970, profiling denotes giving a summary description or a report on not just a person but also an organization—especially structural characteristics. The first *Oxford English Dictionary* example of *profile* as engaging in *profiling* is from 1989 and relates especially to racial profiling. This is the case even though the Federal Bureau of Investigation's (2012a) Behavioral Sciences Unit was created and engaged in certain kinds of profiling in the early 1970s, while there are other examples of scientific profiling going back at least to the mid-19th century (see the following section). From 1992, *profile* denotes optimal analysis, especially of a problem. This is something profilers attempt. Interestingly one other usage of *profile* goes back to 1970, wherein the profiler by definition postures, that is, acts or pretends to be something he or she is not. I do not choose to provide references for the following statement, but profilers have been accused of profiling and known to have profiled in this manner.

1.2.3 CONTEMPORARY SCIENTIFIC HISTORY OF PROFILING

I will share only a few examples of this history (covered in more detail in, e.g., Canter & Youngs, 2009, Chapters 2–4; Turvey, 2011, Chapter 1). What might be original in this section relates to what I wrote in the preface. Profilers create stories linking events to some event of interest. So what follows are some events leading to an event of interest—where profilers are today. However, I submit that there is controversy about not only where profilers are today but also what happened to get to this point, again assuming this point is known. So I critique a few examples of the last 200 years and then highlight features of the better profiling textbooks of the last 10 years.

Often, contemporary scientific histories of profiling feature some text on the pre-diction, post-diction, and peri-diction of *witches*. These histories suggest that the event of interest, being a witch, may not have existed in any absolute sense, so profiling efforts were doomed from the beginning and may still be doomed. They could also suggest that profilers back then were biased and ignorant, unlike those of today. Some of the events associated with being a witch probably yielded many instances of false accusation, even if witches did exist—given alleged witch indicators such as having a pet; being a woman who had not borne children even untimely ripped from the womb as Shakespeare's Macduff; having some blemish, spot, or birthmark; or being a woman who lived alone. Again, there's often some implicit self-congratulation about how we're progressive and scientific now, although to his credit, Turvey (2011) rightly suggests that religious inquisitions have continued and have continued to follow what he calls a *pseudo-rational attribution*. Here a societal problem is blamed on a group within a population, and rules are developed to give the blame and punishment process some legal authority. I object only to the *rational* part of the term, given that there are irrational, illogical, and emotional phenomena at play behind the rational and that the pseudo may be so great that any pretense at the rational dissipates.

While Turvey (2011) hopes we can "avoid similar pitfalls" (p. 18), I've lost hope or maybe never had it. Pseudo-rational attribution whether imbued with sincere belief and buy-in or cynically employed as a weapon of power is alive and well across various governmental, organizational, and social regimes. This is the case for small entities like a pair of humans or many nuclear families and for entities as large as the United States and the People's Republic of China. Anytime someone is being made an example of for the good of others—or better yet for some idea or some other abstract entity like the organization, nation, or society—the witch trial may be alive and well supported by what I'll call, following Turvey, *pseudo-rational profiling*. The profiling task, then, becomes linking events to another event of interest—often in the service of social and political power. And this becomes a theme throughout this book, that profilers look for evil to explain evil as opposed to thinking in terms of a 2 × 2 matrix of good and evil causes and consequences or in transcending good and evil as in Nietzsche's (1966) rejection of traditional morality altogether for some healthier approach that has many perspectives but at the same time is not relativistic.

A successful demonstration of this idea might be the American historians Paul Boyer and Stephen Nissenbaum's (1974) *Salem Possessed: The Social Origins of Witchcraft*. The authors note that social envy was a key to 17th-century witch allegations within Massachusetts—in that less powerful members of Salem's social establishment were accused by lower-prestige citizens who had an ongoing quarrel with the victims. What might have varied across cases was how much accusers and victims each bought into the accusation at specific moments as the adjudication continued—from sheer cynicism to being caught up in forces beyond awareness or understanding. Falsely accused by others, true believers in their own guilt may have shown psychological dynamics similar to victims of 20th-century show trials and of 21st-century false self-confessions.

A Frenchman, Francois Eugene Vidocq (1775–1857), may have helped popularize the systematic collection and analysis of as many events as possible for the development of linkages (either associative or causal relationships) between and among them and then with a *specific* criminal event of interest, a *kind* of criminal event of interest, or person or types of people engaged in crime. These events and linkages may be seen as constituting the profiling of people, situations, and their interactions. He also is credited with developing undercover agents to help collect this information for analysis and then for action to deter and decrease the probability of specific crimes.

However, what he actually may or may not have done is questionable. Morton (2011) writes that one might do best to compare Vidocq's claims and many claims about him to Casanova's memoirs and take his deeds (as one might take the sexual exploits claimed by the late basketball great Wilt Chamberlain, who had sex with 20,000 different women) as apocryphal unless shown otherwise. Edwards (1977) seems to take Vidocq more at face value. On the other hand, readers from the intelligence, security, and law enforcement worlds may find a sense of déjà vu when contemplating the possibility of an individual fabricating information about others and himself in a manner contributing to that individual's material well-being, self-esteem, and fame. Attempting prudence and avoidance of litigation as I did in the preface, I write only that such public discourse about some contemporary profilers is still with us today. And any claim for Vidocq's originality of concept, collection technique, or mode of analysis most often is associated with a lack of historical knowledge. For example, the use of undercover agents is described in treatises over 2,000 years ago from India (Shamasastry, 1909) and China (Duyvendak, 1928).

Hans Gross (1847–1915) wrote one of the first books (Gross, 1911) significantly using scientific psychology in forensic contexts including profiling. He helped popularize nonverbal communicative events as linked to deception, a topic covered in depth in Chapter 9. He also helped popularize the belief that criminals are psychologically very different from people who are not identified as criminals. Even if these differences could be validated, at issue would be the possible causes. Could it be that the label of criminal or the sanctions on criminal behavior leads to differences or some assumed intrinsic or developmental psychological sources? Wouldn't there be differences among these differences for different people, crimes, situations, and so forth?

Importantly, Gross (1911) stressed that what we now call profilers get into serious trouble the more inferences as opposed to sense-based observations are used. An example of becoming enmeshed can be found in in Cronbach and Meehl's (1955) nomological nets. This has had a huge impact on profiling and in methods of criminal investigation based on and reifying *just the facts* and empirical data as the be-all and end-all. The problem is that perceiving an observation without inferences is beyond the human. (Readers might try this and email or call me if they think they succeed in observing without inferring. They may then have demonstrated that they are beyond the human or that I am incorrect about the human.)

In American psychiatrist James Brussel's obituary in the *New York Times* in 1982, details were given of some of his most important work, including clients George Metesky, the so-called mad bomber, and Albert DeSalvo, the Boston Strangler; and the fact that he held the office of assistant commissioner in the New York State Department of Mental Hygiene. In my reading of profiling histories and discussions with profilers, however, the Metesky case (involving about three dozen explosions in public places in Manhattan between 1940 and 1956) is by far the most significant component of this psychiatrist's fame. Did Brussel create a profile so accurate that it was the crucial piece of analysis leading to the mad bomber's capture—an example of post-dictive profiling and, perhaps, peri-dictive profiling assuming the culprit was identified in the middle of a bombing spree? Many in the general public and some among profilers thought so and some still do. The truth seems to be otherwise.

Following Delafuente (2004), Ewing and McCann (2006), and Brussel (1968), I submit that Brussel's profile had little, if anything, to do with identifying the culprit. In fact, it may have led to many fruitless investigations of innocent people and a number of hoaxes and false bombing threats among the public. His putative contributions seem much more significant as an example of urban mythology. It also highlights the impact of an old parlor trick that psychologists term the *Barnum effect* (cf. Rosen, 1975), in which events including preferred behaviors and inferred thoughts and feelings—probably the case for many people of a certain subpopulation—are linked together with common types of logic and are then presented as a unique pathway to an event of interest for specific individual. In this case, many bombers of the time were male, so the perpetrator was probably male. A buttoned, double-breasted suit was common apparel for men in those days, so the bomber might wear one and or at least own one. (Readers should watch entertainment films made and set in the 1940s and 1950s involving spectators at a ball game and check out the attire in the stands.) Not all bombers have *sexual problems,* but in an era imbued with crude popularizations of psychoanalysis and Sigmund Freud, it would not be a stretch to assume so and then that the culprit might live with an older female relative. (Brussel apparently used handwriting analysis, especially the rounded bottoms of each written *w* of the perpetrator's written warnings that otherwise were characterized with straight lines and points.)

Besides the Barnum effect, other effects implicated in what seems to be at first blush successful profiling, whether of Brussel's work or that of others, include the Rainbow Ruse, the Jacques Statement, and the Fuzzy Fact. In the Rainbow Ruse, profilers include both some event and its opposite as associated with some event of interest. So someone can be quiet but can be quite boisterous as well in the *right* situation. (Who can't be?) In the Jacques Statement, profilers will include the various *dictions* (pre-, post-, and peri-) that are characteristic of people of a certain age for someone whose age is known. (Nothing wrong with this, but special profiling expertise is not needed.) In the Fuzzy Fact, profilers offer some diction so large or general that it might be hard to contradict, as in she may be from Detroit, or some urban area, or somewhere close to one, or certainly has some familiarity with urban lingo or style. (See Rowland, 2008, for even more such effects.)

I'm by no means indicting Dr. Brussel here but instead the mythology that has been made out of his work. He certainly was described as the real thing of what otherwise were just fictional creations—for example, the powers of the mind of Sherlock Holmes and the *ratiocinations* of the detective prototypes of Edgar Allen Poe. A less noted aspect of Brussel's work with the Metesky case is that he suggested the profile be publicly disseminated to draw out the perpetrator. This may well have elicited additional information leading not only to a breaking of the case but also to many hoaxes and false confessions.

Now what follows is a look at the most recent history of profiling. David Canter and his associate (Canter & Youngs, 2009) in the United Kingdom provide one contemporary example of applying statistics to comprehensive data collected on criminals and criminal behavior. I have been very interested in their integrating statistically analyzed data (pp. 81–118) with the construct of personal narratives (pp. 119–138) so that (1) explanations of crime from the perpetrator's point of view may receive some empirical support and (2) presumed action patterns of crime useful in criminal investigations are developed. The essence here seems to be that criminal actions can be profiled through narrative themes—useful for prediction, post-diction, peri-diction, understanding, and influence. (Chapter 6 contains material on narrative.) If I understand their work correctly, they also believe that additional characteristics (both internal and external events) of a criminal already apprehended or on the loose can be developed through applications of deductive and inductive logic.

Canter (2011) more recently seeks to establish what he calls *profiling equations* not in the mathematical sense, but as consistencies in human criminal action. Some law enforcement personnel might call these *modi operandi*. I believe that the attempts to emulate scientific methods with information collected and analyzed, to employ narrative analysis or other conceptually based methods to identify empirically supported themes, and to use logic to generate additional events useful in prediction, post-diction, and peri-diction is where profiling is at the moment. The problem to be considered through this book, however, is whether scientific methods so valuable to the physical and life sciences methods are significantly so for the psychological, behavioral, and social sciences.

A focus on the cognitive activity of both profilers and interpreters of profilers is a cardinal feature of Alison and Rainbow's (2011) collection of multiauthored chapters by authors, almost all affiliated with professional organizations from the United Kingdom and none from the United States. Much of this work is on the cognitive expertise of profilers and geographic profiling specialists (pp. 72–159). As important is the impact of verbal and quantitative expressions of probability within profiles on the degree of uncertainty attributed to these profiles arrived at by people reading and otherwise using them (pp. 206–227). This work actually involves profilers profiling the consumers of their profiles (wittingly or otherwise) by choice of language related to certainty of specific statements. Alison and Rainbow also describe the impact of heavily researched heuristics (mental strategies to problem solve in situations of uncertainty, ambiguity, and, often, time pressure) on profilers (pp. 228–249). Chapter 4 discusses examples of this work (see also the chapters on the logic and metacognition of profilers in Petherick, 2009).

Turvey's (2011) textbook, already in its fourth edition, broadly covers *behavioral evidence analysis*—which I interpret as inferring internal and external events from external events, viz., physical, documentary, or testimonial evidence (p. 123) as applied to crime. He provides sections on real and alleged victims, offenders, and crime scenes—thus focusing on the person and the situation. There certainly seems to be an implicit expectation within Turvey's work that much of practical value can be accomplished through his approach to prediction, post-diction, peri-diction, understanding, and influence. I'm not sure this is the case for two reasons. One comprises the materials I've summarized in Chapter 2 on profiling validity. The other comprises the arguments of Meehl (1954), Dawes (1994), and Faust (2012) that I've already alluded to. (If simple statistical models are usually superior to expert judgments, and so little of the latter exists, and even what does exist may need to be updated as people change, what's left for profiling experts to do?) Nevertheless,

I commend Turvey's work for its seriousness of purpose, its lack of creative but outlandish speculation, and its accessibility for investigators and legal adjudicators.

Finally, Harcourt's (2007) *Against Prediction* presents several ideas that influence the contemporary history of applied scientific profiling and that suggest the difficulties in demonstrating profiling's validity and utility (see especially the discussion in Chapter 2 of Kydd, 2011; Press, 2009). The first is that putative indicators of some event of interest—the indicators having the potential to be not only events but also events of interest concurrently or at some other time—bring with them the vulnerability of an error rate. This rate is exemplified by the percentage of perpetrators of the event of interest who are not characterized with some or all of the indicators and the nonperpetrators who are so characterized. Moreover, application of these indicators within a deployed profiling program—such as counterterrorism, counterespionage, and counterdeception—*facilitates* the successful commission of the respective events of interest. That is, people who don't display putative indicators and who attempt to perpetrate events of interest more likely be successful because of profiling. This example of what is called a *false negative* is further developed in Chapter 4.

The second idea is that people who display or engage in events assumed to be indicators of some event of interest—but who are *not* intending to engage in the event of interest—may be noxiously affected by a deployed profiling program. For example, someone selected for an invasive search at an airport because of displaying or engaging in events construed to be linked to terrorism may in the future be more likely to engage in the very event of interest or something else that may be legally or ethically proscribed. This example of what is called a *false positive* is further developed in Chapter 4.

Now, the problem in writing any scientific history, perhaps any history, on the study of human psychosocial events or what is commonly called the human sciences (cf. Polkinghorne, 1984), including profiling, has to do with two tensions. First, as popularized by T. S. Kuhn (1962), is the tension between believing that science or any quest for knowledge is a progressive one based on an accumulation of truth and the jettisoning of falsehoods versus and believing that there are just changes through time in what questions, answers, and methods are popular without any necessary bearing of truth. In the latter case, history may not have direction, certainly not one toward the true, the good, and the beautiful as some idealistic endpoint. The second tension is between the belief that knowledge is possible and that it is only a futile exercise in terror management (Pyszczynski, Greenberg, & Solomon, 1991). That is, as described in the preface, to attenuate or otherwise manage the existential terror of living in an otherwise unpredictable, ambiguous, and unknowable world, people may pursue something called knowledge to develop cognitive consistency, belief in a just world, self-awareness, self-esteem, social identity, impression management, and influencing the worldviews of other people.

Arriving at the contemporary status of the science of profiling and whether profiling is yet a science or should be a science, I assert that there is little *direct* information—based on my review of pertinent scientific the literature to be reviewed in Chapter 2—on the strengths and weakness of the decisions going into the many profiles affecting the lives of the profiled and those who may be affected by them. I also focus on these decisions in Chapter 3 based on the languages used by profilers; in Chapter 4 based on profilers' various cognitive, emotional, motivational, and behavioral phenomena (conscious and unconscious); and more concretely in Chapters 7 through 9 on terrorism, espionage, and deception, respectively.

Humbleness toward knowledge about profiling or anything else in the human sciences is well described in modernized fragments of a poem by Keats (2012) titled "When I Have Fears That I May Cease To Be." It begins: "When I have fears that I may cease to be/Before my pen has glean'd my teeming brain/Before high-piled books in character..." then continues "... When I behold ... Huge cloudy symbols of a high romance/And think that I may never live to trace/Their shadows, with the magic hand of chance..." and ends "... then on the shore/Of the wide world I stand alone, and think/Till love and fame to nothingness do sink." I feel like this sometimes. Do you? Is this why war correspondents like Anthony Shadid of the *New York Times* and Marie Colvin of the *Sunday Times* risked death and found death covering political violence in Syria in 2012? Is this why serious profilers risk if not death then at least the alienation of their peers, potential marital and family problems from putting in too much time on the job, professional burnout, and the guilt of additional fallout from one's inevitable mistakes?

I now ask readers to engage in LO 1.2—to *dec* three examples each of profiling's cultural history, lexical history, and scientific history in the context of a film fragment from *Duck Soup* (Mankiewicz & McCarey, 1933). What elements of the film—images, costumes, the humorous one-liners (at least they are to me), the digs at formal authority, the violations of decorum—are examples of profiling history? A suggestion might be to think about how people of various social statures, genders, and explicit and implicit degrees of power are portrayed.

1.3 POLITICS OF PROFILING

There are political phenomena affecting how and how well profilers engage in the prediction, post-diction, peri-diction, understanding, and influence of events of interest. I describe these in Chapter 4. At present, I intend to describe how politics affects the previously given definitions and histories of profiling.

As popularized by the French philosopher Michel Foucault (1977), there may have been a huge change in how political authorities control masses of people that began several hundred years ago. Throughout most of human history, the most effective power that political authorities had over people was achieved in two ways. First, the authorities used resource-intensive methods of intelligence, surveillance, and reconnaissance (ISR)—analyzed by Foucault before today's ongoing revolution in technology-facilitated ISR. Second, they used the threat and implementation of externally mediated punishments such as death, incarceration, torture, and various deprivations. However, in the last 200 to 300 years, a more effective power has evolved wherein people deploy ISR and the threat of punishment against themselves. How does this happen? Shouldn't people feel free to do what they want as long as there seems to be no externally mediated ISR against them and, thus, no significant threat of punishment? But people began to more strongly believe that they might never really know when and where this ISR was being deployed and employed. And since—and now I'm switching to an individual, present consciousness—one can't be sure if one is being watched or collected on, one develops a behavioral style wherein one acts as if one is always having ISR applied and the threat of punishment looms near. So what has happened? Since continuous and completely comprehensive ISR even today—at least at the time of this writing—has collection and analysis limitations (but see Jacobs and Bullock, 2012), in essence one is doing the political authorities' work. One has internalized the controlling power of the authorities and at least is attempting to comply with the authorities' standards in a manner more effective than externally controlled systems could achieve. In yet other words, one has learned what events are to be approached and avoided (like what in John Frederick Coot and Haven Gillespie's 1934 song "Santa Claus Is Coming to Town" is deemed naughty and nice); one strives toward accurate predicting, post-dicting, peri-dicting, understanding, and influencing oneself as an event and the events one generates and comes in contact with; one becomes a more effective profiler than government-sanctioned profilers.

From a political and ethical perspective, profilers are just part of a control process—the control of others as well as their participation in their own control. And in the support of political authorities, they often receive only what amounts to chump change. As technology approaches closer approximations of continuous and comprehensive ISR, developing linkages among events to predict, post-dict, peri-dict, understand, and influence an event of interest may face unique challenges: on one hand, more information and more sophisticated methods to mine it; and on the other hand the remaining challenge of tapping into internal events such as thoughts, emotions, and motives—especially those that have not succumbed to the *internalization* of *external* control mechanisms.

This analysis may be useful in contemplating the validity of allegations of behavioral scientists engaged in at least generic profiling supporting interrogations bordering on or constituting torture (Shane, 2009) and of professional literature addressing such issues (Nordgren, McDonnell, & Loewenstein, 2011; Suedfeld, 2007). This analysis may also address my own impression of behavioral sciences research on criminal behavior based on applying keyword searches through the *PsycNET Gold* databases (APA, 2012). Similar but not identical to what the preface applied to *books* on profiling, there's much more posted on these databases on illicit substance abuse and street-level selling, street-level and massage parlor-related prostitution, violent behavior that is street level or committed out of rage, and petty theft and vandalism than there is on malfeasance by financial and business titans, high-level political corruption, and high-level war crimes perpetrated by cabals of national and international authorities.

Profiling, in summary, may largely be a tool of power, and profilers may merely be witting or unwitting tools. As a literary illustration, I refer readers to the various drafts of the play *Woyzeck* left unfinished by the untimely death (age 23) in 1837 of the German polymath Georg Büchner. Although the play may be taken to be about a murder, there is a significant focus on how profiling expertise in the service of political authority is employed to dehumanize working-class and lower-class people whose allegedly primitive needs and desires must not be allowed to subvert and destroy civilized manners of acting that are control mechanisms to keep people in line.

I now ask readers to engage in LO 1.3 to *dec* the politics of profiling—especially where (1) profiling can be construed as a control mechanism and (2) internalizing an external control mechanism can complicate profiling. The film fragment for analysis is from *Who's Afraid of Virginia Woolf* (Lehman & Nichols, 1966). The setting is an after-the-party drink at the home of a department chair and his wife entertaining a new faculty member and his wife. How might George and Martha be profiling each other? How is this profiling affecting their respective behaviors? What is the role of Martha's repetition of "Getting angry, baby?" as an event leading to the breaking of a liquor bottle by her George?

2 Challenges of Profiling
Validity and Its Estimation

In the greater Toulouse, France, area including Montauban, a French paratrooper, Mohamed Merah, of North African descent was murdered on March 11, 2012. Two more French paratroopers, again of North African descent, were murdered on March 15. On March 19, a teacher and three children were murdered in a single attack at a Jewish school. What events would be most accurately associated with the murders—the event of interest? A hypothesis quickly arose that all were killed by the same individual. This proved to be the case.

Various experts and the general public were split on two other hypotheses about that individual's motivation. One was that motivating events included an anti-immigration bias, a bias against people perceived as foreign, that is, xenophobia, and some sort of far rightist, conservative ideology. The other hypothesis was that motivating events included an anti-Western bias; an Islamicist political orientation, often denoting an individual who is intentionally distorting or unwittingly misconstruing Islam leading to terrorist behavior; and a jihadi religious quest, often denoting an individual who believes in and acts on a mission to engage in an armed struggle against the enemies of Islam, to convert nonbelievers through noncoercive and coercive means, and to engage in an internal psychological and spiritual struggle to believe and act according to Islam. A further complexity here is that terms like *Islamic, Islamicist, jihadi,* and *Arabic* can be catch-all, derogatory phrases for people who *look like* they're from the Mideast (where I was taught lies the cradle of civilization) are terrorists by definition and are often uncivilized to boot. In essence they become the *Other,* a term significant in the philosophy of the French–Lithuanian Emmanuel Levinas (see *Time and the Other and Additional Essays,* 1987) denoting something that cannot be known or assimilated and that remains unfamiliar. The *Other* becomes even more negatively construed in the field of *critical theory,* such as the work of the Palestinian philosopher Edward Said (see *Orientalism: Western Conceptions of the Orient,* 1978) as often containing crude negative stereotypes of those viewed different from us. What *look like* means in this case might take us too far away from our focus on profiling, even if *look like* may capture the essence of what profiling is.

In any case, the second hypothesis proved to be far more accurate and was coupled with other internal and external events presumably leading to the terrorist event of interest including being emotionally disturbed, volatile, and alienated; having a record of committing crimes including purse stealing and driving without a license; actively engaging images and text on jihadi-oriented websites; using political and religious indoctrination and paramilitary training in Afghanistan and Pakistan; and protesting the deaths of Palestinian children (thus, the killing of presumed Jews) and against the French involvement in Afghanistan and other "Muslim countries" and a French law banning the facial veil in public, thus the killing of paratroopers (Bilefsky & De La Bauame, 2012; Sayare, Erlanager, & Berry, 2012).

Then the second hypothesis was modified as it was posited that the shooter's brother might have been a primary causal agent in the murders (Sayare, 2012). Another modification was that the secular instead of sacred, personal instead of religious (as if the *religious* cannot be *personal*), and French failure to integrate second- and third-generation Islamic immigrants were paramount as events leading to the murders. This modification was supported by discovering an alleged suicide attempt by hanging and a marital divorce both experienced by the presumed murderer—the latter days before the murderous spree began.

In leaving this example, readers might hope that matters would be much simpler, if profiling could be founded on perfect or near-perfect linkages of events to events of interest. What do I mean by this? Well, during an interview, a Tibetan monk claimed that plainclothes police officers infiltrating religious ceremonies could always be identified as such even as they tried to blend in to remain unobtrusive. "They never fool us because they hold their prayer beads with their right hand, and every Tibetan knows to hold them in their left hand" (Jacobs, 2012). As another example, there have been problems at times with how easy federal air marshals can be identified because of Transportation Security Administration rules about the marshals' grooming, dress standards, and time of boarding (Investigative Report by the Committee of the Judiciary, 2006).

2.1   RESEARCH STUDIES

In this section I provide opinions on the validity of profiling—but not any validity and any kind of profiling. As to validity, I focus on (1) predicting two kinds of events, behavioral intentions and behaviors; and (2) post-dicting why people have already engaged in events of interest or are likely to have engaged in such events. This is because most of the extant scientific research focuses on these two areas. Also, I will attempt to make distinctions between *validity* and *utility* related to validity. The former has to do with correct linkages between and among events and between these and an event of interest, the latter with the usefulness of the degree of correctness in problem resolution like solving, understanding, or influencing a crime. (The two are often conflated. On the other hand, I've used the two terms conjoined within a sentence about 10 times up to this place in the book, and I would wager—based on profiling potential readers—that few readers reached for a dictionary and instead depended on their distinctions.)

As Kocsis (2009) points out, the satisfaction of law enforcement consumers with profilers may be taken as evidence of both validity and utility—otherwise why would consumers be satisfied? So, too, the continued use of profiling by various consumers again supports its validity and utility. Yet even satisfied consumers may not be able to specifically point to where a profile made a difference in a specific case. Moreover, beliefs in the validity and utility of profiling can lead to congruent estimates of profiling's validity and utility in specific cases. That is, it must have made a difference because it's supposed to make a difference. (This is a common explanation for why placebos work in medicine.) Kocsis also notes that an unfortunate circle of reinforcement for all of this is nurtured by the mass media popularizing and glorifying profiling in popular entertainment—just as I described in the preface. Yet another caveat is that different studies have different approaches to what does and does not constitute profiling and what might constitute validity.

As to profiling, I focus in this section on people intending to behave, behaving, and having behaved in a *socially deviant* manner. The events here may be criminal or otherwise but will share being perceived as somehow unusual or unwanted by political or social authorities—except for times wherein deviant behavior is encouraged as a political control mechanism, such as opium, not religion, being the opiate of the masses, as suggested by Karl Marx. And, again, I base my opinions in this section on profiling's validity and utility on significant scientific studies.

I have judged these studies to be significant based on three possible reasons. First, they may be published in a prestigious journal, wherein prestigious is operationally defined by some combinations of having a thorough peer review, a high rejection rate, and a high citation rate—that is, other researchers use the journal's articles as a cited reference and often may read them as well. Second, the studies may be based on a review of many other studies in an attempt to derive valid lessons learned about the validity of profiling or at times best and worst practices in carrying out research on profiling. Such reviews often are called *meta-evaluations* and are based on coding studies through a list of meaningful and identical criteria and then subjecting the studies' coded data to various statistical procedures. Third, I view some studies as significant because I just find them clever as thought experiments or empirical studies or applications of logic to the practice of profiling.

The first study was published in the *Proceedings of the National Academy of Sciences* and was chosen because I believed it met the first and third significance criteria just mentioned. William Press (2009), a computer scientist and integrative biologist at the University of Texas at Austin, wrote about using profiling as a valid means to justify secondary screening for only some members of a population, all of which would be subjected to some primary screening—even including the possibility of using ethnicity or nationality in predicting events of interest like terrorism. (Here note that ethnicity and nationality are subject to change and thus are events.) He specifically was interested in whether using *prior probabilities*—statistically derived probabilities for (1) people associated with specific events who already have committed the event of interest, (2) people associated with the same specific events who have not yet committed the event of interest, (3) people not associated with the same specific events who have committed the event of interest, and (4) people not associated with the same specific events who haven't commit the event of interest—would help lead to optimal accuracy. The problem here, as Press points out, is that prior probabilities are rarely if ever known for real situations. But he went ahead in his study and assumed an *ideal* case of completely accurate prior probabilities and of secondary screenings concentrated on the individuals with the highest probability of committing the event of interest.

He then demonstrated that even with this ideal approach—one that that would never pertain to an actual situation—uniform random sampling of the entire population would be just as efficient in generating the most optimal accuracy in identifying would-be bad actors, such as terrorists, and not those who act badly and who can't act on in the entertainment world. This is because through time and through multiple screening situations, screening resources would be wasted on the repeated screening of people who had the highest probability for committing the event of interest *but who had no intention of committing that event.* He went on to recommend a mathematically optimal strategy called s*quare-root biased sampling*—the geometric mean (for our purposes here a measure of central tendency or some typical value)—between profiling based on prior probabilities and uniform random sampling. The way he sees it, secondary screenings would be distributed broadly, although not uniformly, over the population. What I call *strong* profiling—based solely on the quantitative linkages between and among events and some event of interest—would not be optimum.

The next study published in *Terrorism and Political Violence* also meets the first and third significance criteria. Kydd (2011), a political scientist at the University of Wisconsin at Madison, focused on a specific profiling problem—how large numbers of people can be screened most efficiently to discover those who may engage in terrorism. He showed how complicated this problem can be through several thought experiments. Those sending a terrorist for an attack need to make calculations based on how likely their agents may or not be detected as having terrorist intent. They need to worry about instances of suicidal terrorists being detained by good counterterrorism tradecraft and technology or turning themselves in shortly before an attack because of a change of heart or mind. They need to worry about how likely their agents may or may not engage in terrorism if undetected by security authorities—problems including a weapon or explosive not working or some unexpected and serendipitous event impeding an attack. Terrorist senders need to have an accurate understanding of what security authorities look for and how they act when implementing antiterrorism and counterterrorism plans and programs and, implicitly, many other contingencies including the likelihood of terrorism even if detected. (An example of this last might be activating a suicide vest and causing multiple deaths after being detected but before being incapacitated or during apprehension and detention.)

Security authorities need to make similar calculations based on similar contingencies such as how accurate an understanding *they* have of the understanding of those sending agents to commit terrorism have of what security authorities look for and how they (security authorities) act when implementing antiterrorism and counterterrorism plans and programs based on such an understanding. Reading this last sentence, one should be able to see how the complexities can easily enough get out of hand. I'll share that I've been involved in developing many such chains linking sequences of likely intrapsychic elements and likely resulting behaviors leading to further likely perceptions and so on in the context of ongoing situational changes. And all the associated events may vary in degree of interdependence. (I remember one presentation in particular wherein I discussed all of this and seemed to elicit derision both because the complexity was denied and because it was accepted but is resolution was deemed improbable. What do you think?)

Kydd (2011) posits that any equilibrium in the system of those sending terrorist and those protecting against them would be only momentary because of the many dynamics and complexities just alluded to above. My reading of Kydd's article is that unless one is blessed with the predictive powers of Cassandra, a deep undercover mole who is *in* on terrorist deliberations, or yet again accurate technical collection means unknown to those plotting terrorism, both sides may revert often enough to completely randomized procedures. (Readers who wish they were like Cassandra may ponder her dual fate of always being right and never being believed.)

Thus, those supporting terrorism will randomize choices of agents and methods, while those seeking to deter and apprehend before terrorism occurs will randomize screening and other procedures. Discerning readers will quickly grasp even further complexities. For example, there are the effects on observers of the tarantella (literally, a fast, upbeat dance) between antiterrorism, counterterrorism, and terrorism—with *antiterrorism* denoting activities to make terrorism less likely and *counterterrorism* denoting resolving any aspect of an ongoing terrorism plot. In addition, sometimes there are no explicit senders; that is, terrorists send themselves. Moreover, randomization may affect terrorism propensities not only of terrorists but also of people who before randomization were not intending to engage in such activities and after randomization now are. (As to this latter point, readers may remember my discussion of Harcourt, 2010, in Chapter 1.) After reading Kydd, I arrive at a concluding question. How can the development of profiling lead to better security in an ever-changing, dynamic field of human internal and external events? In other words, any profiling book, even this one, may be obsolete before it is published. (A grim thought as I write, made less grim by my belief of the moment that one is at least morally and ethically obligated to attempt resolution of challenge.)

The third study published in *Psychology, Public Policy, and Law* meets the first importance criterion. Woodhams and Toye (2007), at the time, respectively, a psychologist at the University of Leicester, England, and a member of the Division Intelligence Unit of the Surrey, England, police, studied profiling wherein commercial robberies might be judged to be committed by the same individual. Judgments were based on (1) assumed behavioral similarities between and among crimes and (2) inferences about who might have committed the crimes based on what the alleged perpetrator might somehow *look like*—a phrase just used in the discussion of the previously described March 2012 terrorism case—based on elements of the crimes committed. (Theoretically, the *look like* could include anything from size, strength, desires, and needs to unconscious perceptions, behavioral track record, and financial status.) So here situational events and events about a person or people would be judged to be homologous (i.e., have some sort of similarities) based on derived or assumed statistical relationships, inductive and deductive logic, intuition, respected opinions of others, and so on.

Woodhams and Toye (2007) also assumed that the homologies may be valid and bearing utility if *legal*, not scientific, criteria are met. For *legal*, they use U.S. Supreme Court criteria based on the *Daubert v. Merrell Dow Pharmaceuticals* case. I both paraphrase and elaborate upon these criteria to share that, therefore, the profiling data must (1) be viewed as *scientific* as determined by the judge of a case, (2) be relevant to the case at hand as determined by the judge and rest on scientific foundations, and (3) rest on sound scientific methods such as (a) being based on empirical data; (b) having the potential for the results to be falsifiable, refutable, and testable; (c) having been subjected to peer review and published; (d) having a known or potential error rate; (e) having standards and controls concerning its operation; and (f) being generally accepted by a relevant scientific community. Two major implications of all of this are that what's scientific is decided by people who aren't scientists and that what's scientific seems to be characterized by Kuhn's paradigms (see Chapter 1 in this volume) that may bear more on ritual as opposed to truth.

Woodhams and Toye (2007) found that there was some support for profiling demonstrating that individual commercial robbers offend consistently. That is, each robber *seems to tend to* have—these multiple qualifiers represent my attempt to capture for the reader *my* reading of this study's analysis—a special way of robbing. Robbers also were found *to tend* to be inconsistent from each other when robbing. That is, they *may be more consistently than inconsistently inconsistent* from each other. However, the hypothesis of a homology between offender and robbery type—that components of the crime should somehow match characteristics of the person—was *not* supported. Because it's been at least *my* impression that homology is strongly assumed and supported as approaching gospel truth by the stories and plots of mass media and various entertainment vehicles—especially investigative procedurals like the *Law and Order* (2012) franchise—many loyal viewers of the show may question Woodhams and Toye's findings and even their expertise. This has, of course, no necessary bearing on whether they're right or wrong but more on the relationships among reality, hyperreality, and make-believe intimated in the preface.

The fourth study, also in *Psychology, Public Policy, and Law,* meets the first and second criteria. I'll also add that the author, John Monahan (2012), a psychologist at the University of Virginia, has influenced my thinking significantly by his many years of carefully written scholarship and research on psychology and the law. After reviewing many works on the psychology of terrorism, Monahan concluded that prediction, post-diction, and peri-diction of terrorism—not just any presumably deviant behavior—has four main challenges that have not yet been resolved. First, there's a need for a more careful definition of what is being studied—whether anything considered terrorism or specific types, roles, phases, and purposes. Second, there's a need for more careful decision making about which criteria might be valid and useful for profiling violent behavior in general and are still so for violent terrorism. Third, he asserts that "... there is little existing evidence supporting the non-trivial validity of any individual risk factors for terrorism ...." (Readers might at this point wonder who are all those terrorism experts discussing such putative factors on television interviews, at public hearings, and, most influentially, on crime shows focusing on terrorism.) Finally, I read Monahan to conclude with something quite pessimistic. To validate some profiling instrument, researchers would need access to known groups of terrorists and nonterrorists from the same population. Only one big problem here would be that even individuals who have engaged in terrorism may be quite different by the time they're accessed; those who will engage may be quite different before, during, and after; and only a few have been caught in the or right before it (e.g., a few Palestinian suicide bombers caught right before the act in Israel) and seem to have been or be available—with an accompanying challenge for the use of inferential statistics.

Of the six main approaches to *risk assessment,* or predictive profiling, described by Monahan (2012), then, all have significant problems, and the reasons for this will become apparent for those who read Chapter 4. Here are the five. *Unmodified clinical risk assessment* comprises the profiler selecting and weighting factors and arriving at some estimate, all of which may be different for different individuals studied. *Modified clinical assessment* involves the use of some formal list of factors, and all may be used, but *how* they are and should be weighted for a specific individual may remain quite ambiguous. *Structured professional judgment* involves a formal list of factors and a way to weight each individually, but not whether some factors should be weighted more or less than others and whether or how one should sum the contributions of each to some overall estimate. *Modified actuarial risk assessment* involves a formal list and rules for weighting and combining weightings of the relevant factors, but there's still room for some more subjective judgment about unusual events and an unusual event of interest for a specific case. *Unmodified actuarial risk assessment—* that includes everything described in the modified version but proscribes more subjective judgment—is often thought to be the gold standard for individual risk assessment, but at the time of my writing this book there's nothing specific for terrorism.

Monahan correctly points out that (1) there's no current research that systematically compares these five approaches—again, there's apparently no data for the sixth approach—and (2) (citing Kroner, Mills, & Reddon, 2005) the validities of the existing actuarial approaches related to violent behavior often are similar—because they may all involve factors like criminal history, "irresponsible lifestyle," psychopathy and criminal attitudes, and substance abuse-related problems. These factors are taken from more generic crime behaviors that may have little to do with many types of contemporary terrorism. These conclusions underline the concerns of Meehl (1954), Dawes (1994), and Faust (2012) that seem to still apply to any claims of valid and useful profiling.

The fifth study meets the second importance criterion. Snook et al. (2007), the lead author of whom was a psychologist working at the Memorial University of Newfoundland, state they were motivated by what they claim was the increasing use of "criminal profiling [CP]" in criminal investigations despite scant empirical evidence that it is "effective." (I take *effective* to be some combination of validity and utility.) Based on this motivation—itself a self-profiling assumption—they completed what they term a "narrative review" and a "2-part meta-analysis" of the published CP literature. A narrative review in this case seems to be analyzing the text of CP studies for implicit and explicit assumptions, inferences, and logic. (I read this as Snook et al. applying their own versions of common sense to the text of the studies—an interesting state of affairs given their finding that the CP literature rests largely on commonsense justifications. How many *common senses* are there?)

Results from the first meta-analysis suggested that "self-labeled profiler/ experienced-investigator groups" did not outperform various comparison groups in predicting various offenders' cognitive processes, physical attributes, actual behavioral violations, social habits, or history, although they were marginally better at predicting "overall offender characteristics." (Those "self-labeled profiler/experienced-investigator groups" are, once again, those folks *experting* through the mass and entertainment media including the pitching of educational products to rid the world of the statistically deviant. Am I an expert? I submit to readers that I view myself only as a lifetime student, but perhaps I communicate this because I have access to other profiling-independent revenue streams to support my version of the *good life*. And hoping that the reader will tolerate one further tangential remark, the vagaries of *expert* versus *student* and the material and psychological strivings of those seeking a certain expert status and of those bestowing it are deftly described in the American author Herman Melville's (1996) description of how one attains and loses literary fame, *Pierre or the Ambiguities*.)

Results of Snook et al.'s (2007) second meta-analysis suggested that self-labeled profilers were not significantly better at predicting various behavioral violations but outperformed comparison groups when predicting "overall offender characteristics," cognitive processes, physical attributes, social history, and habits. I read this to mean that the experts might do better with whether someone has freckles than whether that someone has strangled somebody. If freckles become a threat to humankind, this may reap some reward.

The sixth study, by Kocsis (2003), an Australian psychologist whose writings I have read and much appreciated, is somewhat long in the tooth, but I am advocating that much more work like it needs to be done. I also view it as a mini-meta-evaluation, as it attempted to help answer the question of what areas of expertise, such as skills, knowledge, and aptitudes, might lead profilers to be most accurate—which presumes that there's some accuracy toward which the skills and so on can be applied. Kocsis linked areas of expertise that might be associated with valid and useful profiling with a group of people *presumed* to possess or display each area. So for intuition, he identified a group of psychics. For highly logical and objective reasoning, he chose science undergraduates. (I hope it was the top half of the class from a good school.) For an understanding of the human mind, he chose psychologists. (Please spare me the gratuitous, if not ribald, humor. There's a 1962 film *Follow That Dream* starring Elvis Presley, who outwits a corrupt social worker emulating a psychologist in courtroom drama. And then there's the venal plaintiff attempting to emulate a psychologist in the 1947 film *Miracle on 34th Street*. Then again, maybe *emulating* is the problem, and the *real* psychologists are OK.)

But back to areas of expertise presumed linked to valid and useful profiling. For three different kinds of investigative experience, three different groups of law enforcement personnel were chosen varying in length and kind of professional experience. Along with yet a few other areas of expertise and groups allegedly exemplifying them including a group of profilers with actual profiling experience, a table of data was created depicting the profiling accuracy of the different groups for different types of profiling events. These events included physical characteristics of alleged perpetrators, the behaviors constituting a crime, and the social habits and history as well as cognitive responses of alleged perpetrators.

The good news for supporters of profiling and those wanting to believe in its validity and utility is that the profilers were more accurate than the other groups across the board. I want to point out that there are no indicators of statistical significance in the study, and the scores are standardized in a manner making it difficult—at least for me—to figure out how accurate in an absolute sense the profilers were. As well, Kocsis (2009) pointed out that while profilers may demonstrate high degrees of accuracy, they also may demonstrate high degrees of statistical variance—perhaps because there's so much variance in what it takes to self-identify or be identified as a profiler.

Also, the good news for undergraduate readers of this book is that the science students did second best overall with their greatest weakness in cognitive responses—an empathy issue for science students? The psychologists were third best overall with strength in physical characteristics and the biggest weakness in cognitive responses—maybe the psychologists embraced a radical behaviorist orientation (see Chapter 3).

Looking back at this and similar work, Kocsis (2006, 2009) concludes that profiling is most associated with understanding human behavior and applying logical and objective methods when interpreting case material. The reader may wonder whether such a conclusion begs the question of what contributes to valid profiling. And although there are issues that need to be addressed with the experimental methodology—to his credit, most noted by Kocsis himself—I advocate that ongoing professional accountability of profilers for the accuracy of the components of their profiles might be useful for rewarding and assigning profilers, if not for developing a knowledge base of validity and effectiveness advocated by Meehl (1954), Dawes (1994), and Faust (2012) (see Chapter 10).

A more recent study by Kocsis (2010) meets the significance criterion of being a meta-evaluation. It's also interesting because he critiques Snook et al.'s (2007) study for having reviewed and included studies in *their* meta-evaluation that were of poor quality and, thus, would potentially skew conclusions about profiling. He also critiques Snook et al. for (1) equating the work of police personnel in general with profilers—something Kocsis (2003) tried not to do in his work; (2) improperly accepting data from yet another, older study (Pinizzotto & Finkel, 1990) as applying to expert profilers; and (3) assuming researchers who are not involved in profiling or proving profiling advice are more objective in analyzing research data on profiling. (My view is that both profilers and nonprofiler researchers are mixed bags on types of subjectivity and objectivity manifested.)

Kocsis (2010) makes an interesting distinction with what he calls the *nomenclature illusion*. My reading of this distinction is that labeling the same profiling process with different names and different profiling processes with the same name can lead to artificial distinctions in the perceived credibility of these processes among scientists and others including readers of profiling and profiling-related books. It also can lead to hopeless complexities in carrying out meta-evaluations of profiling research.

In this book, I purposely am aggregating different labels with overlapping processes—for example, investigative psychology, psychological assessment, sociopsychological criminal profiling, crime scene analysis, behavioral evidence analysis, criminal profiling, crime action profiling, criminal investigative analysis, criminal actuarial profiling, geographic profiling (cf. Palermo & Kocsis, 2005)—as examples of a generic profiling process. But in all fairness, these different labels often denote somewhat different specific processes and profiling goals. For example, *criminal profiling* may involve making predictions about the probable perpetrator of a crime based on collected or assumed behaviors exhibited at a crime (Kocsis, 2009), while criminal actuarial profiling may involve developing aggregated characteristics—I would call them internal and external events—describing a type of person who usually engages in a specific type of crime. This is ultimately an empirical question that can be resolved with careful operational definitions of labels that currently are inconsistently defined and used in scientific and popular literature.

Kocsis's (2010) overall conclusion is that caution is warranted in using profiling, that its knowledge bases needs to be further developed, that integration of sound studies from multiple profiling traditions would be most valuable, and that researchers need to carry out studies with significant ecological validity—focusing on the kinds of people and situations most proximal to real profiling in the real world. These conclusions also are supported by Alison et al.'s (2003) meta-evaluation, who found that for 21 actual investigative profiles developed by "experts," a significant majority of inferences about the characteristics of perpetrators was *not* supported by tangible and relevant evidence.

Saks and Koehler (2005) published an article that meets all three criteria—based on analysis of others' data and treated in a clever fashion. They clearly identified problems not just with profiling but with many examples of alleged forensic knowledge applied in courts. They specify the basic challenges—almost all involving a lack of adequate data—when asserting that some indicator or indicators can uniquely identify person as intending, committing, or having committed some behavior of interest—what the authors call *discernible uniqueness*. The same applies to some indicator or indicators identifying small homogeneous groupings of such people. Indicators of most interest to profilers would include characteristics of hair, bullets, handwriting, footprints, bite marks, and fingerprints. Many of these indicators and characteristics are often thoughts of as more reliable, valid, and useful in legal adjudication than psychological characteristics. Yet they're found wanting, a conclusion that should render unsurprising recent conclusions from the Defense Science Board (2012) that "There is no silver bullet to stop ALL targeted violence" (p.2) and that "There is no effective formula for predicting violent behavior with any degree of accuracy" (p. 2). (With what I consider to be an unfortunate bias and hope for physical explanations, this report also posited that "Over the long-term, screening technology related to biomarkers [from the neurosciences and genomics] has potential" (p.2).)

The authors' dramatic empirical findings are based on wrongful convictions in 86 cases wherein DNA analysis was employed as a primary ground truth that the individual convicted should not have been. Representative findings show that eyewitness testimony contributed to wrongful conviction in 71% of these cases, false confessions in 17%, police and prosecutorial misconduct combined in 72%, and false/misleading testimony by forensic scientists in 27%. Saks and Koehler's article suggests that in addition to the reliability and validity issues of indicators, adjudicative process issues further complicate the quest for prediction, post-diction, and peri-diction. This is even more the case in that once salient information like false confessions are introduced into an adjudicative process, the information from such confessions contaminate choices on what other information will then be collected and how already collected information will be interpreted and re-interpreted (Kassim, 2012)). The most significant contamination encompasses confirmation biases and corroboration inflation making the world conform even more to one in which the false confession is true and the true false.

In another study, a report sponsored by the Office of the Secretary of Defense and developed by the MITRE Corporation (JASON Program Office, October, 2009) that meets the first and third importance criteria, expectations for profiling are much more modest, even pessimistic. This may be because the events of event interest presumably occur at a much lower frequency even if with a much higher probable impact if successfully accomplished, viz., terrorism through weapons of mass destruction and other events labeled as rare (WMD-T). For these rare events there are little, if any, historical data from which to establish profiling validity, unless readers might be predisposed to make huge leaps of generalization and faith—greater than anything the 19th-century Danish philosopher Søren Kierkegaard might have advocated even in the dreaded leap toward truth faith in God—among various terrorist acts or yet other statistically deviant acts.

JASON—not the individual associated with the Argonauts and Medea, although this individual may have been the source of the name, and not the character associated with the *Friday the 13th* horror film series, but a group of highly esteemed scientists who are not formally affiliated with the U.S. government but who advise it on scientific and technology issues usually with security implication—concluded that it is not possible to validate predictive models of rare events perpetrated by humans and that one should not rely on unvalidated models for important decisions. JASON also concluded that collaborative research would probably not contribute to profiling validity, not because there's lack of collaboration among researchers but because there are problems coming up with appropriate metrics—units of measurement and so on. Moreover, JASON warned of the tendency to engage in premature development of profiling models without appropriate data. Finally, JASON could not differentiate levels of profiling expertise between people with significant experience with events of interest (WMD-T) and academics bringing analytic expertise to these events of interest. My conclusion after reading this study is that profiling psychological, behavioral, and social events may be hopelessly more complicated than profiling physical phenomena whether prediction, post-diction, peri-diction, understanding, or influence is the desired endpoint.

Whether prestigious journal, meta-evaluation, or clever thought experiment, empirical study, or application of logic, the results of research studies suggest that profiling is less than the general public and some experts seem to think. (See Bloom, 1999, 2001, 2003a, 2003b, 2010a, 2010b for theoretical support of this conclusion and Salfati, 2011 for a contrarian opinion.) Is this only because people have a need to believe in profiling to ward off the terror of mortality, have unknowingly substituted hyperreality for reality, or have placed positive depictions of profiling from mass media within themselves as suggested in the preface? Or maybe the financial, psychological, and social benefits for well-marketed profilers stand in the way of working toward reinforcing a type of false consciousness on the general public and others. An alternative perspective would be that the sorts of research studies carried out on profiling have been inappropriate for its subject matter. As I intimate in Chapter 4, the sorts of epistemological and methodological approaches so far applied to profiling may be much more valuable for the physical and life sciences than the psychological, behavioral, and social. In any case, profiling *is* practiced and is used to help arrive at important decisions. The rest of this chapter as well as Chapters 3 and 4 provide additional information on the challenges of profiling. Then Chapters 5 and 6 describe the essential tasks of profiling regardless of theoretical and practical approaches and techniques. Chapters 7 through 9 provide examples of what go into the completion of these essential tasks for events of interest bearing on terrorism, espionage, and profiling. Chapter 10 points the way toward profiling's future. All the while, like the story of the sword of Damocles as described by Cicero in his *Tusculan Disputations* (1927/45 BCE), the unfinished business of research support for profiling validity and utility hangs over the whole enterprise. Ironically, Cicero attributes the story to an incorrect tyrant—Dionysius I, not Dionysius II. What misattributions are profilers making?

I now ask readers to engage in LO 2.1 to *dec* at least four main findings on the validity and utility of profiling based on scientific research studies. Please do this in the context of a film fragment from *The Unknown* (Thalberg & Browning, 1927). In this film, a carnival knife thrower, Alonzo the Armless (Lon Chaney), amazes the crowds by throwing knives and shooting a rifle with his feet at Nanon (Joan Crawford), a scantily clad female target. Unbeknownst to her, he actually has arms kept tightly bound to his torso. Nanon cannot bear to have men touch her with their arms and hands, so she feels comfortable with Alonzo, who is in love with her. Alonzo blackmails a surgeon to amputate both his arms so that he can win the love of Nanon. When he returns from the surgery to claim her, he finds that she has been able to "cure" herself with the help of Malabar (Norman Kerry), the circus strongman. I find the film fragment extraordinary, with Nanon showing her happiness to Alonzo by letting Malabar put his hands all over her and Alonzo showing *his happiness* by laughing in feigned joy—or is it hysterical or insane laughter having nothing to do with joy? Given profiling's issues with validity and utility, how does one identify indicators of how people really feel—events associated with events of interest?

2.2　SOCIAL DEVIANCY

Although I have already noted that profiling can be applied to crafting linkages between and among any events and some event of interest, of most interest to the general public and most experts are events that are socially deviant. Events are ascribed as socially deviant in two main ways—as statistically uncommon and as intrinsically bad. As to the statistically uncommon, there's much more interest in the bad than the good. Thus defining *bad* becomes a paramount enterprise. (I qualify this last statement by noting there has been a move within scientific psychology in recent years toward positive psychology—that is, the study of what is good as opposed to bad (Seligman et al., 2005). This move has not yet significantly affected the theory and practice of profiling, however.)

Bad may refer to what's illegal. However, some things that are legal may still be bad at least to some people—for example, license to discriminate *against* people of a specific ethnic group as long as that group is not one's own. And some things that are illegal, by the federal government, may not be considered bad by at least some people including state and local officials—for example, using marijuana for medicinal purposes. *Bad* may refer to what's unethical or immoral, but people often differ even within themselves through time about how to define these terms and what they are based on. *Bad* may refer to some inferred intrinsic badness or presumed bad consequence—both obviously unhelpful and circular in reasoning—leading to stigmatization of specific events and the individuals alleged to have caused them. Finally, *bad* may refer to transgression of rules, regulations, expectations, and custom that may transcend legality but threaten balances of political power and who holds and wields it. It's to some people's advantage for themselves and others to think, feel, be motivated, and behavior in certain ways and not others. Depending on what kind of *bad* is at issue, profilers might find constraints on what hypotheses about individuals and situations will be believed or at least accepted by others inside and outside the scientific, legal, and entertainment communities.

The same sorts of constraints on profilers relate to social and cultural beliefs about the etiology of the *bad*—that is, how did the bad get that way? Given an event of interest is a thought, feeling, motivation, or behavior, should profilers be looking for other events that may link to it as (1) a characteristic of an individual, e.g., some psychopathology; (2) the social context, such as a breakdown in neighborhood support for law-abiding behavior or plentiful opportunities for the individual to copy *bad* behavior from role models in the neighborhood or some cyber-environment; (3) some functional aspect of individual psychology, such as the desired consequences of the event of interest for the individual; or (4) intentional political authority via direct external coercion or via the more elegant shaping of an individual—the latter so that there's self-coercion to engage or not engage in events of interest and what may be associated with them? Profilers' own beliefs that may transcend research findings and concurrently shape interpretation of these findings can lead to a self-censorship of what is allowable to believe about the absence or presence of *bad* events and corresponding events associated with them.

In essence, profilers may be walking around with their own versions of Dante's *Inferno*. According to Dante, being indifferent to moral and ethical issues earned one a place in hell but in many ways was the least sinful in the eyes of God. The lustful and wrathful were perceived as progressively more sinful. Flatterers even more so, but not as much as thieves. The worst—Cassius, Judas, and Brutus—were traitors. I believe that profilers each have their own version of circles of hell—some consciously, some not—affecting the kinds of events chosen to be investigated and to be more likely believed in regardless of the findings of research.

In fact, profiling may actually lead to social deviancy. For example, Adler (2001) argued that laws against child pornography increase an objectifying gaze onto children—that is, reinforcing the notion that children are sexual objects even as it proscribes looking at them that way—and thus further sexualizes them. In the same way, profiles of victims and of crime scenes reinforce the notion that certain people and situations are imbued with a potential to be used as a vehicle for some crime and lead to a higher probability of the very crimes that profiling is intended to help deter or manage for some larger public benefit.

Thus, the profiling of social deviancy poses several challenges. The same event of interest—for example, external behavior—may be construed as deviant or not by the same or different people at the same or different points in time. Explanations for deviancy and its putative causes supported by political authorities may constrain profiling options. The distribution of profiles of various deviancies whether from individuals or situations may increase not only their deviancies but also the probability that they occur.

There are two last challenges that have so far not been mentioned in this section. First, the cultural consumerism contributing to the mass fascination with the profiling of deviancy may shape profilers' decision making and motives. Profilers' may develop profiles with events associated with the event of interest that are themselves more deviant, as this may sell better to others and to other profilers based on the buy-in to profiling's mass depictions containing the bizarre and grotesque. Second, as *bad* may be caused by or lead to good, and good to bad, so too deviancy with the *normal*. An analogy would be how the objective qualities of stressors, for example, the physical impact of improvised explosive devices (IEDs) or the sight of one's comrades in arms being mutilated, are associated with myriad subjective construals and with positive and negative outcomes varying from anxiety, depression, substance abuse, and suicide to psychological growth experiences reinforcing hardiness and rock-solid character (Weiss, 2010).

A literary example of this last point is the life of the 19th-century Swedish playwright, painter, photographer, musician, and alchemist August Strindberg. First, read a quote from one of his autobiographies (Strindberg, 1913/1886) on his childhood. "Hungry and afraid, afraid of the dark, of spankings...afraid of being in the way... of being hit by his brothers, slapped by the maids … caned by his father and birched by his mother...he could do nothing without doing wrong … the safest things was simply not to move …. It had effectively been dinned into him that he had no right to exist …." And thus the beginnings of a creative genius, not a serial murderer nor chronic psychiatric inpatient.

I now ask readers to engage in LO 2.2 to *dec* at least four main challenges in profiling socially deviant events of interest. Please do this in the context of a film fragment from *Rebel Without a Cause* (Weisbart & Ray, 1955). The star of the film, James Dean, plays Jim Stark, whom some might call a sensitive *juvenile delinquent.* In the fragment, he may seem to have a better idea of what is right and wrong and what to do about it than his parents played by Jim Backus and Ann Doran. At issue is a *chickie run,* actually a generic conflict (chicken game) from game theory, wherein both antagonists prefer not to give in, but the worst possible outcome is when neither gives in. In the film, Jim and his rival Buzz race stolen cars toward the edge of the cliff. Buzz gets his leather jacket sleeve caught on his inside door handle and goes over the cliff, while Jim bails out in time. What to do about Buzz's death is the focus of the argument in the film fragment.

2.3 LESSONS FROM LITERARY CRITICISM AND HERMENEUTICS

Another challenge in documenting the validity of profiling relates to *where* the profiler should be looking for validity. Although there are choices of profiling language (see Chapter 3) and many other options bearing on basic epistemological approaches, argumentation methods, heuristics of social cognition, statistical reasoning, deception analysis, interdisciplinary close reading, and the profilers' political environment (for all of this, see Chapter 4), there are four overarching choices popularized by the American literary critic Morris Abrams (1953) and the French philosopher of hermeneutics Paul Ricoeur (1981). (Remember, hermeneutics is the study of the interpretation of text.)

The first is an *expressive* choice. It suggests that an individual's life is like an artistic work and that artistic work is an expression of the artist—the individual. All aspects of the individual—thoughts, feelings, motivations, and behaviors—constitute an artistic work (or a text) and are expressions of yet other events within the individual. One might also assert that some event of interest is associated with the expression of salient characteristics of some *situation*. The focus in either case is on the expressions from the assumed agent, person or situation. In essence, the expressive choice is self-recursive in that it repeats the process of what lies behind an event and then what behind this. Another way of communicating this is that there's more than an association between events and these with an event of interest—there's also a sharing of expressed meaning. A common profiling interpretation might be that the deepness of a knife wound in a corpse might be an expression of the perpetrator's rage—especially when it's not necessarily the most efficient way to effect a murder. Or the polyrhythmic sensations of loud drumming, the body heat of masses of people dancing in an enclosed space, and the stroboscopic flashing of lights are expressed by the polymorphous sexuality of a rave event of interest.

The second is a *pragmatic* choice. It suggests that whatever an alleged perpetrator might have done, the meaning behind it is constituted by the effect of what has been done on us. In a case of espionage, how the case strikes us—cognitive, emotional, motivations, and behavioral effects *on us*—is that case's meaning. It's been my observation that many profilers seek to develop profiles based on an *expressive* choice, but underlying this is a *pragmatic* choice. It's as if there's a social consensus that a perpetrator's acts must meaning something about the perpetrator, and the profiler must turn in such a product even if this is actually a cover for what it means for the profiler. So nasty guy must be behind an act that strikes us as nasty.

The third is an *objective* choice. Various internal and external events of an individual or of a situation—the external events of a situation would be exemplified by those of *other* situations or those of people—have their own meaning irrespective of anything about that individual or situation. This seemingly contradictory statement denotes that (1) events by their very structure bear meaning without any necessary relationship with anything else and that (2) events and their associations with other events—please remember that any event may become an event of interest depending on social needs and the referral question posed to profilers—also bear meaning without any concerns for the *expressive* and *pragmatic* choices already described. It's as if the individual is as Shakespeare wrote in *Macbeth* (1607), a poor player, a puppet strutting on some stage in some theater to some audience. The audience will persist in expressive and pragmatic choices but to understand the player and puppet one must seek the holy grail from its *playerness* and *puppetness*. Or it's as if the substance and dynamics of the situation itself—perhaps the magic environment of Shakespeare's *A Midsummer Night's Dream* (1596)—not the players in it tell the real story. This is an uncommon approach in today's profiling, and I'm not sure why. It would seem to depend on huge amounts of statistically analyzed empirical data or some trans-scientific intuitive knowing, neither of which seems to be in our profiling world today. This it might seem to yield a threatening picture of our constraints on knowing and difficulties in legal adjudication including admissibility of profiling data. In theories of literary criticism bearing on attempts to interpret text, this approach has been called the *new criticism,* and the text it seeks to interpret including descriptions of human behavior and of situations is viewed as a self-contained, self-referential aesthetic object. Aren't we all self-contained and self-referential to a degree, even if not especially aesthetic except when we dress up?

The fourth is a *mimetic* choice. Just as a work of art might or its creator or audience might all attempt to get at how the world really is, the events and events of interest stemming from an individual or situation are assumed to contain or represent meaning about the wider world—often enough, some eternal conflict between good and evil or other timeless dichotomy. But this would not necessarily be an expression of the individual's perceptions of the world. In fact, in Ricoeur's (1981) work, there often is tension between what someone intended to express by effecting various events and what the meaning of the events turns out to be. Most often with the mimetic, people and situations are vehicles or vessels for larger trends and phenomena that might even be unknowable to profilers and the rest of us.

Abrams's (1953) book *The Mirror and the Lamp* is so titled because these four approaches can be collapsed as follows. They work either as (1) a *mirror* and reflect to various degrees of accuracy individuals, situations, and those larger trends and phenomena of the world or (2) a lamp and help us see via light what otherwise would be dark—even what may have been reflected mirror-like but with more or less light seem to be different than first perceived. Profiling may have both consequences, but one is never sure. As Ricoeur (1970) wrote, "Hermeneutics seems to me to be animated by this double motivation: willingness to suspect, willingness to listen; vow of rigor, vow of obedience" (p. 27). Transposed to profiling, readers are encouraged to march on bravely in their tasks at supporting the validity and utility of a profile with a concurrent double motivation of believing and suspending belief. Or as Beckett ended *The Unammable* (1978), "You must go on, I can't go on, I'll go on."

As a concrete example of the abstract material thus far, I offer what the French literary critic Gustave Lanson popularized as an *explication de texte* applied to something as culturally suspect as a fragment of early rock and roll, *Chantilly Lace* (1958). Near the end of the first minute of the song, the crooner, the Big Bopper, seems to be on the phone with a girl attempting to engage in what psychologists call *affiliation behavior.* All we hear is his end of the conversation. "What's that baby? … But … but … but … oh honey … but … ok baby, you know what I like." And near the end of the second minute, "Pick you up at eight? … And don't be late? … But baby I ain't got no money honey … ha ha ha ha ha … you know what I like." What about what *he's* saying leads us to interpolate what *she's* saying? This is a profiling exercise wherein attaining validity and utility is made even more difficult by the fact that she' not saying anything at all—although rock scholars may point out that Jayne Mansfield answers him 8 years later in an even more sorry cultural product, *That Makes It* (1966), wherein we only hear her and must assume *she's* talking to *him.* In an *expressive* choice, we listen and infer about the Big Bopper's intentions. In a *pragmatic* choice, how the song makes us feel—what would we be feeling if we were singing like this—is where we get out interpretation In an *objective* choice, the song itself somehow yields the meaning through its various characteristics—sounds of a saxophone might suggest some lewd intent. In a mimetic choice, what we hear somehow characterizes the world—maybe of the mindlessness of boy chasing girl chasing boy, the *corso e recorso* (self-repeating circle of events) of the 17th- and 18th-century Italian philosopher Giambatista Vico. So back to Beckett (1978): "You must go on, I can't go on, I'll go on."

I now ask readers to engage in LO 2.3 to *dec* the four main hermeneutic approaches to profiling. Please do this in the context of a film fragment from *All About Eve* (Zanuck & Mankiewicz, 1950). And you have many choices. You may focus on Bette Davis playing Margo Channing whose career and life may have seen better days and on her line "Fasten your seat belts. It's going to be a bumpy night." Or on Anne Baxter playing Eve Harrington whose career and life seem to be on the way up. Or on Marilyn Monroe playing Miss Harrington and her quote "Why do they always look like unhappy rabbits?" (Monroe's cameo is my favorite because she's showing her talent for comedy and playing against what became her common public stereotype as a *sex bomb*.) While the film is titled *All About Eve*, knowing Eve without the context of the others or the structure and dynamics of common social situations may not be possible.

3 Challenges of Profiling
What Is Being Profiled?

3.1 LANGUAGES OF PROFILING

Even profilers disavowing any theoretical affiliation or theory itself use language to think (actually my inference is that they think, and think in this manner, as thinking is unobservable) and communicate. And theoretical assumptions permeate language. What follows are five different languages of profiling, their assumptions about human psychology, and how—when salient—the psychology interacts with biological and social events. The goal for readers is to understand the languages outlined herein and how they might be applied to profiling. Whether the concepts and theories are true in some absolute sense is largely irrelevant. What *is* relevant is how useful they are in navigating social life in general and in the profiling quests for prediction, post-diction, peri-diction, understanding, and influence. As American psychologist Brad Piekkola (2011) wrote, "The language for personality need not be consistent with personality." That is, whatever may be happening may be at least partially inaccessible to language in that language may be both a knowledge facilitator and constraint. This could bring readers to consult philosophical skeptics from the Greek Gorgias to the French Jacques Derrida as part of profiling training. And I do advocate for philosophical training for profilers in Chapter 10.

To further show my ambivalence with language as a vehicle to knowledge even as I think about and write this book with language, I offer a quote from the Belgian author Luc Sante (2012) in his review of an edited volume of the letters of the Beat Generation icon William S. Burroughs—"He [Burroughs] believed that language was a virus that had achieved equilibrium with its human host, and that 'blocks' of language and thought enforced convention, making it necessary to find techniques … to break the patterns" (p. 21).

3.1.1 PSYCHODYNAMIC LANGUAGE

Let's begin with a look at "Closer" (1994), a song written by Trent Reznor and performed by Nine Inch Nails. I'm not sure who he may be thinking of, but that someone may be in for some extreme loving—some mixture of sex and violence. That someone is going to be violated, desecrated, penetrated, and treated like an animal. The insides of this someone are to be loved as if to the point of evisceration. Whomever Reznor may be taking on—the role(s) of sexual aggressor and object of aggression—are going to be radically transformed in body and soul. To use the parlance of both sadomasochism and some homosexual subcultures, we have a top (penetrator) and bottom (penetrated). But the more they are involved, the more one segues into the other. Each controls the other, even as each loses control. And communion with God may be the result. Do you wish to line up as a new convert to this religion? The sex, violence, and extreme intensity of the text to my mind magnified by the beat behind the lyrics are suggestive of the first profiling language and its implication beyond abstract conceptualization.

This language has been popularized by Sigmund Freud (1986/1886–1939) and his disciples. And I'm not using the term *disciples* loosely. In Spring 1919, Freud gave a gold ring to the small number of those whom he believed were his closest colleagues and called the group the Secret Committee (Grosskurth, 1991). There are six colleagues who along with Freud are seen in a photograph of the committee available through Psychoanalytic Electronic Publishing (2012). I've long had three reactions to the photograph. First, Freud hoped to stack the committee to 12 to emulate Jesus and his disciples. Second, this was a marriage of sorts with many ironic implications for someone whose view of healthy personality was founded on what he termed a genital stage of heterosexuality reached through resolving a much earlier attraction for one's mother, resentment toward one's father, and an even earlier penchant for what he termed *polymorphous perversity*. Third, I am curious as to whether in this *marriage* the disciples are multiple wives for Freud, Freud is the mother or mother substitute for the disciples, or the whole lot is a band of brothers united through killing some primal father or sharing some primal mother. In any case, I have studied the purest of psychodynamic writings, termed *classical psychoanalysis*, for many years without becoming a disciple, acolyte, significant other, or camp follower and without grabbing even a brass ring.

Given that Freud's psychodynamic writings stretch over about 40 years—usually encompassing the late 1890s right up to his death in 1939 and always depending on how one identifies what is termed *psychodynamic*—the meaning of his most common concepts is less than certain. Ironically, even the most vehement critics of everything Freudian unwittingly or otherwise may think in a Freudian manner, because his work and that of those working in his tradition have so permeated Western cultures. And this is the case, even as these critics rightly assert that according to common scientific tenets little of psychodynamic note has been validated. (The counter of psychodynamic supporters, of course, is that common scientific tenets often are not relevant here. And the counter to this is that surely one must rely on more than just the assertion of some expert. So the world turns.)

So what follows are the most relevant psychodynamic constructs for profiling. But I first will add here that I've already used the descriptor *Western* several times and wish to underline that my take on profiling as a whole and on its languages specifically is grossly underinformed by Eastern and other non-Western traditions. This is an egregious failing on my part, one I share with colleagues and associates and one I hope will be rectified by future generations of thinkers and writers about profiling. At issue are not only profiling approaches but the who, what, where, when, why, and how of profiling. So, back to psychodynamics.

In *psychodynamic, psycho-* denotes a psyche or mind, while -*dynamic* characterizes something as active, with varying degrees of energy, as having varying forces, pressures, aims, or presumed consequences that may be in conflict. Although psychodynamic was similarly used by the English philosopher G. H. Lewes at least as far back as 1874 (OED, 2012) and, as we'll see, the Greek philosopher Plato (2008/380 BCE) posited something very similar in *The Republic* over 2,000 years earlier, Freud popularized this approach to the mind that has been used by 20th- and 21st-century profilers.

Again, my contention is that even profilers who claim to focus only on *behavior* and not *mind* are employing *their* psychodynamic minds in arriving at and acting on their claims and working with the minds of people they interview, interrogate, and talk with to obtain behavioral information. The profiling implications of psychodynamic are that an individual can change with time, may always be changing, or may be in the throes of various forces continuously changing in content and intensity. A challenge is to surmise what combination of intrinsic *internal* variability interacting with various *external* events leads to change associated with an event of interest. On the other hand, a profiler also may jettison the construct of a mind and just keep the assumptions about dynamics as characterizing the potentialities of human behavior or of situations. (I believe it's significant that major theorists in a very different field—economics—also assert that dynamics are crucial in profiling economic moments and phases with huge impact on human functioning, such as the *self-regulatory forces* of the Scottish Adam Smith, the *class conflict* of Karl Marx, and the *creative destruction* of the Austrian Joseph Schumpeter.)

The terms *structural* and *economic* delineate the dynamic possibilities. Following Plato and like many other psychological theorists, Freud most often posited the mind as having three *structures*. The first is a problem-solving, executive managing, mostly rational, logical, and conscious structure. The Latin term from Freud's German text now incorporated into the English language is the *ego*. By *logical*, I mean in the sense of common deductive, inductive, quantitative, modal, and abductive logics: *deductive* as in the "if event X, then event Y"; *inductive* as in arriving at a general conclusion about event *Y* based on specific examples *X1, X2,* through *XN* of that event *Y*; *quantitative* as in making valid statements on *all, some,* or *none* of various events that may or may not be related; *modal* as in making valid statements about the *necessity, possibility,* or *impossibility* of various events; *abductive* as in giving it one's best shot based on various thoughts and feelings about some event. Aware or unaware, profilers are using these five logics and perhaps others permeating through explanations of how events are associated with an event of interest. Chapter 4 provides specific examples and comments on common logics.

Profilers might use concepts identical or similar to this first structure, the ego, in declaring whether some event of interest occurred by mistake. Perhaps, appropriate attention to security procedures was not followed and this led or may have led to a pile of classified information being taken home—wittingly or unwittingly. Perhaps one lost a proprietary formula as opposed to giving it to a competitor.

The second structure, again from the Latin of the German text to English, the *id*, pertains to what is mostly irrational, illogical, instinctual, unconscious (of which we can't be aware at all or can be only with great difficulty or fortuitous serendipity), without reason or, instead, with a very peculiar kind of reason. (The more I've thought about terms such as *rationality, reason, logic,* and their alleged opposites, the less I'm sure what these and their alleged opposites mean. A deep but leisurely study of the OED might suggest all involve applying some inferred guiding principle or process of the mind that leads to some desired end or valid judgment. I then think of the folks who claim to be attempting to do this and may actually be doing this—folks who end up being detained, incarcerated, tortured, and murdered at the hands of formal political or informal social authority, that is, by their alleged peers or formally constituted superiors for allegedly not doing what they are doing or doing what they are not doing. French psychoanalyst Jacques Lacan (2006/1953–1981) advocated that the *unconscious*—what Freud equated at times with the irrational and illogical and at other times with easily understood sexual and aggressive instincts—was just as rational and logical, just different kinds with a language all its own. The id is largely of a sexual and violent nature, but, to Lacan, what Freud termed the unconscious part of the id—if one assumes all the id is not unconscious—is really something about which we are always experiencing a loss but aren't aware that we are and something for which we unknowingly launch all sorts of activities in an attempt to understand and experience what we never can. Lacan calls this something the *imaginary.*

Why is this distinction so important for profilers? Profilers often come up with assumptions about hard-to-control and hard-to-understand needs, desires, and motives of which an individual may or may not be aware. Whether they are composed of and fueled by sexual and aggressive content needing to be fed or by some sense of loss, some imaginary, needing to be filled may have quite a bit to do with identifying what may increase, decrease, or maintain future events of interest. Especially in Lacan's case, an individual may be involved in extremely (socially) deviant behavior in an effort to fill an emptiness through sex, drugs, radical changes in life, commitment to God or a political ideology, abandoning oneself to a revered mentor, self-medication through exercise, terrorism, espionage, or deception. In Freud's case, an individual may ultimately be a two-trick pony—which is fine, if that's all the tricks there are.

A third structure of the mind according to Freud relates to morals, ethics, and conscience. The Latin term from Freud's German text incorporated into English is the *superego.* Often the superego is associated with one's upbringing; less often one seizes control of the development of this structure and becomes one's own person—even if seizing control may be the result of one's upbringing. But I read Freud as intending the superego along with the ego and id to interpenetrate, interrelate, forming alliances and breaking them in immortal combat. Without the right balance of structures, the reality of and potential for life success as defined by each individual or by various societies, micro-societies, groups of people, and friends and associates may be low, socially deviant, defined in a peculiar fashion, or outwardly normative but inwardly precarious.

Sometimes I think that the association of balance of structures with success or some positive normality or normativeness—whether by Freud or other psychodynamicists—is an implicit misapplication of Aristotle's Golden Mean. Aristotle (1999) seems to suggest that only a minority of people live a life of balance resulting in living a life of excellence according to basic virtues. What's at issue for psychodynamicists and profilers is whether balance leads to being part of the herd or going a more unusual way—and whether this unusual way is desirable or undesirable. And

Plato's description from *The Republic*, I believe, is more evocative of this point with a three-structured mind depicted as a charioteer (something like the ego) attempting to steer a course by controlling both a black horse (something like the id) and a white horse (something like the superego). Without the appropriate skill and balance, the mind may be headed far off the appropriate path or for a fall.

Another construct of psychodynamic language, the *economic,* relates to the amount of energy each of the three structures may have at any moment and is predictive of which combinations of the three structures are in precarious control. The profiler, then, has some ready-made inferences over what sorts of internal events might lead to an event of interest. These would include mixtures of sexual and violent instincts that are partially out-of-control, hopeless attempts to get to some ineffable *somewhere* to fill an ineffable emptiness, excessive strivings to meet an impossibly high standard of good, and rigorously analytic and emotion-free approaches to manipulating people as candidates for associations with events of interest. Again, given that the three structures are interdependent, even standards, reason, and logic may be permeated to a degree with instinct. I often think here of examples like causing severe punishment in the alleged name of the good or employing brilliant and incisive analysis to cut someone down.

Freud also uses the term *genetic* referring to a series of developmental stages and challenges most people pass through, that is, one's history is important; the child is father/mother to the man/woman. (Later on, genetic will take on another meaning, referring to a molecular unity of heredity of a living organism, viz., stretches of DNA and RNA that code for components of proteins, and chains of RNA that serve a biological function in living organisms. But now back to Freud.) Freud emphasizes a foundation of psychosexual gratification wherein the amount of stimulation, control, and sensation of physical areas like the mouth, sphincters and anus, and genitals early in our lives lead to predictable psychological themes and adult character types. (I'm not sure whether the derision this idea receives from some commentators should count as its support or lack thereof.) A useful variant of this is the work of the German developmental psychologist Erik Erikson (1993/1950) identifying a sequence of not psychosexual but psychological challenges most people pass through, again with predictable consequences dependent on whether the challenges are adequately negotiated.

Profilers may find psychological challenges, themes, and adult character types useful in helping to identify sources of socially deviant behavior like leading a life (1) of terrorism to resolve the need for a stable self-identity and a sense of order, (2) of espionage to feel one's life is one of achievement and praiseworthy (by one's self and one's handlers), and (3) of deception to satisfy a need for intimacy with others by rejecting it, thus forestalling any disappointment if someone does not deliver as one wishes. Maybe the sources go back to too much or too little physical stimulation of some body area long ago (Freud) or to still wrestling with a challenge of figuring out who one is (Erikson). Many Eastern physical strategies of enlightenment like yoga and some variations of kung fu are predicated on physical movements and postures that allegedly lead to psychological maintenance and change.

I'll now cover just three more groupings out of many psychodynamic terms useful for profilers. One grouping is *fear* and *anxiety.* According to Freud, *fear* may be a warning signal that something is wrong in the external world or with one's consciously experienced internal world needs to be resolved. Anxiety, however, is often *consciously* experienced but ultimately relates to the *unconscious* dynamics among the three competing mental structures (ego, id, and superego) as they affect an individual's internal and external events. A big problem for the profiled and profilers, however, is that it may not be obvious whether fear or anxiety is a motive force associated with an event of interest. Also, a superstructure of conscious reality based on fear may be balanced on a substructure of unconscious or at best partially conscious reality based on anxiety.

Another grouping is that of *defense mechanisms*. My reading of Freud is that these are unconscious processes leading to dynamic compromises among the three mental structures and their contents. The compromises are of expression, that is, how closely internal and external events, especially perceptual ones, mirror what actually sets them in motion. Why can't expression occur directly and completely accurately? Because this would be a threat and would generate anxiety if it occurred, thus the compromise. So some kinds and intensities of aggression are not directly expressed through bloodily killing someone but indirectly through carrying out root canals as a peridontist (*sublimation*); through sincere but incorrect rejection of the notion that aggression ever occurred (*denial*) wherein one is not feigning but believing the rejection; through expression toward someone or something different from what is actually the primary target like kicking the dog as opposed to eviscerating one's boss (*displacement*); or showing deep love for someone one hates (*reaction formation*).

For defense mechanisms to be operative, one actually has to be unaware of what *really* is going on. One really feels the love for the person one really hates and feels none of the latter. The biggest problem with this state of affairs is the assumption that there are many, many expressions that people apparently can't handle. It's one thing to not have the mental capacity to tap into or perceive certain mental events, if for no other reason than there may be too may to attend to at any one time. It's quite another thing to be shocked by these events if directly expressed—especially in a world with the most extremes experiences at our fingertips. (Can it really be the case that one can handle the latest article on the sexual abuse of young children but not that this might have happened to oneself? But somehow choosing to experience events coming from outside is deemed much less threatening than having access to the same stimuli from inside.)

The last psychodynamic grouping involves *relations*. Freud's contribution is the popularization of *transference*. *Transference* describes how we relate to people we meet based on their similarities and differences to people we've met earlier who have been emotionally significant in our lives in varying degrees. In essence, we transfer the past to the present so that the present resembles the past, and thus the present becomes a key to one's past or that of someone one may be perceiving. Profilers may find this useful in predicting, post-dicting, and peri-dicting situations wherein an individual has a life history of being the victim of one abusive relationship after another. Transference also helps answer the question, "Haven't I seen you somewhere before?" To some degree the answer is always yes.

Object relations—popularized by *neo-psychodynamicists* defined as theorists heavily influenced by Freud who then contribute elaborations or changes that they term innovations—studies how individuals view and relate to any people or things in their lives. Each person or thing in an individual's life as perceived by that individual is termed an *object*. My reading of object relations theory is that we perceive people and things not just in terms of their so-called objective or real characteristics but also in terms of images we carry that are based on intrinsic developmental factors interfacing with early experiences. So what we perceive are actually objects fused together out of the objective and real and these images. An object may be perceptually constituted as many components, such as good and bad, loving and mean, friendly or threatening, vibrant and deadened, just some components, or one component. In this last case, a person may be overly idealized as in the first blush of love, or a thing may be perceived as the exemplification of pure evil. People also differ in how dichotomous or varied the various components constituting some object may be. This has relevance for profilers in terms of how many perceptual possibilities a person has in viewing others and how some people have a very rigid and constrained perceptual set toward just some others, for example, people of a certain physical stature, skin color, or hairstyle.

Woe to someone who is or believes that he or she is romantically involved with a person accurately ascribed as manifesting a *borderline personality disorder*, because one feature of this psychopathological term is often viewing one's romantic partner alternatively with pure love and hate yet at other times as constituting multiple components of love, hate, and many additional components as well. An individual also perceives himself or herself as an object. So objects are relating to objects, and the same people and things may be perceived very differently by different people and by the same people at different times.

Object relations are often very primitive and even frightening early in life according to theorists like the Austrian psychoanalyst Melanie Klein (1987). Examples might include viewing a body part of a human object, like a mother's breast, as seeking to devour one thereby terminating one's very existence. Profilers might use this information in linking attempts both to join the military and law enforcement and to engage in various criminal enterprises. One interpretive approach uninformed by object relations might be to assume the individual has a single-minded purpose, and the military and law enforcement attempts were just vehicles to facilitate criminal intent. Another interpretive approach informed by object relations is that the individual has been struggling to create a situation wherein there's a capability to confront and be victorious over a very threatening world—whether through legal or illegal means is secondary. This last statement might be applied to the introduction to Chapter 2 on Mohamed Merah. Merah's challenge may have been to navigate within a world with components perceived as bad or evil, others as good and even holy—thus, the swings from supporting legally constituted authority to seeking to violate it.

Stemming from psychodynamic theory and research is another *relations* concept, *attachment*—as with all psychodynamic terms a tropic or figurative construct, not necessarily implying any correspondence to or reflection of an assumed objective reality. For example, Mary Ainsworth et al. (1978) collected data supporting at least three models of how a child may have established an ongoing emotional relationship, an attachment, to a parental figure. My reading of their work is that each model serves as a foundation for all other emotionally significant relationships—especially love relationships—including those occurring when the child becomes an adult and throughout life.

Ainsworth et al. labeled the first model *anxious-ambivalent*. Here the child–parent attachment is characterized by the parent being perceived by the child as inconsistent in managing that child's emotional needs and in doling out affection and attention, or punishment, in specific situations. (The child may perceive this inconsistency as applying just to him or her, to some other children, to all children, to most people, and so on.) This type of attachment is exemplified by the child becoming very upset when the parent leaves the room in the presence of another adult. (Upset is often defined by amounts of yelling, crying, and latching onto body parts of the parent.) The predicted adult relationship style with emotionally significant people including those making up one's love life would be characterized by jealousy, obsession with the object of one's affection, and very clinging and cloying behavior.

The second attachment model is labeled *avoidant*. Here the child–parent attachment is characterized by the parent being perceived by the child as not welcoming, even rejecting, attempts at reassurance, physical contact, and affection. This type of attachment can be exemplified by the child *not* becoming upset when the parent leaves the room in the presence of another adult and then ignoring the parent's return. As an adult, the individual might not even perceive many, if any, people as emotionally significant but instead might be perceived as distant, cold, and uninterested in close relationships. (Such an individual might make a great accountant, intelligence analyst, engineering specialist as opposed to manager, or other professional wherein personal relations are not primary.)

The third model is labeled *secure*. Here the child–parent attachment is characterized by the parent being perceived by the child as predictable, aware of the child's emotional needs, and nurturant and caring when appropriate. (Of course, it's the *when appropriate* that is difficult to implement, especially when there's a large disparity between how the child perceives and what might actually be appropriate in some ultimate sense.) This type of attachment can be exemplified by the child being initially upset when the parent leaves the room but being easily comforted by the remaining adult and happily acknowledging the parent upon the parent's return. Such individuals as adults often experience long, stable friendships and romantic relationships and view loving and emotionally close relationships as a significant part of life.

In conclusion, psychodynamic language seems to have permeated Western societies and cultures, even among people who oppose its relevance to human nature and its validity and utility for prediction, post-diction, peri-diction, understanding, and influencing human events. Profilers who knowingly or unknowingly adopt this language in their own choices of what data to collect, what to analyze, and what to communicate are using the following assumptions: that people are continuously in conflict and changing; that what looks like a consistent external presentation may mask a very different internal one, and the converse, that conflict may often be between good and bad, even if according to Nietzsche beyond good and evil; that a very relevant question is why don't we do more bad, not why someone does bad with the rest of us in seeming bafflement about it; that the potential for the sublime and for evil reside in all of us; above all that events of the present are imbued with events of the past. Here I often think of Picasso's painting of the *Weeping Woman* (1937). The face has many angles and colors. I interpret the face as the sum total of everything that has happened to the woman up until that moment and all potentialities she harbors for those with whom she'll come into contact. This is just so different from the common first impression many of us derive from the sight of a new person. Even as one may gaze at a face of someone well known, there may well be new facets each time. But were they always there, or are they new, or did we change not them? Would it be a dream or nightmare for profilers and the profiled to perceive in this manner?

3.1.2 CONDITIONING LANGUAGES

From the film *A Clockwork Orange* (Kubrick, 1971) comes the following quote by the protagonist, Alex. "One thing I could never stand was to see a filthy, dirty old drunkie, howling away at the filthy songs of his fathers and going blurp blurp in between as it might be a filthy old orchestra in his stinking, rotten guts. I could never stand to see anyone like that, whatever his age might be, but more especially when he was real old like this one was." The difficulties involved in deciding which components of the quote might serve as stimuli and which as responses, deciding which components may cause or help lead to others, and choosing something called aversion therapy in seeking to change Alex for the better all set the stage for our next profiling language.

The cardinal assumption within the conditioning languages is that the precipitating *antecedents* and subsequent *consequences* related to how one functions are crucial in profiling events of interest. In one version, *radical behaviorism*, profilers might need not even posit what's happening within someone's mind or, indeed, whether there is such an entity as mind. Instead, an individual's internal (e.g., physiological) and external behaviors occur based on internal and external stimuli happening before these behaviors appear as well as the various consequences resulting afterward. It's almost like the person is secondary between precipitating stimuli and consequences or is merely a playing field for them to engage in life. It's as if inner psychology doesn't happen or doesn't matter.

This goes against the common notion popularized by the French philosopher René Descartes, who wrote that the one thing people can know about themselves is that they think. In radical behaviorism, no one thinks, or we just don't care if anyone thinks. (I've always wondered how radical behaviorists write textbooks without thinking or whether they just sit back and let the stimuli and consequences take over.) One radical behaviorist, John Watson (1930), wrote, "Give me a dozen healthy infants, well-formed, and my own specified world to bring them up in and I'll guarantee to take any one at random and train him to become any type of specialist I might select—doctor, lawyer, artist, merchant-chief and, yes, even beggar-man and thief, regardless of his talents, penchants, tendencies, abilities, vocations, and race of his ancestors. I am going beyond my facts and I admit it, but so have the advocates of the contrary and they have been doing it for many thousands of years" (p. 82). He seems to have believed this even if he admitted not having the facts, and many long-suffering parents wish he were correct. I wonder how he knew he didn't have the facts or knew anything at all including being comfortable with the rationale that he could be beyond the facts for thousands of years just like his presumably wrong-headed opponents.

There are less radical versions of behaviorism wherein inferred thoughts, feelings, and motivations constituted by words, images, and various sensations occurring before, during, and after behaviors interdispersed with stimuli and consequences also play a role. In fact, some behaviorists define *behavior* to include thoughts, feelings, and so on or use phrases like cognitive-behavioral (Meichenbaum, 1980) or cognitive-affective system (Mischel & Shoda, 1995) to better illustrate what's in play in prediction, post-diction, peri-diction, understanding, and influence.

For profilers, there are two main versions of the various behaviorisms whether radical or not: *classical or respondent conditioning* (Staats, Staats, & Heard, 1961) on one hand and *instrumental or operant conditioning* (Skinner, 1936) on the other. The story on classical conditioning is that there are stimuli—that is, various events including combinations of behaviors, thoughts, feelings, and motivations of an individual or individuals that individual interacts with as well as various external and internal physical stimuli—that spontaneously and automatically elicit some other event. For any specific stimulus that does this, other stimuli may elicit similar events contingent on how similar the latter are to the former or close they are spatially or temporally to the former.

In a profiling context, a hairstyle coupled with a specific hair color and skin color and some body type may be enough to elicit events coupled with sexuality and violence—for example, a rape-murder. An assumption here is that multiple rape-murders might occur depending on how many times a perpetrator comes in contact with these or similar characteristics—that is, events leading to an event of interest. A perpetrator with an unusually evocative imagination might not need the actual contact, nor would one whose perceptual processes are such that much *unlike* a preferred target seems to be much *like* it. Another assumption is that potential targets who often change how they look through clothing, hair, makeup, and diet and exercise choices in cases not involving racial and ethnic characteristics may be increasing their safety—unless the perpetrator is looking for people who frequently change their look or for people primarily of a specific race or ethnic background. A third assumption, of course, is that the distinction of how similar or close stimuli are actually makes a difference in what events occur during the stimuli's presence or after they are present. The problem here is, given that any stimulus can be characterized in many different ways, what aspects of similarity are actually functionally related to what event occurs and how would one necessarily know this about oneself or anyone else? As the Scottish philosopher David Hume (2003) opined, all we know for sure are the temporal, spatial, or other relationships between two or more events, not how they actually affect each other.

The story on operant conditioning is that, while stimuli may elicit various events, what's as, if not *more*, crucial are the consequences to whatever is being elicited. If the consequences are positive/negative, there's a greater/lower probability that the event will occur again. However, by this logic, knowing ahead of time what is positive or negative may not be possible. Things become a bit more complicated because a positive consequence may be so in two ways. It's somehow intrinsically positive (often called *positive reinforcement*) or intrinsically less negative (often called *negative reinforcement*, that's right negative, even though it denotes a appositive occurrence). And a negative consequence may be somehow intrinsically negative (often called *punishment*) or intrinsically less positive (often called *omission training* wherein something positive is partially taken away for some unit time or lost altogether). There's much confusion over what being intrinsically positive or negative means, which is why long-suffering parents or judicial officials may not be able to effectively apply this to their problem children and citizens, respectively—or if they do whether they can validly know that their use of one of the four main operant conditioning approaches is responsible for what then occurs, such as little Johnny growing up to be an axe murderer or wielding an axe to chop down a cherry tree and then becoming a great U.S. president.

And I need to describe the problems with *punishment* in more detail. To many members of the general public, punishment is a negative consequence to a behavior that will decrease that behavior's probability of future occurrence. To many psychologists and behavioral scientists as well as some members of the general public who employ punishment to others for education, socialization, interrogation, or entertainment, things are much more complicated. First, punishment may be both a stimulus leading to some event and a consequence from that event. (And this is also the case for the other three operant conditioning approaches). Second, punishment may have no behavioral effect on an individual, if that individual has no alternative behaviors including *no behavior* to engage in. Third, when punishment occurs or is applied, it may be associated with any of multiple internal and external events from feelings of hatred or love to wearing some ghastly hat or wearing nothing at all. (Again, this is also the case for the other three operant conditioning approaches.) To identify which of all these events has been, is becoming, or will be the target of punishment—or any of the other approaches—may not be possible. It's not like life and one's functioning remains held in abeyance until an operant conditioning approach is applied. Fourth, the longer the time stretches between some behavioral event and punishment, the less effective or less identified a consequence may be. Fifth, punishment may not occur or be consistently applied to all instances of some event of interest. The consequences of this inconsistency may vary from the event of interest increasing or decreasing in frequency and intensity—or not changing at all. There may be equally variable consequences for other events occurring at the same time, before, or after the event of interest. Again, it's not like life and one's functioning otherwise remains held in abeyance. Sixth, punishment—even if occurring or consistently applied after all instances of some event of interest—may be spontaneously mixed with other negative and positive stimuli or consequences, so that a pure consequence and, actually, the application of something that might be pure punishment may be quite unlikely. Seventh, it's difficult to identify what actually qualifies as punishment either *before* or *after* an event of interest occurs. This is the case for the individual to which punishment allegedly occurs or is being applied; the individual allegedly applying self-punishment or punishment to some other individual; and profilers studying individuals in an attempt to predict, post-dict, peri-dict, understand, and influence. The same applies for estimating both the quality and quantity of punishment. (Crude examples of punishment as pleasure in sexual masochism or of sincere attempts of giving pleasure being perceived by their target as aversive, such as the kisser of the kissed having foul breath, are only the tip of an iceberg of a social world more unknowable than readers might think.) As an eighth and related point, punishment may lead less to direct effects on some event of interest than on conditioning an individual to (1) conceal that event's occurrence even while that event continues in frequency and intensity; (2) punish others as a way of life based on the premise that those with more power should use that power as punishment on people with less power; and (3) change conceptions of self-identity, self-esteem, and degree of control over one's social world—including the helplessness, hardiness, and their converse that one may attribute to the self—as well as conceptions of the nature of that social world.

The complications of punishment are significant for profilers in several ways. Extreme situations such as physical, emotional, and sexual abuse occurring in early childhood are often used to partially explain some extreme behavior occurring much later in life. The alleged effects of punishment may be part of calculations leading to penalties given to individuals after criminal conviction by political and social authorities. On the other hand, as Pinker (2011) described, punishment can weaken empathy and sympathy for others; attenuate, inhibit, or otherwise modify control of violent tendencies; and prime individuals after experiencing punishment-related fear to react with hot and cold rage to enemies and others wrongly presumed to be enemies. Related to these assertions is research by White (2011), who popularized *developmental affect control theory* to help understand and influence serial murder—viz., that the serial murder functions as self-medication to alleviate intense feelings of discomfort regardless of the discomfort it transiently causes for (1) victims and, in a more long-lasting fashion, (2) survivors of the victims. This last may especially occur when an individual assumes enemies are manifesting some vulnerability like lowered defenses or deactivated offensive capabilities. If all people are perceived as enemies or potential enemies, all who seem weak are in big trouble. As to violence, readers should note that Pinker believes people in general are becoming less violent because of macro-trends such as a human social evolution from living as hunters and gatherers to living in more stable settlements; the rise of centralized political authority over larger numbers of people; and a greater respect for individual rights. I confess that I find this hard to accept as I look over what has occurred during my lifetime—from the murders and rapes and assaults and batteries in the daily newspapers; wars, insurgencies and counterinsurgencies; and genocides, war crimes, and crimes against humanity often perpetrated by centralized political authority.

Other useful constructs from conditioning languages include *habituation, sensitization, vicarious conditioning,* and *social learning.* In habituation, the presumed effect of a stimulus and actual consequence on an event of interest decreases with time. In sensitization, it increases. In vicarious conditioning, neither stimulus nor consequence needs to directly be applied to an individual for events of interest to be modified. Instead, an individual is indirectly conditioned through watching the direct conditioning of someone else (Bandura, 1969). Bandura also noted that people choose the social environment in which they are directly and indirectly conditioned just as environments have an effect on people and their choices. This assumption of *reciprocal determinism*—that mental phenomena, individual behaviors, and the environment (or situation, a term at times used equivalently with environment) concurrently interact—seems useful in developing a rich understanding of why various events of interest occur. I view social learning as an expansive vicarious conditioning. Here there is more focus on the conditioning of internal psychological events such as motives, drives, and expectations about life as well as external behaviors. In Dollard and Miller's (1941) version of social learning, approach–avoidance, approach–approach, and avoidance–avoidance conflicts often are deemed significant in understanding behavior. For profilers, what influences an individual to approach or avoid something, how many events concurrently have various approach and avoidance effects, and the cumulative strengths of these events may help predict, postdict, peri-dict, understand, and influence behavior. Such language seems helpful in studying an individual's attempts to stay straight or jump off the proverbial wagon whether the event of interest involves illicit drugs, alcohol, rape, murder, theft, or terrorism, espionage, and deception—yet again, staying in one's covenant, following the straight and narrow, keeping one's nose to the grindstone. Readers should note that Dollard and Miller (1941, 1950) and Dollard et al. (1939) attempted to put psychodynamic languages into conditioning languages to afford ease of research, analysis, and subsequent application to human nature—especially for such approach and avoidance conflicts fueled by inner forces or those from the external situation and their interaction. (I believe that their attempt significantly succeeded in making psychodynamic insight more accessible to a larger audience.)

Rotter's (1954) version of social learning theory and Mischel's cognitive-affective personality system (Mischel & Shoda, 1995) focus on the conditioning of expectations—an individual's perceived likelihood of achieving various goals; the size, quality, and quantity of the consequences upon achieving or not achieving goals; and what goals and reinforcement one should seek to achieve. (The same applies to how the individual perceives others.) Profilers may find significant value in how normative and statistically deviant expectations may link up. To seek human intimacy is normative; to seek it through killing them to later eat them at one's leisure is not. To engage in the web of small deceptions that reinforce a cohesive social world—for example, telling people how great they look when they don't look so great—is normative if, perhaps, unappealing and not virtuous in the Aristotelian sense of having an outstanding soul, even sinful in some variants of Judeo-Christian dogma. To live a lie as to whom one really is and how one really feels even among our alleged loved ones and close friends may be something quite different. As the French philosopher and novelist Albert Camus (2008) wrote, "How could he preach justice, he who has not even managed to reign over his own life?" (p. 112). Is this how profilers should practice their craft?

I believe that the conditioning languages were developed primarily to counter the many problems of psychodynamic languages with scientific validation. In the process, however, many of the important scientific assumptions related to conditioning languages have been unanswered or answered in error. Profilers should take note of the differences between something scientific, something scientistic (an exaggerated belief in what science can deliver), and something that is knowledge in casting around for valid and useful information in specific cases.

3.1.3 Trait Languages

Just like yesterday for some. Like ancient history for others. Remember the lyrics of the 1965 hit "The Boy From New York City," performed by the Ad Libs?

They comprise a set of attributes, descriptors, essentially words suggesting that a special young man thinks, feels, is motivated, and behaves in a specific way. We can expect whatever is the hippest or coolest—Plato's Ideal Form taken to a new low—from him. And why? Because he lives in a great penthouse, wears a mohair suit, has money, and has physical features compatible with what an attractive male should look like or try and emulate. Or maybe nothing else matters, if he has these four characteristics. What events of interest might these events be associated with? Are descriptors profiling-relevant?

Imagine all the different words you can use to describe people. Many of them are adjectives like *good, bad, quiet, saintly,* and *vicious.* Others are used as adjectives in that they describe something—even if they are phrases containing verbs like *look* and *satisfy*: "He's always looking for action"; "She's never satisfied with anything she's got." Whether adjectives or words or phrases used as adjectives, we're dealing with descriptors, again, words describing people and even things that we have relationships with, for example, those of us who name our automobiles or keep pet rocks. Now think a step further, for now just in the context of people. Some of these words may apply to all people, some to some people, some unique to an individual.

With this introduction, trait languages are based on research with three main goals. First, out of all the possible descriptors, which ones are most germane for understanding a specific individual, a certain group of persons, or all persons at various points or interludes of time? Here, understanding includes what internal and external behaviors people may engage in, have engaged in, or are engaging in—that is, our old friends prediction, post-diction, and peri-diction. Second, is there one group of descriptors that can be used to best understand all people all of the time? Third, how do traits and situations interact?

As to the first goal, the degree of association between various descriptors and yet other descriptors or, better yet, between and among all of these as events and events of interest continues to be studied. For example, Khurana et al. (2012) studied the relationship among memory, initiation into sexual activity for adolescents, and two traits, one of which was *sensation seeking.* In this study, sensation seeking was defined similarly to that of its popularizer, American psychologist Myron Zuckerman (2009)—"the need for varied, novel, and complex sensations and experiences, and the willingness to take physical and social risks for the sake of such experiences" (Khurana et al., 2012). Readers might attempt to guess or already think you know the relationship between sensation seeking and when (how early) adolescents initiate sexual activity, but many of you will be wrong. It turns out, at least in this study, that sensation seeking may lead to *later* not earlier sexual initiation, because this trait supports working memory ability, which also is associated with *later* sexual initiation. I am impressed with this study because too much of trait research can be illustrated by a presenter (who will remain nameless) at a conference who found that the descriptor *hyper* was associated with behavior that was, "well ... hyper."

As to the second goal, many statistical analyses deriving associations between and among descriptors and between and among these and actual internal and external behaviors have come up with different traits and different numbers of them pertaining to specific events of interest for all people. About 45 years ago, one consensus based on the work of American psychologist Raymond Cattell was that the correct number of traits that together could fully describe all essential aspects of people was 16 (cf. Conn & Rieke, 1994). Here *traits* were labeled with the phrase *primary factors* and names in noun form like *dominance, warmth,* and *liveliness.* More recently, a significant consensus based on the work of many psychologists including Ernest Tupes, Raymond Christal, and Lewis Goldberg and then popularized by McCrae and Costa (1997) has been that the right number is not 16 but 5—corresponding to *openness, conscientiousness, extraversion, agreeableness,* and *neuroticism.* The general public and national security officials often weigh in with two dichotomous traits in noun, adjective, or verb forms—friendlies–enemies, good–bad, or people like me–people not like me.

As to the third goal bearing on the interaction of traits and situations, answers have cycled from traits being much more significant than situations, situations much more than traits, and both being important to either one or both being important depending on the circumstances. The thinking is that some situations have such a strong pull on people that traits may not matter much, such as the situation of being bombarded with noxious, loud noise (as defined by the bombardee). And some traits may be so significant for certain people that they will seemingly have a significant impact on behavior regardless of the situation, for example, the intense trait of being fearful and thus experiencing fear regardless of whether one's house is being invaded, one is alone in a beautiful, bucolic Shangri-La, or whether one is yet again in an impregnable, urban pleasure dome.

Here are some complexities about traits that profilers need to keep in mind. First, although one can come up with a definition for a *trait*, the definition usually suggests that a trait is something immutable or close to it, often something one is born with, often a hand one has to play through life. In actuality, traits may change through time based on interactions within an individual's biopsychosocial life space. Traits that seem to help identify and resolve threats and exploit opportunities may stick around and become even more ingrained. Traits that don't help or don't seem to help in these ways may weaken and even drop away, if there are viable alternatives.

Second, traits may be applied to inferred psychological processes, internal physical processes, external behaviors, even to groups of people and organizations, various social situations, and larger historical and cultural phenomena—examples of the last being the Golden Age, the Jazz Age, the Gilded Age, and the Renaissance. However, most trait research has been focused on individuals. Profilers may find that as traits beyond those applying to the individual are better studied, a more comprehensive conceptual and empirical base may facilitate prediction, post-diction, peri-diction, understanding, and influence.

Third, because a word and others that may be synonymous with it may have the same or different meanings at the same or different times, capturing what an individual from another historical time (that may be as short as a moment) was thinking or feeling or how they were behaving may be quite difficult. The immediate application to traits is that assigning a descriptor to an individual at one time founded on data collected and analyzed at a time different from the time in which an event of interest has occurred may be quite problematic. This accompanies the problem of developing associations between a trait to thoughts, feelings, motivations, and behavior of an individual based on information collected from people different from the individual to which the information is to be applied. (Unfortunately, the last two problems are intrinsic to what is called *nomothetic-based, psychological assessment*—a generic variant of profiling applied directly to individuals. In this sort of assessment, what seems to be a general trend regarding a trait for groups of people who themselves are differentially like an individual in all ways, some ways, and in no way are applied to that individual. This sort of assessment also seems to be mistakenly based on the assumption that traits are or should be ahistorical, asocial—in the sense of being present regardless of who else or what else is interacting with an individual, whether other people, cultural and economic trends, and so on.)

Yet another problem with *traits* is that each may vary not only in terms of how much of it may characterize, be manifested by, or possessed by a person but also of how much importance it may have in helping to shape behavior at any specific point in time. The late psychologist Gordon Allport (1937) used terms such as cardinal, central, and secondary in decreasing order of importance to classify traits. Even if an individual ranks high on a trait compared with other people, this same trait may rank low in terms of that individual's other traits. This also becomes an issue if one engages in profiling to develop estimates of a group's modal character (e.g., a group of murderers or murderous investment bankers) or a country's national character (e.g., how the French differ from Americans and whether the latter should be eating French fries or Freedom fries). A related point is that there may well be more variability on a trait within a group of murderers or of French citizens than between each of these groups and some other group like investment bankers or Americans.

There's also a problem with how traits are usually measured for a specific individual. As opposed to ascribing some absolute value of a trait for an individual, psychologists and other trait assessors measure how similar or different an individual is on a trait compared with other people. Thus, what's really being measured is an individual difference not an individual quality (cf. Lamiell, 1991). Parsing the distinction by claiming that an individual quality is an individual difference begs the question of whether assessors—and by extension, profilers—have derived any information at all about an individual one seeks to understand. As importantly, traits often need to be integrated into some sort of whole-person concept so that profilers can best understand some event of interest. But even if absolute values of traits for an individual could be developed, profilers would still need to know how the traits mediate and moderate associations among themselves and with other internal and external events bearing on the event of interest. Although such an attempt is the quest of formal psychological assessment, even here the fruits of over 100 years of fairly systematic research have yielded at best partial success.

The challenge here, again, is that predictive, post-dictive, and peri-dictive statements based on people in general who may be quite different from an individual of interest to profilers are necessarily interpreted as applying to that individual by the most commonly used assessment devices, such as variations of objective instruments like the MMPI (Lee et al., 2012) and projective ones like the Rorschach (Wood et al., 2010). This has much to do with controversies bearing on the validity and utility of these instruments and the shortfalls in logic applied to empirical approaches (Millon, 2011).

A final problem with traits is what Canadian philosopher Ian Hacking calls *historical ontology* and *dynamic nominalism* (cf. Sugarman, 2009). *Historical ontology* may refer to how concepts like the *trait* or specific traits—and their various denotations and connotations—rise and fall and otherwise change throughout intellectual history. The question is as concepts and their meanings vary through time, is reality also varying in this manner? Or do various historical eras help contribute to the opportunity for variation in concepts and their meanings without any necessary correspondence to or reflection of that era?

Dynamic nominalism may refer to how our concepts and the labels for them interact with the persons and things to which the labels are ascribed. As Sugarman (2009) writes, "… In describing ourselves psychologically, we humans are uniquely capable of reacting [to labels others give to us or we give to others or ourselves] in ways that can constitute or reconstitute a relation with ourselves" (p. 6). In other words, traits change us as we change traits—a significant complexity for profilers using trait languages to understand people including identifying the kinds of people who may have committed some event of interest. Labeling people may affect the intensity, frequency, and kind of events of interest that are occurring and will occur. Labeling people may as well influence the elicitation of information provided by an individual and by people about that individual, thereby affecting how profilers (1) associate events with events of interest that already have occurred and even (2) estimate whether these events of interest have occurred at all.

Now in what follows, I apologize for only citing in passing some of what I have in mind about research establishing the validity and utility of traits beyond the *individual* to *situations*. There are traits of historical eras often labeled as stages and phases of history posited by idealist philosophers such as Giambattista Vico (the ages of Gods, Heroes, and Humans) and the Germans G. W. F. Hegel (the stages of actualization of the Spirit) and Karl Marx (stages based on socioeconomic conflict including Primitive Communism, Slave, Feudalism, Capitalism, Socialism, Communism). These historical traits presumably have an impact on social behavior and inferred psychological processes accompanying them much like Freud's psychosexual stages might. In fact, idealist philosophers who study history speculate on abstract phenomena that, if they exist, would help predict, post-dict, peri-dict, understand, and influence human behavior—usually against the backdrop of cultural trends, economic change, war and peace, and social change through time. Come to think of it, this may be what criminal profilers, even those who most protest to the contrary, may be up to, even if on a much smaller scale.

Both idealist historians and profilers can find stages, phases, and traits of eras or other less expansive situations most valid and useful that change in a specific direction across the life course of an individual or of human generations. Philosophers find that this direction is linear, usually progressing toward the support of human perfection—viz., Hegel (the Spirit actualized as some state of pure reason separate from the passions) and Marx (some state wherein each person takes according to need and gives according to capability). Others find the direction to be cyclical—viz., Vico's three phases passing from dependence on Gods, Heroes, and Humans and then fragmenting back into a dependence on Gods.

However, other authors called postmodernists, such as Derrida, assert that the whole enterprise of identifying stages, phases, and traits to situations or to people is doomed to *aporia*—that is, a maze we can't escape because of (1) the interdependence of words especially with their opposites, (2) the ever-changing meaning of words wherein any specific meaning is but a soon-to-appear and soon-to-leave trace, (3) the links between and among words having more meaning than specific words themselves, and (4) the absence of some independent center of unadulterated meaning and truth. A related contemporary perspective that can be traced back at least as far as the classical Greek skeptics like Gorgias—and that readers might note is becoming a motif of this book—is that all attempts at understanding and influencing situations or the people within are just doomed. Doomed because we are incapable of knowing anything or because the world is inherently unpredictable even to attempts from probabilistic estimates or models of chaos. (As an attempt at gallows humor, I add that profilers usually are looking less for someone's redemption than perdition or damnation—and so may be doomed either through success or failure.)

But discounting postmodernists and skeptics for a moment, let's get back to applying traits to situations. Another example of this would be analyzing social environments and social climates for events affecting human internal and external events along the lines of seminal work by Rudolph Moos (1973)—an American psychologist born in Berlin, Germany, who had a harrowing escape from Nazi Germany and, presumably, knows a thing or two about the effects of situations on individual and group behavior.

He studied the interactions of what he termed ecological variables including geographical, meteorological, architectural, tempero-spatial, and other physical variables on yet a number of other entities. These include behavior settings; various dimensions of organizational structure; collective, personal, or behavioral traits of individuals within the social environment; dimensions of psychosocial phenomena and organizational climates separate from but interrelated with organizational structure; and various conditioning contingencies impacting on human functioning. (We see here interactions with trait and conditioning languages.)

As Moos (2012) pointed out, what he termed the social climate is the "personality" or sum total of traits of a social environment, be it a family or work area. Like people, some social environments are more or less friendly, supportive, restrictive, and controlling. All aspects of the social climate are nonexclusive, overlapping, and mutually interrelated—and take us far beyond studying the impact of human traits on other human traits, various internal and external events, and any specific event of interest such as terrorism, espionage, and deception. The rather dismal results from research studies described in Chapter 2 might be partially explained by the dearth of application of this broadened perspective of trait to data sets that are interpreted to support profiling.

Traits are so commonly used by profilers and the general public in making sense of the world. I hope readers now appreciate that the trait construct may mask significant complexities in the sense it furnishes.

3.1.4 PHYSICAL LANGUAGES

In 1981, the English–Australian singer Olivia Newton-John scored a hit with the song "Physical" written by Steve Kipner and Terry Shaddick. The lyrics describe the desire of one person to get beyond the mental to a physical, sexual encounter with another. An intimate restaurant and a suggestive movie have not been enough. Some sort of meeting of the minds might have occurred, but there's nothing left to talk about. Nothing left to talk about, that is, unless bodies talk instead of minds. After all, we have many natures including animal nature, not just the rational. Has the quest for social appropriateness neutralized an essential part of human nature? Can we profile based solely on logic? The lyrics and accompanying campy video of Newton-John and various men working out at a gym suggest that profiling languages centered on the psychological and abstract elements of the behavioral and social can take us only so far.

Maybe there's something as important, even more basic and essential, to human nature. Maybe there's a significant *physical* foundation to the prediction, post-diction, peri-diction, understanding, and influence of events of interest. Here *physical* refers to some combination of events related to physics, biology, and chemistry often bearing on genes, neuroanatomy, and neurophysiology. The physical characteristics of a crime scene and of various situations will not be covered here—just one example of the latter being putative effects on human functioning of nonionizing electromagnetic radiation (NIEMR) as in the waxing and waning of concern about Soviet and Russian bombarding of the U.S. Embassy in Moscow with NIEMR (Pollack, 1977).

A physical foundation for profiling makes sense. Most scientists, political and social authorities, and members of the general public believe that an individual must be alive to think, feel, be motivated, behave, and be influenced by other social and, recursively, other physical events. In another sense, a primary, physical foundation for all internal and external events is a stretch. It's one thing to claim that a neurotransmitter, serotonin, may be affected through an antidepressant or antianxiety medication—some selective serotonin reuptake inhibitor—and a consequence may be a decrease in clinical depression or anxiety. It's another thing to claim that levels of serotonin cause depression or even that various chemical features of the medication are responsible for a decrease in clinical depression. Other explanatory possibilities include partial spontaneous remission, the attention from a human agent—like the medical doctor writing prescriptions, a certain type of placebo effect wherein a patient's beliefs that a chemically active substance will have a specific effect increases the probability the effect will occur, and putative healing effects of assuming the social role of a patient (Angell, 2011).

Moreover, given that talking and self-talk therapies—psychotherapy, cognitive-behavior therapy—also can be associated with decreased clinical depression, what are we to make of this? That the causal foundation of human psychology is talk and self-talk? But then again, talk and self-talk have physical consequences; thus, the field of psychosomatics and also of research wherein social experience including psychotherapy leads to improved clinical consequences with associated neuroanatomical changes no different from those allegedly effected by medication (Martin et al., 2001).

The complexities involved in using physical events to explain some social behavior is illustrated in some contemporary work on the genetic foundations of autism and autism spectrum disorders. For example, on April 4, 2012, research studies were posted on the online site of the prestigious journal *Nature* (Neale et al., 2012). The studies collectively suggested that the presence of several gene mutations significantly increased the probability that a child would develop autism. These mutations are called *de novo* mutations, because they are not inherited but are assumed to spontaneously occur near to or during conception—thus the use of *novo,* meaning "from the beginning" or "anew." It turns out that, in one of these studies, two genetically unrelated children with autism in one study had *de novo* mutations in the same gene. This mutation did not occur in children without an autism diagnosis. In another study one child with autism had the same mutation in the same gene. In this second study, two children with autism were found to have the same *de novo* mutation in a different gene. A third study found support for findings of the first two and for the possibility of *de novo* mutations in yet other genes. One conclusion from the third study was that—while most if not all people have at least one *de novo* mutation—children with autism have a slightly higher rate with more severe effects. All three studies also found that the probability of *de novo* mutations increased with parental age and seemed to be significantly higher for the DNA of male than female parents.

Readers, if you made it through the preceding paragraph, you may feel perplexed. And you should, because there are significant complexities in interpreting such findings. There may be other *de novo* mutations with higher and lower probabilities of occurrence and varying degrees of severity. Mutations that are inherited may lead to greater or lesser severity than *de novo* mutations. The various interactions between (1) genetic mutations and various genes on one hand and (2) the myriad biological, chemical, and physical interactions among the expressions of mutations and genes leading to some eventual phenotypical (observable, often external) expression (i.e., autism) on the other hand may be much more significant than the direct expressions of the mutations and genes themselves. And all of this occurs within a biopsychosocial environment that may mediate, moderate, or otherwise influence what the end results might be for a specific individual. As Lieutenant Larry Turner (played by Patrick Waltz) exclaims in the 1956 film *Queen of Outer Space*, when learning from the beautiful Talleah (played by Zsa Zsa Gabor) that he and his crewmates are the only men on a planet of lovely women, "Wow!" The wow factor in interpreting psychological and behavioral consequences of the physical can be quite significant because of the complexities, intricacies, ambiguities, and incompleteness of data.

A related take on genetic explanations of socially deviant and stigmatized behavior is that large numbers of very rare genetic mutations may have the most explanatory power in understanding the appearance of such behaviors (Tennessen et al., 2012). But because the mutations are so rare, research at the moment may be prohibitively complex and costly to identify the various combinations associated with specific behaviors. So, what previously was a common assumption that more common mutations are associated with common deviant and stigmatized physical and psychological expressions is being seen as less likely than the case for a significant role for rare mutations.

For readers including profilers wondering about this change in perspective, note that an additional complexity is that many of the most significant rare mutations may have first appeared recently and in specific human subpopulations. There are two implications of this. First, these rare mutations may first have to be identified for different genetic subpopulations. And second, variations of what is commonly called *natural selection* in evolutionary theories have not had time or the opportunity to affect the frequencies of these mutations based on the latters' adaptive qualities. (See the later discussion of the evolutionary psychologies.)

The overall, interpretive point for profilers is that *biological reductionism*, wherein the search for events leading to an event of interest (before, during, or after that event of interest) is reduced to the identification of a physical property or phenomenon, is most often a highly simplistic quest. (As but one example, there are still many unanswered questions about what constitutes "junk" versus functional content within bits of DNA as recently popularized by a series of studies published by the ENCODE Project Consortium in *Nature* [Berstein et al., 2012].) There are some cases like phenylketonuria—in which a mutation in the gene for the hepatic enzyme phenylalanine hydroxylase occurs so that the amino acid phenyalanine cannot be metabolized to the amino acid tyrosine—which can lead to progressive mental retardation. However, the search for genes and various physical interactions leading to acts of terrorism, espionage, and deception is doomed. For the most part, scientists working in the field of the biological foundation of psychology are aware of this. Profilers often may not be and might attribute a murder or rape to a gene or neuroanatomical or neurophysiological anomaly (cf. Lyons, 1968).

On the other hand, there certainly are neuroanatomical anomalies due to birth, injury, or medical intervention leading to both predicted and unpredicted psychological consequences for cognitive, emotional, and overall personality functioning. These consequences can serve as intermediary events associated with yet other events and with some event of interest. The most likely consequences bear on behavioral impulsivity with sexual and aggressive foundations, cognitive styles of information processing, difficulties in learning common social contingencies, and emotions like anger arousal (and its controllability). And the hottest area these days has to do with the *still forming brain* of adolescents and what associated ethical, moral, and legal implications ensue when criminal behavior occurs (Beckman, 2004).

Another set of languages within the physical languages of profiling is that of the evolutionary psychologies. I term these generic evolutionary psychology perspectives (GEPP). (As a caveat, I coedited a textbook on this topic [Bloom & Dess, 1993], but with the mission of an educator, not as a proselytizer, iconoclast, or slavish devotee to some paradigm.) According to many of these psychologies, there are but three main assumptions when predicting, post-dicting, peri-dicting, understanding, and influencing external and internal human events and events of interest from a feeling to some complicated social behavior with consequences for the masses. First, an event occurs impelled by some motivated goal like obtaining some material asset or achieving and implementing power over other people. Second, an event occurs reactive to various components of internal or external environments from fear to extreme temperature to bizarre social practices like being *friended* online by people. Third, an event occurs randomly or yet again as something that just happens because it's somehow associated with another event that is related to achieving a goal or reacting to some aspect of an environment. Readers should note that there are degrees of interdependence among these assumptions, and these assumptions can be fragmented into a larger number or further reduced and integrated. My reading of eminent popularizers of evolutionary theories explaining human behavior suggests that all human psychology including the events of interest studied by profilers may be founded on some complicated mix of altruism, cooperation, competition, domination, reciprocity, defection, and deceit (cf. Gould, 1986; Wilson, 1975, 2012).

In all the aforementioned cases, the idea is that what we see from and infer about people, what we and they actually feel, think, and act like, *works.* That is, human functioning constitutes our best attempts—coupled with some surprising or unintended efforts—at achieving goals and reacting to our external and internal lives. This exemplifies being *psychologically, behaviorally,* and *socially* adaptive. But what about people who seem to be failing miserably? It's still the best they can do at the time.

And there's a saving grace for these failures. Because what's most important according to the physical languages, is being *biologically* adaptive. As we shall see, psychological, behavioral, and social failures in many cultural contexts may actually be biologically adaptive successes. And the cultural successes including the top 1% of various economies may be the biological failures.

How is this? Biological adaptiveness is associated with having a higher probability of surviving to an age range within which one can engage in procreation and be able and willing not only to engage in procreation but also to help the fetuses one has helped create come to term and thrive and survive to an age range compatible with *their* procreation, ability and willingness to bring fetuses to term and thrive, and so on in a great chain of life.

As I, and maybe some of you, read the June 14, 2012, newspaper article (Cowell, 2012) about a political uproar in the United Kingdom on the legality of same-sex marriage, an ineluctable issue would involve same-sex sex. How is this adaptive? Why is it part of or still part of the human repertoire? Why are some people exclusively same-sex-sex oriented? One answer of the GEPP is something called *inclusive fitness* or *kin selection.* The story here is that such people are still more likely to engage in various supportive behaviors for other people who share, if not fully, than partially some genetic identity. In essence, humans can be ultimately construed as vessels containing genetic material—with people as throwaway cameras with only the film (genes) of significant value. What's important is how much of our genetic material similar to it make it into the next human generation, the generation, and, presumably, ever after or until humans are no more. Exclusive heterosexuals and homosexuals are biologically adaptive to the extent that they are successful in the amounts of their respective genetic material that rises and is maintained through procreation and throughout generations. And the other types of adaptiveness are—to follow the Marxist model of cultural superstructure on an economic substructure—residing on a biological substructure.

Of course, through the wonders of technology or some deus ex machina (something out of the blue that may occur through some seemingly miraculous or statistically deviant intercession), procreation (and in vivo and in vitro fertilizations) may be tossed aside as efficient genetic multipliers for something still to be conjured up—maybe a holographic fist bump between two cyborgs, maybe some variant of Dr. Frankenstein's experiment with a DNA/RNA swab and nuclear fusion, but certainly not anything like the sex scene between David Bowie as the alien Newton and Candi Clark as the human Mary Lou in the 1976 film *The Man Who Fell to Earth* directed by Nicolas Roeg. And I've experimented with variants of game theory applications in which either the exclusive heterosexuals or homosexuals are the victors in genetic propagation depending on assumptions including the odds on bisexuals, asexuals, transsexuals, yet other *sexuals* still unnamed and not part of contemporary public discourse on sexuality.

So getting back to the motif of what constitutes life success, the cultural, especially economic, winners can be losers and the losers winners. While religion and opium (and related psychoactive substances) are often thought of by many critical theorists as imprisoning the poor and middling with the quest for a heaven in another world or some magic carpet ride of the moment, procreative sex may be the ticket to the victory of biological adaptiveness.

But wait, there's more. There seems to be a significant time lag in that GEPP theorists assume it takes long periods of time for biological adaptiveness to evolve from one set of characteristics to another. As the story goes, today's adaptive psychological phenomena are associated with what *worked* during the time most humans were living in hunter-gatherer cultures—the primacy of these cultures ending about 10,000 years ago. We're prisoners of our past and will not live to see which of all the internal and external human events of today's present soon enough to become and tomorrow's past will become adaptive in the GEPP sense.

Now for the qualifiers of the previous description of what is significantly responsible for internal and external human events. First, there is no claim that people are consciously motivated to behave solely, largely, or even at all in the service of what it will take to maximize how much of the human biological future will contain genetic material identical or similar to their own. (I *have* met a few people who seem to be consciously attempting this, but they are not needed to support the claims of GEPP.) Second, although biological adaptation defined by maximal survival of genetic progeny may be significantly behind the frequency and intensity and timeliness of human internal and external events, there's no assumption that other events—the psychological, social, cultural, economic, ethical, or moral—are not significant as well. Third, there's still room for quicker changes in human psychology and behavior not through the pace of genetic developments and mutations, but through social, cultural, and other historical trends and anomalies. Fourth, the GEPP do not require biological determinism. That is, the internal and external events studied by profilers are the result of biopsychosocial interactions, not just biology. As I muse on human nature in the context of GEPP, I'm most often troubled by the notion that we're significantly wired (even if not totally wired) to confront the threats and opportunities of the present and future with the psychological disposi- tions of the past. Lastly, not everything in human biological, psychological, behav- ioral, and social functioning is nor should be deemed adaptive. Some characteristics of functioning may appear and stay through human generations just because they're part of the human infrastructure necessary for adaptive characteristics to appear, be maintained, and function.

As an aside, I add that people may actually use profiling languages as integral to their *own* self-descriptions as well as that of others and how *they* feel, think, and act. Sometimes these languages contain content that is *genetic* in both senses—as historical and developmental and pertaining to genes and biological adaptiveness. For example, in her notebooks and journals, the American public intellectual Susan Sontag wrote the following about an anonymous lesbian lover. "... C. doesn't see herself as the product of her history, but the vehicle of her nature. For me, I am the product of my history ..." (Sontag, 2012).

In conclusion, I believe that the physical languages including GEPP describe some constraints within which human functioning operates and some parameters about what is possible and how likely. They provide limitations on what sorts of hypotheses profilers should consider in their work.

3.1.5 EXISTENTIAL AND HUMANISTIC LANGUAGES

The film *Braveheart* (Gibson, 1995) borrows from events at the time of a 14th- century Scottish hero. One fictional quote from the hero, William Wallace, follows. "Ay, fight and you may die, run and you'll live. At least a while. And dying in your beds many years from now, would you be willing to trade all the days from this day to that for one chance, just one chance to come back here and tell our enemies that they may take our lives, but they'll never take our freedom." A presumed significant event associated with events of interest is *the big idea, a vision, something bigger than ourselves*—here, freedom. Even bigger is what is captured by the construct *episteme*. This can denote whatever *justified true belief* might be for all people or an individual (Plato's usage) or the implicit and explicit infrastructures that are the foundations for how we perceive and believe (Foucault's usage). The various versions of such significant events are termed existential or humanistic languages.

In fact, so far along in this section on profiling languages, readers might be excused for thinking that these languages do not capture the whole person before, during, or after an event of interest has occurred. Instead, we have unconscious instincts, condi- tioning paradigms, verbal descriptors, and biological phenomena. How about a focus on what's most importantly on many people's minds? How about the big ongoing issues and how they affect various internal and external human events—especially events of interest to profilers? Well, it's time for the existential and human languages of profiling to step up. The premise here is that such issues—for example, the mean- ing and purpose of life, how much control we have over our lives, the role of hap- piness and how we become happy, what's fair in life and what's not, an individual's unique take on present and desired reality—are crucial to understanding and influ- encing people. (Admittedly, not all people have big ideas and anything that might qualify as a vision. These people may not even be able to conceive of something bigger than themselves, and if they can, don't want to.)

The most popularized of the existential and humanistic languages is that of the American psychologist Abraham Maslow (1943)—although this was also anticipated by the German philosopher Immanuel Kant (1963/1784). Kant wrote (somewhat cumbersomely) that humans are a realization of nature's plan to bring forth a perfect state so that the potentialities of humans can be fully developed. Maslow's version is that after lesser needs are satisfied, self-actualization becomes or should become the primary purpose of one's life. Although seemingly intended to be liberating, interpreters have been bogged down on what self-actualization means—in a society with a rule of law that may constrain thought and behavior, what one should be free to do, and how free one should be in defending it.

For example, based on the work of German philosopher Martin Heidegger (2010), Binswanger (1975) attempts to explicate what it means to *be in the world*—including the awareness of one's bodily sensations and appearances, one's continuous interactions with other people and things, one's sense of spirituality or place in some not completely understood universe, and one's very sense of awareness of being aware of all of this. One related construct is *thrown-ness*—the time, place, and situation into which one is born and in which one lives. This refers to one's awareness of living in a world in which there are facts as well as of the facts themselves and yet again of awareness of interactions among these facts. Another important construct is *angst* (*anxiety*)—feelings of discomfort when confronting life and making choices—much different from Freud's *anxiety* reactive to unconscious psychological conflict. One also lives in *bad faith* (Sartre, 1958) when one ignores or discounts this—especially if one does not engage in choice. In fact, this last is *not* possible according to Sartre, because when one does not choose one can only choose not to choose.

These are Western-oriented constructs. *Eastern* big-issue and vision constructs include embracing the goal of approaching a serene selfless state unbuffeted by needs, desires, and the quest to satisfy them. (Is the quest for a serene selfless state an attempt to satisfy or transcend needs and desires? And how might one know one has attained a selfless state if there's no self to know and if knowing implies boundaries with someone or something differentiated from something else?)

Then there are Western and Eastern assumptions about whether people are basically good or bad and whether some sense of self-actualization or self-dissolution should be the focal point of a full and rich life. Finally, there are various cultural differences in how individually or collectively oriented one's life should be, the rigidity with which one should or shouldn't comply with social values, and how complexly a tapestry of big ideas should be woven in one's life—that is, one big idea or vision versus many. (As many readers have experienced, there are people for whom the be-all and end-all is one big idea, such as feminists with the status of women, dialectic materialist with economic inequities, hipsters with a degree of *hipness*—coolness, being *in the know* or *with it*.)

Here are some implications from a profiler's perspective. First, the association of big ideas with events of interest has face validity in terms of the phrase *they deserved it*. A terrorist bombing the Great Satan, a treasonous official doing it not for the money but for ideology, and someone living a lie with a spouse who believes the spouse at fault for being such an innocent in a world of predators are all examples. Of course, not all people with such beliefs may engage in the event of interest. Thus, the other languages of profiling can become fruitful as well.

Second, the database from which big issues and visions are identified and used in specific profiling cases must be handled with cultural sensitivity. Here I do not just refer to the bromide that what applies to one racial, ethnic, or national group may not apply to another. I also refer to there being many cultures within cultures, so that even in the United States there may be not only the red states and blue states related to political issues but also various geographical distributions of personality traits. For example, Rentfrow, Gosling, and Potter (2008) found that people living in Massachusetts and Montana are in the lowest quintile on the trait of extraversion, while those from Utah and New Jersey are in the highest. In the same way, there are differentials nationwide, internationally, and globally on big ideas and vision that are common to survey research (cf. Pew Research Center, 2012; World Values Survey, 2012).

Third, the association between big ideas and visions and events of interest may be complicated by the construct of *double consciousness*. There are two classes of meanings for this construct. In one class, people are aware of themselves and also of how they look through the eyes of others—especially the eyes of those who view themselves as superior because of the others' presumed inferiority based on economic, racial, ethnic, religious, national, or gender status. DuBois (2012) popularized this for African Americans in the United States. Fanon (1967) modified it for the *dark-skinned colonized* especially in Africa and the Caribbean who had lost the vitality of native culture and embraced the culture of the colonizer. So which consciousness is operative at any point in time?

In the other class, the person in the inferior position actually swallows the big ideas and visions of the people in the superior position. They believe in their now *natural* (!) inferiority based on incorporating the artificial distinctions of those who have more power. For the contributions of DuBois and Fanon and for other types of double consciousness that in the context of this book I will only mention—for example, state-dependent learning (different states of consciousness linked to different situations), multiple personality and dissociative disorders (often but not always with some competing mental processes compartmented off), intrapsychic splitting related to borderline personality disorders (often the best at the time adaptation to severe early psychological trauma)—pain and anguish can be cardinal experiences associated with events and events of interest including those of terrorism, espionage, and deception.

The upshot for profilers here is that what one's big ideas and visions are, how they are addressed, and how they are associated with other events and events of interest may be quite difficult to ascertain. This is also the case when individuals who employ variants of the Islamic Shiite principle of *taqiyya* are the target of profiling. (Taqiyya comprises both the hiding of one's sectarian identity and the commission of lies in the service of protecting the Shiite community, and I cover profiling and deception in greater detail in Chapter 4.)

A historical illustration of big ideas and visions or their lack relevant to the profiling of terrorism has been described by many Japanese commentators analyzing the sarin nerve agent attacks of March 20, 1995, by a religious cult, Aum Shinrikyo, which killed 12 and sickened thousands of people employing subway transport. I do recognize that informed commentators may term any group of people steeped in any religion or lack thereof a cult. But as described by reporter Marvin Fackler (2012) in the *New York Times*, there's Japanese belief in "… the continued vulnerability of … youth to cult leaders who fool them with promises of some greater cosmic meaning …."

In conclusion, profilers—wittingly or otherwise—choose from among a small number of languages whether in making associations from (1) a person or situation to some event or event of interest that has not yet occurred or (2) an event or event of interest already occurred to a person or situation with implications for the who, what, where, when, and why of perpetration. These choices may be further illustrated by the following questions. How much should profilers generalize from how people seem to be in general to how an individual might be in a specific situation? What will be the comparative contributions toward some event of interest of events characterizing an individual versus those of a situation? When should inferred psychological states be considered as having more association with some event of interest than external behaviors or larger social and cultural events? What is the shelf life or perishability of scientific information purportedly suggesting associations among various human events—given that concatenations of beliefs, attitudes, opinions, and expectations of and about people and situations may change much more quickly than essential aspects of physical objects? How to best handle *reactance*—that people may consciously and unconsciously change how they function based on whether they believe that they are being observed by others—and its threat to the validity of profiling validity and utility? Even the best knowledge on prediction, post-diction, peri-diction, understanding, and influence about an individual's reactance may be easily stymied by that individual's belief that this knowledge is being applied to that individual—much as the validity and utility of a psychological assessment instrument may be compromised by the assessee's reactance to the assessment situation. An additional issue is that individual's knowledge of profiling knowledge about specific people, their acts, and related situations—much as the validity and utility of a psychological assessment instrument may be compromised by an assessee's (1) reading and understanding of that instrument's standardization and interpretive manuals and (2) subsequent choices of whether to fake good, fake bad, or not fake at all.

I now ask readers to engage in LO 3.1 to *dec* the five main profiling languages. Please do this in the context of a film fragment from *The Godfather* (Ruddy & Coppola, 1972). In the fragment, the Michael Corleone (played by Al Pacino) engages in a risky deception along with Enzo the Baker (played by Gabriele Torrei) to protect his father Don Corleone (played by Marlon Brando) who's bedridden after an assassination attempt. After the deception works, Enzo's hands are trembling and he can't even light a match for a cigarette. Michael's are steady; he notices this and stops for a moment of self-reflection. What might be the best language to describe this moment of self-reflection, this inferred mental self-dialogue?

3.2 PROFILING SCHEMATICS

A picture says a thousand words. Actually, this statement that may be attributed through Chinese ideographs to an emperor of the Xia dynasty (circa 2,000 BCE) and denote something like *a picture's meaning can express ten thousand words* (Lester, 2012). Either way, as an education and training technique, I offer the following schematics (diagrammatic pictures) to help profilers best appreciate implications of profiling languages. That is, out of all the events and events of interest that may become significant in a specific profile, which should be inferred through the profiling languages and then chosen? I am suggesting that keeping the meanings of each of the schematics in mind before, during, and after profiling development allows students and professionals to at least be asking the right questions about what to look for and what interrelationships might be significant.

The first schematic is heavily influenced by the research tradition of German-American psychologist Kurt Lewin (1936) termed *topological* or *hodological*. The first construct denotes the study of the characteristics of continuous places, spaces, or locations as their shapes change and the interconnections of their components. The second construct denotes the study of paths. Lewin used both terms to represent the characteristics and dynamics of an individual's *life space*—viz., the individual's psychological environment expressed as something that may be continuously changing and through which an individual navigates with multiple interactions. The life space may be constituted with perceived events and events of interest within and outside of the individual.

The ellipse in Figure 3.1 may depict the life space. If it were empty, the life space would be devoid of psychological functioning. Instead, it contains a number of compartments, each pertaining to some interest, image, belief, feeling, goal, facilitator or resistance, and so on. What each compartment pertains to, the number of compartments, and the thickness of the boundaries between and among compartments indicating how easy or difficult it is for compartments to interact may continuously vary as well. The boundary of the ellipse itself may vary in thickness and suggest how easy or difficult it is for interactions and effects to occur between the individual and various external events. For a specific individual, there can also be life spaces within life spaces. Depending on the thickness of the boundaries of each life space, there is more or less interaction between and among what people might call different parts of the mind and implications of how aware an individual might be about their total psychological environment. Lines ending with an arrowhead have been added to Figure 3.1 to depict mental forces that might be able to make it through even fairly impermeable compartment boundaries. And, also, spheres or other shapes depicting agentic subjects (some psychological entity seeking some kind of desired consequence) can be drawn at the source of a line with an arrowhead leading to some end point—a target or object of the source paired with some desired consequence. The length of lines and their breadth have implications for how powerful these events may be in leading to other event events. Thus Figure 3.1 depicts not only specific kinds of motivation, psychological facilitators and resistances, and an individual's mental complexity.

Lewinian schematics are valuable in depicting an ever-seething morass of thoughts, feelings, motivations, and behavioral possibilities. Although Figure 3.1 depicts a snapshot moment in time for an individual, with the aid of today's computer graphic design capabilities the figure would more realistically be continuously changing with boundaries varying in thickness, the number of compartments

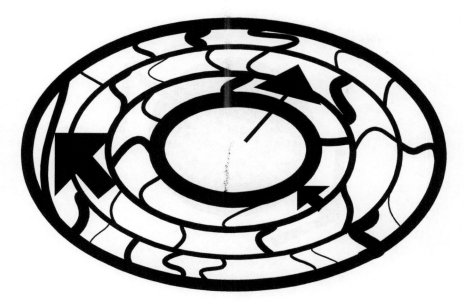

FIGURE 3.1   Lewinian schematics.

changing, the length and breadth of arrowheads, and the number and shapes of sources from which the arrows initiate. A profiler could note on a Lewinian schematic how aware or not an individual might be of internal and external events, how likely or not adaptive and nonadaptive goals can be identified and attained by the individual, and how the external and inner worlds are perceived with implications for an individual's behavior. (Similar schematics can be developed to depict continuously changing characteristics of situations as well.)

As a profiling exercise, I've asked students and professionals to develop schematics on fictional individuals like Lady Macbeth at different points of time or nonfictional characters like former Federal Bureau of Investigation (FBI) special agent Robert Hanssen leading up to a decision to engage in treasonous behavior or yet again some criminal case involving an escalation in violence through time.

I developed the second schematic based on a rereading of an article by the American psychologist M. Brewster Smith (1968) on the relationship between personality and political behavior. As depicted in Figure 3.2, different three-dimensional shapes represent the psychological individual and could again be segmented into various components and boundaries accordingly. (The Lewinian schematic may be two- or three-dimensional, and actually both Lewinian schematics and that inspired by Smith could be hyperdimensional.) In any case, the three-dimensional shapes are each traveling along an axis. The shapes (and their sizes) can change into all possible other shapes and sizes moment to moment, and the shapes of the respective axes can as well (their lengths assumed to remain infinite length). The change in shapes and sizes may be due to events external to them, internal to the shapes, or various interactions. Again, with computer graphic design capabilities one can depict something close to continuous psychological change for an individual. Again, I have

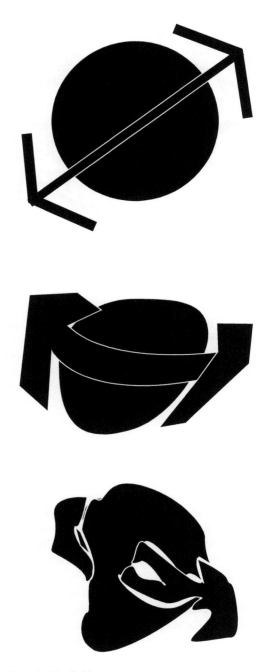

FIGURE 3.2   Psychological individuals.

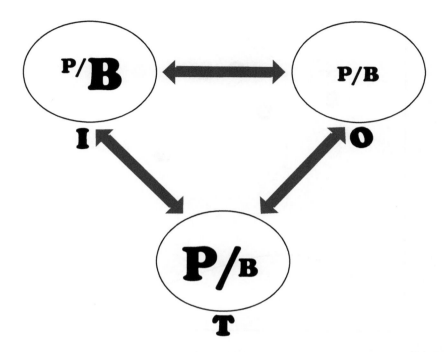

FIGURE 3.3 The interpersonal world.

asked students and professionals to psychologically depict fictional and nonfictional characters through time, especially through periods of crisis.

The third schematic (Figure 3.3) is intended to depict the interpersonal context in which an individual lives and functions. The I, T, and O stand for initiator, target, and object, respectively. Any individual can initiate some action, be the target of some action, and be the observer of some action—often if not always concurrently. (There can be combinations of multiples of each in a specific situation. And instead of *individual*, one could plug in some group, organization, or other entities as well.) The P and B of the initiator, respectively, stand for perceptions broadly encompassing any combination of intrapsychic elements and the behaviors that the perceptions lead to, which in turn affect the perceptions and behaviors of a target, an observer, and the initiator at some later time. The essential value of this schematic is reinforcing profilers' expectations that besides internal and events stemming from the individual and various situational events, there are two other kinds of agents—targets and observers—who can impact on the initiator. And it's important for readers to note that any person or larger number of people can function concurrently or sequentially as initiator, target, and observer. This might be more easily seen through computer graphics wherein (1) the letters P, B, I, T, and O would continuously change in size, depicting which are more operative at that moment and (2) the length and width of the double-headed arrows would change, depicting what interactions are most salient at any moment. Applying this diagram before, during, or after the development of a profile could allow profilers to better account for the various events leading to some event

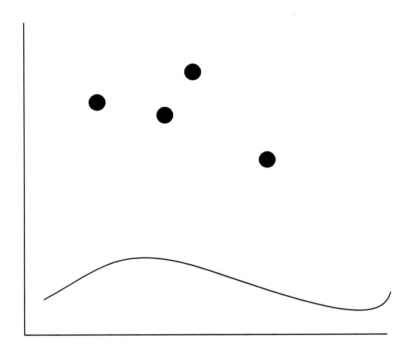

FIGURE 3.4   Four events and an event of interest.

of interest. Some hypothetical examples could involve sequences of interpersonal behavior leading to an individual's betrayal of trust, the surveillance of an individual coupled with deceptive interventions leading to that individual's demise in a terrorist assassination, and the classic sting operation.

A fourth schematic helps illustrate what is being profiled in a more relativistic way. The dots in Figure 3.4 each depict an event that might contribute to some event of interest. For example, a psychological slight (event) might contribute to an intention toward implementing a deception operation to bring down the individual who has committed the slight (event of interest) even unbeknownst to that individual. (Think Shakespeare's Iago and *Othello*.) This event and other relevant events each have at least two probabilities—that of each occurring and that of each having the presumed effect if it occurs (following Kydd, 2011). Figure 3.4 contains four such events each occurring at a moment in time with the curve underneath suggesting the probability through time that the event of interest may occur based on each event's weighting contributing to the event of interest through time and any moderating and modulation effects of the interactions of the four events bearing on the appearance of the event of interest. Figures 3.5 and 3.6 each contain more relevant events with varying individual and interactive contributions to the appearance of the event of interest.

Now for a few other profiling implications of Figures 3.4 through 3.6. At any point in time, a larger number of events may not be associated with a greater probability of the appearance of the event of interest. Also, the probability of the appearance of the event of interest may vary independently of various combinations of events, because the latter are only a sample of an infinite number of events. Although not

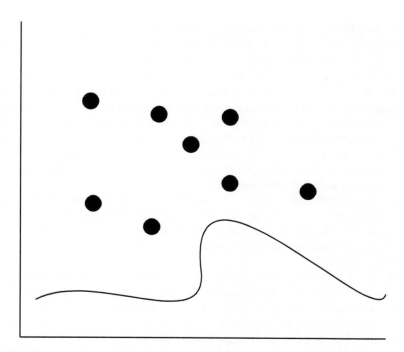

FIGURE 3.5   Eight events and an event of interest.

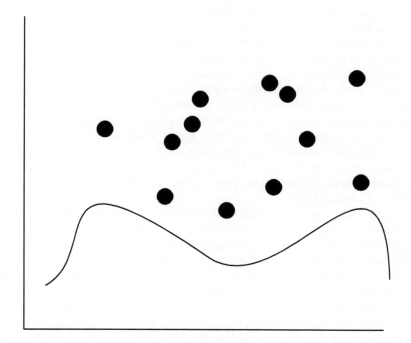

FIGURE 3.6   Twelve events and an event of interest.

shown, the probability of the event of interest appearing at a specific point in time may be greater than that of any and all events that may be associated with it. From the perspective of profilers, Figures 3.4 through 3.6 also illustrate the waxing and waning of events' contributions to an event of interest—a phenomenon more complex than the assumption of static and unidirectional relationships between events and events of interest. This could be optimally illustrated through computer graphics and an ever-changing distribution of dots as events and an ever-changing shape of the curve depicting the probability of appearance of the event of interest. (A further complicating factor is that the dots, presumably, affect the probability of other events and events of interest as well, some of which will affect the curve of the probability of the appearance of the event of interest.)

The next two schematics, Figures 3.7 and 3.8, each depict a hierarchy of the kinds of life challenges—opportunities and threats that affect human motivation—confronting any individual. They each also serve as a checklist for what may or may not be positive and negative, strong and weak, managed well or not in an individual's psychological life.

In Figure 3.7, there are three main *areas* that an individual is continuously confronted with—all the operations (activities) an individual may engage in, all the research and development (knowledge-based procedures) an individual may use to support operations, and the intelligence, (information) supporting operations and research and development. Each of the three areas has three *domains*—a structure, a function (or purpose), and a process (how it's accomplished). Each combination of operations and domain is supported by three kinds of *resources*—money, material, and personnel (the individual and others contributing knowingly or otherwise to areas and domains). And each resource can be characterized by four *properties*—time (how long it exists or functions), type, place (or location), and quantity/intensity. Figure 3.7 yields 108 classes of individual functioning related to profiling. By analyzing these classes as to their adequacy or lack thereof, profilers can identify the sorts of events that may relate to some event of interest. I have used versions of Figure 3.7 to develop plans to influence an individual or individuals in the context of applied research in the laboratory and in the field. Comparably, profilers might use versions to speculate on the who, what, where, when, why, and how of events of interest. These speculations could help shape the work of investigators. (Yet again, computer graphics would depict the continuous changes in these, for example, by ever-changing size differentials between and among the hierarchy of words in what I call the *life hierarchy*.)

Figure 3.8 shows my interpretation of well-known work popularized by Maslow. The various levels of the triangle from bottom to top depict a hierarchy of needs for an individual. Allegedly, it's more difficult to satisfy higher needs if lower ones are not adequately met. Also, needs higher in the triangle are assumed by Maslow and most of his interpreters as higher in terms of personal, social, and cultural value. (An example is that reading Plato is *better* than eating, drinking, sex, and maybe rock and roll, too). It may be the case that an individual's life could be partially illustrated by continuous movements up and down within the triangle—whatever they're most focused on or are being impelled to focus on at a specific moment (again best depicted through the miracles of computer graphics). Readers might imagine

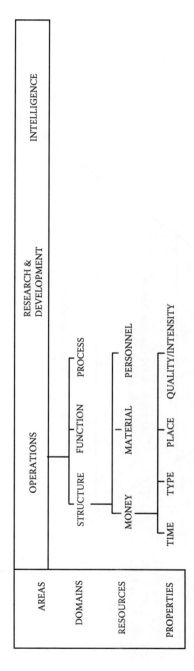

3 Areas × 3 Domains × 3 Resources × 4 Properties = 108 Classes of Military Behavior Ripe for Deception

FIGURE 3.7 Classes of behavior ripe for deception.

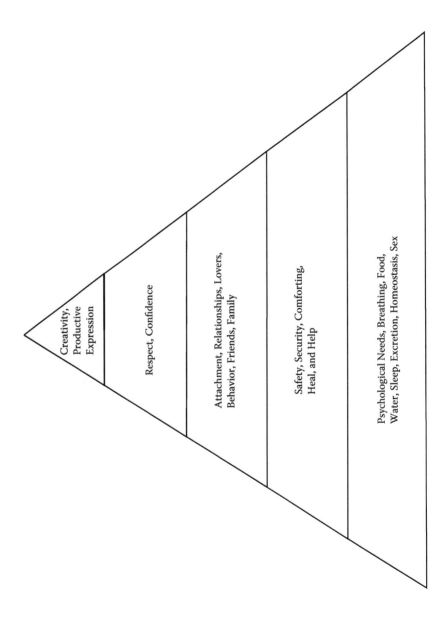

FIGURE 3.8   One version of Maslow's hierarchy of needs.

Figure 3.8 to be continuously changing as to width, breadth, and permeability within boundaries so that different needs could affect others. Profilers might collect and analyze the events related to satisfying needs or attempts at satisfaction. These, in turn, would be or could bear on events associated with a specific event of interest like a terrorist act or intention to engage in espionage.

Two further points about this interpretation of Maslow's work. First, there is nothing magical or even true about the *triangle* of needs—most authors usually use the term *hierarchy* or *pyramid*. I'm somewhat bemused that I'm using a version of something that (1) I first studied in an introductory psychology class many years ago and (2) to my mind has no special empirical support. Yet many within the general public are aware of the triangle, and, presumably, their version of it may be affecting their lives. Second, many formal instruments of psychological assessment like the MMPI and Rorschach are available to provide information that may directly bear on life opportunities and challenges and how much they are focused on and how easily they can be negotiated. But most of these require special training and certification to use ethically, to eke out whatever validity may apply, and to identify the often sparse amount most germane to profilers. (This is still a significant controversy in that most members of the Society of Personality Assessment—to my mind the premier eponymous organization in the world—would, I believe, advocate these instruments' value supporting profiling, while many individuals who consider themselves expert profilers and consumers of profiles would not. This takes us back to issues including the comparative value of internal versus external psychological events in profiling.)

I now ask readers to engage with LO 3.2 and *dec* the schematics just described and apply them to profiling. Here the context is a film fragment from, yes that's right, *Snow White and the Seven Dwarfs* (Disney & Hand, 1937). In the fragment, Snow White meets the seven dwarfs for the first time. She's already walked through their home while they were out. And as she sits up in bed after awakening from a nap and finds them all lined up at the foot of the bed, she's able to identify each one. It seems like she's using facial expressions and clothing in her correct identifications. But the exercise for this LO is to apply at least one aspect of each schematic for each correct identification. How might Snow White have used these?

3.3 THE CYBERWORLD AND PSYCHOLOGY

By the time research has been accomplished on any aspect of human psychology, it already risks becoming out of date. This may be the case to an extent much more than in the physical or life sciences. So the validity and utility of the associations between and among various events and some event of interest need to be continuously questioned, even if seemingly well supported by scientific databases.

At the time I write this book, such questioning may be even more the case because of the advent and proliferation of contemporary technologies constituting the cyberworld. There are desktops, laptops, notebooks notepads, and smartphones with online access and a burgeoning number of applications—the Internet, mobile computing, game consoles, virtual reality, artificial intelligence. Social networking capabilities such as Facebook, Twitter, instant messaging, texting, virtual chatrooms, and microblogs already have been implicated, perhaps too much so, in the radical, if ephemeral, changes of political regimes constituting the Arab Spring. (As of this writing, the latest returns are that they may contribute to shaking things up more than any long-lasting social, cultural, economic, and political changes.) They also are viewed both as threats to political order and as opportunities to preserve or strengthen that order—primarily through surveillance and deception operations—by governments as diverse as the People's Republic of China and the United Kingdom (thus the countercreation of Movements.org and CyberDissents.org; Shane, 2012a). Social networking capabilities have been implicated in the recruiting and baiting of terrorist operational and support cadre, sting operations against pedophiles and other sexual predators, cyberwar, anarchist hacking, cybercrime, and the great game of finding romance for the narcissistic and lonely hearted. But what about moving from the macro—the political, social, and cultural—to change in individual, inter-personal, group, and organizational psychology? For example, is the increased use by law enforcement and others of cell phone tracking and autotracking by various technological means already shaping the behaviors they seek to identify and monitor (e.g., trysts, drug sales)—changing these behaviors' frequencies and modi operandi? Is the increased use of deceptive online images and communications affecting how we deceive, how likely we think deception is, our own tolerance to deceive and accept it in others? (As I write this sentence I think of the recent deceptive image of an alleged special operations unit of the Syrian opposition paramilitary posing with what turns out to be toy guns; Chivers, 2012.) Yes, this sort of thing happened before the Internet, but what does the increasing ease of doing it suggest about our psycho-logical future? What follows are a number of items suggesting something bearing on significant psychological change is going on—maybe to the very essence of human nature—vital to profilers' assumptions about people and the situations in which they function. (And this is a different perspective than fairly well-researched areas such as how depressed versus nondepressed people act differently online, cyber-addictions, online dating, and so forth. Again the issue is the cyberworld changing psychology not people bringing their psychology to the cyberworld, even if the interaction may affect our psychology.)

Kates (2012) reported on an increase in copycat teenage suicides in Russia attrib-uted, again perhaps with overemphasis, to news media outlets and social network sites. Many more titles originally published in significant mass media outlets on the interface of cybertechnology and psychology with titles like "For Impatient Web Users, an Eye Blink Is Just Too Long to Wait" and "Facebook's Dark Side" are posted by American psychologist Michael Fenichel (2012). Is this a consequence related to basic changes in the will to live, the meaning of life, the essence of human identity, or just creating and marketing what sells?

The MIT Initiative on Technology and Self (MIT, 2012) is directed by Sherry Turkle. Her books cited on the MIT Initiative such as *The Second Self: Computers and the Human Spirit, Life on the Screen: Identity in the Age of the Internet, Simulation and Its Discontents*, and, most recently, *Alone Together: Why We Expect More From Technology and Less From Each Other* suggest that technology may be doing at least as much to us as we may be doing to technology. The MIT Initiative goes beyond the cyberworld to embrace technology in toto—viz., "Beyond cata-lyzing changes in what we do, technology affects how we think. The Internet has emerged as a new context for self-exploration and social encounter; psychopharma-cology, robotics, nanotechnology, genetic engineering, biotechnology, and artificial intelligence—all are technologies that raise fundamental questions about selfhood, identity, community, and what it means to be human" (MIT Initiative, 2012).

There are scientific journals about the cyberworld with titles like the *Journal of CyberTherapy and Rehabilitation* and *Cyberpsychology, Behavior, and Social Networking*. But results are mixed on the changing of human psychology in the cyberworld; if so, how is it changing; is it too soon to identify significant changes; and if there are changes how recalcitrant may they be to still further changes or regressions or reversions to previous states?

And what about trends toward being able to meet randomly online with any other person or persons in the world (with compatible technologies) and being able to click off or not whenever one wants to or not contingent on the other or not and then move onto the next? And the avatars and related simulations of the virtual world. How does this affect the so-called real world and its relevance and impact on one's internal and external events and their impact on other events and events of interests? (This takes us back to the preface and the discussion of Baudrillard, 2008, and hyperreality.)

So profilers of the present may be seeking to identify the future based on data and interpretations of the past. Something similar was brought to the community of psychologists who engage in formal personality and clinical assessments about 25 years ago. Following Matarazzo's (1986) short editorial in the prestigious journal, *Science*, he posed the challenge of whether assessments based on test/psychological instrument data administered or interpreted via computerized systems would have similar or different validity and utility than—at least at the time—traditional non-computerized formats. Attempts were made by many other psychologists to answer this question with a general consensus being that there was enough similarity to find the computerized data and interpretation of value as long as they were not used in isolation—the same caveat that applies to traditional administration and interpreta-tion (Butcher, Perry, & Atlis, 2000). I maintain, however, that most assessors and consumers carried on in a business-as-usual mode with research interest in the chal-lenge petering out.

The truth of the matter seems to be that in today's cyberworld hypotheses about what psychological changes have already occurred, are occurring, or will occur often enough are found unsupported. For example, Matt (2011) found that technolo-gies—venues like Skype and smartphones—may *heighten,* not *lower,* feelings of displacement and homesickness for members of diasporas, immigrants, and mobile business people. To Matt, the belief that people can feel at home anywhere in the world via telecommunications is wrongheaded, because it ignores an individual's social need being impeded through the mobility of travel, being unsated through physical separation from family and friends, and being stymied through the psycho-logical loss of one's past.

Zuckerman (2012) wrote that "the Internet has changed many things, but not the insular habits of mind that keep the world from becoming truly connected" (p. 44). To Zuckerman, people are not becoming more similar but more different and jetti-soning borders and differences but instead the converse. This reminds me of a classic finding in social psychology about cooperative interactions facilitating differences on important points (Sherif et al., 1954/1961). Is this finding still applicable to all or some people? Are technology mediated communications increasing or decreasing the probabilities of cooperative interactions? I sometimes think the latter as Americans seem to segregate in news watching among Fox News, MSNBC, CNN, and several other broadcast news channels. But then I go back to read some old newspapers from the second term of U.S. president George Washington and see news segregation was also alive and well. (One important data source for tracking social psychological trends is the multiple-years studies carried out by the World Values Survey, 2012, on sociocultural and political change [read *psychological* change] conducted by a global network of social scientists.)

So, profilers may be operating in a brave new world. Empirical and theoretical research will hold the key to how human nature may be changing—especially as to the development of the self-contingent on social interaction and what the implications for profiling validity and utility may be. But for the moment I ask readers to engage with LO 3.3 and *dec* possible changes in human nature associated with today's cyberworld. The context for this is a film fragment from *Network* (Caruso, Gottfried, & Lumet, 1976). A broadcaster (Harold Beale played by Peter Finch) may have fallen into insanity at the hands of all the pressures of contemporary life. He goes on television live and is able to use the airwaves to inspire people throughout the country to shout out through their windows and from their balconies that "I'm mad as hell and not going to take it anymore." Is the cyberworld making such a possibility more or less likely? How would such a shout-out occur?

4 Challenges of Profiling
Who Is Doing the Profiling?

Should strip searches be allowed of anyone who is arrested for any reason who falls under the U.S. constitution? And is this related to profiling?

In *Florence v. County of Burlington* (No. 10-945), the U.S. Supreme Court answered the first question in the affirmative. In this case, a man was in a passenger seat of a car driven by his wife who was pulled over for speeding. The officer found in a data check that there was a warrant out for the man's arrest for an unpaid fine. It turned out that the fine had been paid. Although a majority of the court found that the man's strip search was allowable, in a minority dissent Justice Stephen G. Breyer pointed out that this would then apply to other cases that had occurred, including a U.S. citizen arrested for driving with a noisy car muffler, one arrested for riding a bicycle without an audible bell, and a nun arrested at an antiwar rally. Justice Breyer's only caveat was that a strip search should be allowed if there were some reasonable suspicion that the arrestee was attempting to hide contraband and, presumably, other proscribed objects like a weapon.

Reasonable suspicion brings us to profiling. What events would lead one to predicting, post-dicting, peri-dicting, understanding, and influencing this? (We need to know what something looks like before we get suspicious that the something will be, has been, is present.) Here's how Justice Anthony M. Kennedy resolved this challenge. He asserted that people detained for minor offenses can be "devious and dangerous criminals," that future terrorists have first been arrested for driving without a license plate and for speeding. He might have added that most future terrorists have watched a bit of television, listened to a radio, or changed cologne brands (see Liptak, 2012, for further details on the case).

The Supreme Court justices were grasping for what information would be relevant for reasonable suspicion and how to make conclusions based on it. Perhaps, the grasping in the majority and in the minority was problematic. In what follows, readers are exposed to materials that may be relevant to grabbing if not grasping the brass ring of valid and useful profiling.

4.1 BASIC EPISTEMOLOGY

How do we know anything? And what does it mean to know? As described in the preface, such questions of *epistemology* are essential to profiling in support of investigations, in court testimony, and in matters far removed from crime including what merchandise to buy and whom to hire who will perform well on the job. What follows are the typical approaches readers may have become aware of through an introductory of philosophy course, some life successes, and their own school of hard knocks. Some of these approaches also were identified in Chapter 2. All constitute the question of *who* is doing the profiling, especially what they bring to the profiling task at hand and how they conceive this task.

But to reinforce the scope of the challenge to arrive at meaning and then whether this meaning is something we know, consider a grouping of words attributed to Trisitan Tzara, often termed a Swiss Dadaist. (I believe that to define Dada or to present a formal citation for the following grouping of Dadaist words—allegedly constructed by clipping words out of newspapers, putting them in a bag, and then drawing them out one by one—would show one does not *get* what Dada means or *know* Dada). *The airplane weaves telegraph wires and the fountain sings the same song at the rendezvous of the coachman the aperitif is orange but the locomotive mechanics have blue eyes the lady has lost her smile in the woods.*

Although often presented as nonsense, the grouping might convey that the contrails of the plane look like telegraph wires; the sound from the fountain near where one is standing looking up at the plane sounds as always like music; nearby there also may be a gathering spot where a certain drink is savored by a coachman and some mechanics with blue eyes, and the lady they're with is about to be in for a rough time. Whether this meaning of the grouping is somehow correct, whether there *really is* meaning, is beside the point. The *point* is that humans seem to have such a pressure to search for meaning that the possibilities are quite large, and all of the following epistemological approaches have defenders claiming merit alone or in combinations.

4.1.1 FAITH

We know something because we believe in it and that we know it. It may even be superfluous to be aware of or posit a rationale. We may have faith in profiling's validity and utility or that there's no God or that she's a proto-punk rocker from a small village near Harare. I term this the *I believe 'cuz* epistemological stance.

4.1.2 AUTHORITY

We know something because that something is purveyed by something or someone else we believe in as the source of knowledge. I have trouble with this one, as I surf through the religious section of channels provided by my DirectTV service. Can the various televangelists all be authoritative if they pose different interpretations of the same scripture and different rationales for why I should send them large amounts of my discretionary income and even what I must have to survive? (The American man of letters Ralph Waldo Emerson posited that *consistency is the hobgoblin of little minds*, but is inconsistency the hobgoblin of big minds?) Can anarchists know anything if a pure anarchist is antiauthority, including the latter's authority? Can profilers correctly know what will lead, led, or is leading to a crime or a purchase if only certain answers are deemed a priori to be authoritative? (Prototypical examples of this include what professional journals will publish, symposia will allow as presentations, professional and general consumers will even consider.) It's lucky for a perpetrator of misbehavior if the draw of the cards yields an investigative authority allowing only several truths regardless of what various events and the event of interest might suggest.

4.1.3 INTUITION

We know something because in our gut it feels right. Philosophers including the Scottish skeptic David Hume have posited moral faculties—actual or figurative human organs that sense what's right and wrong. The generalization I'm suggesting is that we also have faculties about what is *ontologically* the case—that is, that what we think is *is*. Do we go to the doctor for a checkup if the ontological faculties aren't working right? And how would we know they're not working or that we should accept the doctor's prescription and diagnosis? In the U.S. pop-rock music world of the late 1950s and into the 1960s, there was much chatter about who had an *ear*— that is, who sensed what would be a *big hit* and what wouldn't be. As I write this book, the chair of Walt Disney studios has just resigned for—among other putative rationales—not having properly sensed that the science fiction film epic *John Carter* would be a box-office flop leading to a $200 million write-down (Barnes, 2012). Maybe he should have gone to the ontological faculties doctor.

4.1.4 LOGIC

We know something because it rightly fits into what we already know or because its constituent components fit together right. Obviously, this begs the question of how we know the rightness of how things fit together. In any event, I suggest that there are three generic types of logic: *inductive, deductive,* and *abductive.* Using *inductive* logic, profilers come up with a general conclusion based on specific instances. If all liars studied by profilers move their eye gaze to the left and up when they lie (specific instances), then all liars display this movement when lying (general conclusion). Just some of the problems with this sort of logic are that not all liars have been studied by profilers, not all liars may do this and, even if they have been doing it, they may have been doing other things at other times, and may further change in the future.

Using *deductive* logic, profilers assume that if one or more premises are true, then some conclusion or conclusions necessarily follow. Taking the role of profilers, I posit that if a man already has been married six times and has a felony record for physically abusing each former wife, then he is not the right person to marry my daughter. The common analysis here is that the argument founded on the logic just displayed is necessarily *valid*. It also is *sound* if the premises are true. The biggest problem with this sort of logic is that it's a different version of other kinds of logic. To know that the two hypotheses are the case and some conclusion necessarily follows takes us back to faith, authority, inductive logic, and the soon-to-be-described empiricism and experimentalism—each with its own problems. This is even the case with a common example of deductive logic, viz., if all humans are mortal and Socrates is human, then Socrates is mortal. However, this merely constrains what's acceptable as deductive logic not what's acceptable as the reality of a specific case or cases confronting profilers. (Socrates may be immortal, even if all humans are mortal and Socrates is human. Admittedly there are social sanctions for people who push this sort of argument too far, but social sanctions and truth do not necessarily coincide.) A counterargument is that someone who advances such an analysis against deductive logic still lives according to deductive logic, much as a pure skeptic rejecting physical reality usually lives as if physical reality were true if the skeptic is to continue living and not die through falling off the top of a skyscraper or by meditating in a lotus position on the pavement of a busy interstate highway. The counter to *this* is that even if the latter is the case, the analysis is not necessarily false.

Using *abductive* logic, profilers follow a softer version of inductive and deductive logic. The term was popularized from the writings of the American philosopher Charles Sumner Pierce. If profilers use some explanation *x* to account for the already occurred appearance of *y*, they would defend the explanation by asserting that y would be a matter of course if *x* had occurred. So *x* is sufficient or nearly sufficient but not necessary for *y* to occur. The most common example illustrating this is asserting that it rained last night because the lawn is wet in the morning. A corpse found with very fresh blood in the morning might lead to the assertions (each an *x*) that there was a murder, an accident, or a suicide. The job of profilers would then become narrowing down the number of events described as assertions that would lead to *y* (the bloody corpse) as a matter of course. A big problem is when profilers seize a likely *x* as the *x*.

4.1.5 EMPIRICISM

We know something because that something is supported by our senses—sight, hearing, taste, touch, and smell. (Most reputable profilers do not claim to have other special senses like the sixth sense of the eponymous film directed in 1999 by M. Night Shyamalan or the psychic power of, well, psychics—even if tips from the latter are at times accepted and followed up by law enforcement authorities. As will be described in the following section on the validity of Freudian dream interpretation, the fact that some psychics are right some of the time may have more to do with some base rate of chance than special senses.)

Of course, many people including profilers use faith, authority, intuition, and logic when engaged in sensing the world. And, ironically, most believe that they know that empiricism does *not* work in special cases involving, for example, eyewitness testimony, and they believe that they know this through the very use of empiricism. By itself, empiricism is almost useless in that there may be an infinite number and variety of what can be sensed at any moment subject to the vagaries of faith, authority, intuition, logic, and an ever-fluctuating sense of awareness. In fact, *seeing is believing*, even for profilers, often can become *believing is seeing*, especially when the effects of needs, desires, and motivations on the senses is accounted for (cf. Tiedens, Unzueta, & Young, 2007).

4.1.6 EXPERIMENTALISM

We know something because we systematically control what we sense based on faith, authority, intuition, and logic. There often are problems with logistics and ethics as to how often this can be accomplished with the statistically deviant events of interest so often confronting profilers. Another significant issue that has become apparent over the last 50 years is how often researchers are working within a tradition of systematically controlling sensory data so that there's compliance with the parameters of theory and method accepted by many members of a community of experimenters and the consumers of the community's output. The problem is that compliance has taken precedence over the putatively overarching goal—the truth. Here theory and method are assumed to be the optimal vehicle for arriving at truth even if they have not kept up with changes in what might actually be the truth. (The work of the philosopher of science T. S. Kuhn on scientific *paradigms* is relevant here and has already been cited twice in Chapter 1 on the history of profiling science and in Chapter 2 on the validity of a contemporary profiling study.) A related issue for profilers is how often they are scrutinized for following something called *good profiling techniques* as opposed to making a good case for some prediction, post-diction, peri-diction, understanding, or influence of some event of interest as opposed, yet again, to discovering what actually will be, has been, or is the truth. (This is a problem with putting too much emphasis on *Daubert* criteria as described in Chapter 2.)

Experimentalism is a primary component of scientific methods, but readers need to remember that it is employed with other epistemological approaches and is not some pure, isolated process. For example, Hacking (1982), influenced by Australian historian A. C. Crombie, conceived what he calls *styles of reasoning*—mentalities conditioned and increasingly committed by its circumstances (including what is already believed and how and why these beliefs are operative) to expect and to look actively for problems to formulate and solve. These styles of reasoning engender varieties of scientific method. One variety is the embracing of a simple postulate that is a foundation and almost always not questioned but assumed. An example would be that patterns found through statistical analysis of events and events of interest aggregated across perpetrators have meaning relevant to profiling. A second variety is that the experimental exploration and measurement of more complex observable relations is similarly linked to validity for both physical and psychological phenomena. (I have just alluded to the logistical and ethical problems with this and with the validity concerns throughout this book.) A third variety entails the hypothetical construction of analogical models. Here researchers attempt to support the credibility of an explanation for one phenomenon by assessing that explanation's validity and utility for other phenomena that are deemed similar to the first in most if not all crucial respects. Salfati (2011) alluded to the problems in deciding which phenomena should be grouped together in any such endeavor, such as what are the *crucial respects* for various crimes of violence? A fourth variety is the ordering of similarity dissimilarity in the construction of taxonomies without further experimental manipulation. Profilers might do this by identifying similarities in tools of crime, crimes' purposes, or effects on direct and indirect victims. Again, Salfati's work applies, especially her caveat that profilers should be looking more for differences between groups more than similarities within groups. A fifth variety is that the statistical analysis of regularities of populations and the calculus of probabilities are venues to profiling truth. This represents a holy grail, even if it begs the question related to the first style of aforementioned reasoning—whether there is meaning in the results of the analysis. A sixth variety is historicism—here the import of history through stages and phases that are interrelated. Historicism is common to the psychodynamic and conditioning languages of profiling, although the latter usually does not refer to stages and phases.

As I just read the latest reworking of the previous paragraph, I've decided to repeat a variant of how I introduced it. As objective as scientific approaches to epistemology seem to be, their subjectivism is well apparent. In many ways, even actuarial approaches to profiling are only more systematic combinations of faith, authority, intuition, and empiricism. There's more white heat than white light in profiling debates about the overall merits of experimentalism and the relative merits of its varieties.

A peculiar epistemological approach relates to the literary critical theory of Abrams (1953) described in Chapter 2 and to the psychodynamic theories popularized by Freud and his disciples, described and believed to be scientific based on empiricism in Chapter 3. It's called *countertransference*. The meaning of an event, events, and associations of events and an event of interest depend on the reactions it engenders within us—cf. Abrams's *pragmatic* approach. And these are not just any reactions, but unconscious ones—with conscious ones tipping off those with self-insight about what's really happening—engendered so that events and their associations are reacted to as if they were the same experienced much earlier in one's life in important psychological situations. This last sentence is my interpretation of the few times Freud introduced *countertransference* into the psychodynamic literature and of how the term was elaborated upon by later theorists. It's as if we're a mystic writing pad upon which aspects of life are written and registered according to the pad's properties—an extension of "A note upon the 'Mystic writing-pad'" written by Freud in 1925 in which he analyzed perception and its unconscious foundations.

And throughout intellectual history there has been a minority epistemological opinion on advocating the virtues of what might be called dérangement, dérègelement, mysticism, and transcendence. (I do apologize to readers if my long-time immersion in French poets and playwrights along the lines of Arthur Rimbaud, Charles Baudelaire, and Antonin Artaud seizes me for the moment.) These and related states of consciousness are allegedly attained through extreme physical activities such as exercise and diet, ingestion of psychoactive substances, meditative techniques, easier-said-than-done applications of being open to the paranormal if not the Universe, and forced experiments breaking the constraints of common language usage—what the English poet William Blake termed "mind forg'd manacles" in his poem "London" (1794). Many times linked to quacks, charlatans, and con artists, these stairways to heaven (?) also have been sincerely sought and maybe attained by seekers of the truth in creative fields and existential and spiritual quests. Should profilers consider these epistemological approaches?

At times, political and legal authorities have relied on such sources when in crisis or in dire straits, similar to the use of psychics. At times they have been associated with successful prediction, post-diction, peri-diction, understanding, and influence. As I described in the discussion of psychics and will later in this chapter, Freud may have been correct when ascribing apparent success—and he could have meant profiling as well—to inevitable and random conjunctions of an event with an event of interest.

Readers by now have noted the overall emphasis on Western as opposed to Eastern (or other) approaches to knowledge. Here I'll just add that a recent contribution on Eastern (the Nyāya School of India) epistemology (Phillips, 2012) focuses on four sources of knowledge or pramāṇas and two levels of knowledge. The four pramāṇas are perception (conceptual and nonconceptual from memory or directly), inference, analogy, and testimony; the two levels of knowledge are unreflective and certified (justifying the unreflective). In many ways, they denote different levels of analysis from Western epistemologies and are but an example of most profilers' (including your author's) limitations in addressing what knowing is and how to know and know one knows.

I'd now like readers to engage with LO 4.1 and *dec* the various epistemological approaches to profiling. The context is a film fragment from *Do the Right Thing* (Lee et al., 1989). In it Radio Raheem (played by Bill Nunn) shares his philosophy on life, viz., the relationship between love and hate and how the two interact. I hope readers can explain what he means and how this meaning becomes apparent based on each epistemological approach. What's at issue are life philosophies as significant events that may lead to events of interest—like the climactic scene of collective violence near the film's end.

4.2 LOGICAL FALLACIES

Security officers were charged as responsible for 74 deaths at a soccer riot in Port Said, Egypt, in February 2012. The officers were charged at least partly because they "'already knew that [the actual] perpetrators had the intention and the prior determination to attack.... They were certain of it'" (Fahim & Sheikh, 2012). The question becomes *how* and *why* were they certain based on what logic. Even if security officers planned the whole event, how could they be sure the intended perpetrators would act in a specific way?

As another example, a powerful legislator in the U.S. House of Representatives was described as being concerned about reports that Secret Service agents might have been consorting with prostitutes before a summit meeting attended by President Barack Obama in Cartagena, Colombia (Schmidt, 2012). The legislator was quoted as stating, "Things like this don't happen once if they didn't happen before." He might have meant that when people are caught in transgressions—especially those involving vice—they have already engaged in the transgressions before being caught. However, isn't there a first time for such behaviors with, some people getting caught the first time? So things like this can happen without happening before. The legislator went on to imply that probable misbehavior before being caught for misbehavior suggested even more that changes in discipline and increased use of the polygraph needed to be instituted "...so that this can't happen in the future." (The legislator might not have been familiar with federal government-funded studies all of which cite polygraph procedures as bearing questionable validity and utility—at least based on the very scientific approaches I have questioned at the outset of this chapter).

In this section, I describe some specific challenges in applying the previously described logics to profiling tasks of prediction, post-diction, peri-diction, understanding, and influence. I term these challenges logical fallacies, and I do this with some trepidation. As readers might expect by now, one could make the case that socially accepted, approved, and highly valued kinds of logic are no more than the products of socialization interacting with various assumed innate psychological structures and dispositions—and that these logics reflect, represent, correspond to, shed light on, and contribute to power relations between and among people (cf. Foucault, 1990). In other words, they may not be associated with some ontologically based *truth*—something that *is*. But the fact remains that without mastery of appropriate logics, one will usually find interacting with others, identifying and resolving problems, and identifying and exploiting opportunities difficult going.

So in developing associations between and among events and between these events and the event of interest, profilers might—if not should—have the choice of avoiding these fallacies or at least knowing about them. (As we will see, the proposition that *knowing* about fallacies will lead to *not using* these fallacies may be somewhat dubious. On the other hand, profilers may embrace fallacies and find them valuable if they seem to *work* in their everyday decision making often enough and if they correctly infer these fallacies to be associated with the mental activity of people behind events and events of interest related to profiling.)

Logical fallacy 1: I've already intimated that it's a logical fallacy to assuming deductive, inductive, and abductive logics—along with quantitative (bearing on the necessary truths of mathematical procedures and statements) and modal logics (propositions that are presumed true not all but some of the time)—are value-free venues to what is. Yes, there may not be any other choice except some other set of logics with other problems, but as with Cicero's story of the sword of Damocles, logics may pose a sense of dread wherein any moment everything from royal power to the power of a shining light on the world suddenly is over.

Logical fallacy 2: Some Ps are Qs. Some Zs are Qs. So some Ps are Zs. Well, some Ps may be Zs, but they don't have to be. They may not intersect at all. So some Americans are terrorists. Some North Koreans are terrorists. But that doesn't make some Americans North Korean, partialing out those North Koreans who are sleepers masquerading as American and the converse, as well as those presumably very, very few who may be dual nationals through some special legal dispensation. It also does not imply that all terrorists must be American and North Korean, that is, that all terrorists share all characteristics or any characteristics beyond engaging in terrorism. It also does not imply that terrorists may not be something different from American or North Korean. This fallacy had something to do with the American political commentator and stand-up comedian Bill Maher (2002) causing an uproar by suggesting that the acts of the 9/11 terrorists might show some courage while U.S. political decision makers "lobbing missiles from two thousand miles" might be cowards. On the part of Maher and some listeners, some characteristics may have been differentially proscribed from Q or ascribed only to some P or Z.

Logical fallacy 3: If P then Q, not P, then not Q. Just because P can lead to Q, or even that P must lead to Q, does not mean that if P is absent, Q also must be absent. Instead, Q may occur courtesy of other events as well. So if a profiler consults the research literature suggesting that something entitled a sense of entitlement or significant narcissism is associated with committing espionage, other people may still be suspects, even if they cannot be accurately characterized with such terms. And, of course, not all Ps may lead to Q, unless all Ps must do so.

Logical fallacy 4: If P then Q, not Q, then not P. If there's no Q, P may still occur, and there may be another event keeping Q from occurring. Someone with intent to murder may not murder, if there is no means to murder. Or there may be a means to murder, but the surveillance camera is still on at the location where the murder was planned. In this last case, the Q is better defined as a murder that one commits and intends to or does get away with.

Logical fallacy 5: Argument by analogy. P and Q are alike in some or many ways. Therefore, they're alike in some other way. Just because any two entities have similarities, does not mean other similarities need to be shared by the two entities as well. So if someone has many psychological similarities with a group of embezzlers or brain surgeons, that someone may not be an embezzler, brain surgeon, or embezzling brain surgeon. It's been my impression, however, that argument by analogy is a common kind of profiler logic often based on statistically significant differences between two groups of people wherein each group usually is a very small or unknown or unknowable sample of a much larger population.

Logical fallacy 6: Necessary and sufficient conditions. Almost as ad nauseam as correlation does not mean causation, the presence of many events necessary for the appearance of the event of interest may still not lead to that event. Profilers may believe necessary is de facto sufficient if (1) the number of necessaries approaches the number leading to a functional sufficiency or (2) of all the necessaries present, all or almost all the ones that are most vital are present. (In the world of statistics, one might say those events that are most heavily weighted toward a functional sufficiency as opposed to vital.) The danger here is to miss just that intangible something that keeps an athlete with all the physical and even mental attributes from making it in the big leagues or that impedes a film director who fills her work with sexual and violent content from acting on the contact in her personal or social life.

Logical fallacy 7: Begging the question. Just changing terms does not capture a relationship between and among events and their relationship with an event of interest. Claiming an individual is murderous because he or she is homicidal provides no additional value to a profiling task. Neither does associating a theft to the alleged perpetrator having a thieving personality, when that personality is attributed to the theft being profiled. It seems to me that many medical diagnoses fit the bill of this fallacy, even if through some yet to be understood placebo effect begging the question has a palliative effect.

Logical fallacy 8: Confirmatory bias. This is the technical term for making a case versus necessarily finding the truth. Profilers would develop an explanation of how various events might lead, have led, are leading to some event of interest. Then they continue to add events that support the explanation often regardless of the alterative meanings any or all events might also denote, connote, or suggest. The challenge this fallacy poses for the accused is that both one's daily routine and deviations from this routine can be used to support an already existing explanation. Not being able to confirm that one was alone at the time of some bad act when one lives alone and detests being with others poses a problem for this suspect. So does actually being with others during some time at issue—here obviously suggesting that the suspect is guilty because something anomalous in a daily routine occurred.

Logical fallacy 9: Fundamental attribution error or correspondence bias. This is a causal attribution tendency multiply supported through empirical research. Popularized by American social psychologist Lee Ross (1977), the tendency is to be more likely to (1) attribute good things that happen to aspects of oneself as opposed to other people or to situational aspects and (2) attribute bad things to others and aspects of the situation as opposed to aspects of oneself. So students are more likely to attribute their doing well to their intelligence or hard work and their doing poorly to the weather or some human distractor (unless, of course, they've intentionally cheated from a well-prepared person in the first case and an unprepared person in the latter).

Besides the aforementioned examples of logical fallacies, readers will surely note that some of the most important things in life—love and hate—seem not to involve logic but to be associated with many events of interest to profilers. But I'd now like readers to engage with LO 4.2 and *dec* the various logical fallacies as they impact profiling. The context is a film fragment from *Metropolis* (Pommer & Lang, 1927). The fragment is usually referred to by film experts as the "whore of Babylon" scene. *Metropolis* is a silent film, and readers will need to focus on static and moving images in an attempt to associate the various logical fallacies to the attraction of the very rich and elite for the whore's dance and what the attraction and dance might reflect, represent, correspond to, or shed light on.

4.3   ARGUMENTATION

As a context for this section, consider a story recounted by the American psychiatrist Jurgen Ruesch and English anthropologist Gregory Bateson (1987). After a storm on the Javanese coast, a white monkey was washed up on the beach. It was chained to a stone after religious experts concluded that it had been cast out by a god. Much later, the stone was examined by a Westerner, who found that a name and description of a shipwreck had been scratched into it in English, Latin, and Dutch. Smart monkey or profiling blunder?

There are at least two genres of *argumentation* theory—the study of arguments and which of their features are associated with they're being true and being believed whether true or not—relevant to profilers. One is logic, and the other is *rhetoric,* the latter of which involves how best to influence people to accept, if not strongly believe in, a specific point of view or to feel what one wants them to feel. Going back at least as far as the Greek philosopher Aristotle, rhetoric has been segmented into *epideitic* (i.e., what one might use in ceremonies, commemorations, contests, or entertainment), *deliberative* (i.e., what one might use in debate on policies), and *judicial* (i.e., what one might use to help answer questions in legal trials and deliberations). While all three relate to prediction, post-diction, peri-diction, understanding, and influence, the last, the judicial, is of immediate relevance to profilers of crime. The first two are more germane to dueling talking heads on cable news, lobbying legislators or corporate titans about profiling's merits, or mobilizing a crowd the way Antony's funeral oration does in *Shakespeare*'s Julius Caesar.

Unlike a traditional story that begins with *once upon a time*, I'll describe the essentials of deliberative rhetoric from the end, step by step, to the beginning. And the end is some ultimate claim like what kind of person most likely engaged in some event of interest based on events associated them. In rhetoric, this ultimate claim is called the *resolution,* and there may be several resolutions including what may actually have occurred, who may have done it, for what reason(s), and so on.

The resolution is based on *claims.* There are four main kinds of claims—of *fact,* of *definition,* of *value,* and of *policy. Facts* are usually defined as something observable or independently verified. An example would comprise *claims* that (1) a murder was committed by someone with a mask and wearing a black leather jacket verified by a surveillance camera (observable) and (2) a database search yields only one such jacket having ever been made or purchased (independent verification) are associated with the *resolution* that the purchaser is the murderer. Because readers may quickly spot a number of weaknesses with the support for this resolution, other claims may be needed.

There are also claims of *definition. Definitions* involve interpretation—categories, constructs, ways of looking at the world. If we believe that black leather jackets are worn almost always by poor antisocial misfits, by corporate titans captivated by the antisocial misfit persona, and, of course, by the American rock and roll animal Lou Reed, the resolution of who the perpetrator is may become more complicated in that there are more potential perpetrators once the problem of black leather jacket knockoffs is included.

Then there are claims of *value.* Values involve the subjective judgment of worth. What's worth more—materially or aesthetically? A diamond or a baseball? Men or women? One god, another god, or no god. Values claimed to relate to someone may lead to how likely that someone might be to want to murder, to risk murder, to murder a specific person. The person who becomes identified as the black-leathered murderer—constituting the resolution—may be one who is valued by the self and others as someone who would more likely engage in such a heinous crime. This might lead to further resolutions of motive as in *she couldn't control her murderous impulses* or *it's her pleasure and she just likes to do things like that.*

Finally, there are claims of *policy.* Even if one values certain behaviors, one might still have a style of engagement with the world that precludes engaging in what one highly values or dictates engaging in what one doesn't highly value. At least consciously, psychological masochists might fit the bill as a likely black-leathered murderer engaging in sadistic play. Or for a different scenario, an honorable schoolboy chooses to act in a manner contrary to policies on self-management and preferred behavior.

Continuing with rhetoric, readers should note—as a matter of self-management constituting self-policy—that there also are *warrants*. Warrants are inferences linking *claims* to *resolutions* and various events to each other and to claims and resolutions. In other words, warrants form the interstices of the rhetorical structure. If Mary highly values killing (a claim) and murders as a matter of policy when there's a need to self-medicate for existential emptiness (a claim), we state as a resolution that she most likely committed murder in a specific situation like the street corner where the murder took place. The warrant might be that she hadn't murdered in a while and was due, because, ironically, tension from existential emptiness was building up and she hadn't done anything of high value lately. Then there was that black leather as fashion statement and her just having read the American intellectual provocateur Camille Paglia's dismantling of Lady Gaga for killing sex by flaunting its accoutrements.

A common warrant might include *signs*; the tremors displayed in the murderer's left arm were similar to those displayed by Mary when she engages in some self-celebration before actually killing someone. Another common warrant might be *analogies*; the actions of the murderer recorded by the surveillance camera look like figurative murders of people during the winning of arguments through cutting their legs off. And warrants could include gross *inferences* about what events generally or specifically cause various other events, as well as other commonplace beliefs or urban mythologies about how the world works. As much as one struggles to show independent demarcations among types of warrants, there is significant interdependence and a straining for boundaries to keep from breaking like the proverbial levee.

Profilers should be continuously assessing and reassessing the validity and utility of their resolutions and the claims and warrants serving as the foundation. And readers can simulate this by engaging with LO 4.3 to *dec* the components of rhetoric as applied to profiling. The context for this is a film fragment from *Of Human Bondage* (Berman & Cromwell, 1934). A club-footed, neurasthenic aesthete played by Leslie Howard falls for Mildred Rogers, an uneducated, vulgar, and low-class waitress, played by Bette Davis. As they hurl accusations, as one or both seem to be more bound together the more one or both struggle to leave, their observers (you, readers) can employ rhetorical constructs and create an argument as to what is the nature of human bondage and on what is it based. Spoiler alert: By the film's end, happiness awaits one of them, an unhappy death the other.

4.4   SOCIAL COGNITION AND UNCERTAINTY

All people, not just profilers, live much, maybe all, of their lives challenged by differences between how they would like things to be and how they are. To modify these differences in a desirable direction, people need information to discriminate among events. Which present opportunity, which threat, which both or neither? Also, to exploit and manage opportunity and threat, people need information. However, such information is often, if not always, incomplete, ambiguous, partially contradictory, and less than optimally construed. Moreover, the time to decide and act on opportunity and threat may seem inadequate, and unlimited time may not always be an ally in this endeavor—especially when one has maximized the value of one's capabilities.

So, in the context of evolutionary psychology at least, what seems to have transpired is the development of *heuristics*. (In contemporary intellectual history, the groundbreaking work on *heuristics* was carried by Allen Newell and Herbert Simon (1972) and further developed and popularized by Daniel Kahneman (2011) and Amos Tversky (Kahneman, Slovic, & Tversky, 1982). Simon and Kahneman each individually received Nobel Prizes for their work, so readers might want not only to understand *heuristics* and their application for profiling but also to contemplate why this work would be of such value warranting a top intellectual kudo. Then there's the issue of why Newell and Tversky did not receive Nobel Prizes. Tversky died of metastatic melanoma before the Nobel was awarded to Kahneman. (The Nobel Prize is not awarded posthumously.) Newell died 14 years after Simon's Nobel was awarded but did receive other prestigious awards including the Turing award with Simon and the U.S. National Medal of Science right before he (Newell) died.

With the historical smoke clearing, I'll share that heuristics are conscious or unconscious mental strategies to solve a problem most often in a social context involving people and resources. They help identify what information may be relevant, how much information may be enough without processing the infinite amount of events the world presents to us, how information should be linked together, and a decision on what may be an opportunity or threat and how to exploit and manage them. The decision may not—actually, will not—be optimal (even if *optimal* could be appropriately defined) but one that *may* have claims to be satisfactory under the circumstances.

Now, some readers may think that developing and employing heuristics are exactly what profilers are attempting to do. However, heuristics more often than not are *not* intentionally developed but are characteristic of thinking to resolve problems in many social situations, regardless of what profilers and other people think they may be up to. It's also crucial for readers to note that although heuristics by definition may satisfy some parameters of how to resolving issues and, again, are not optimal, these strategies should not be viewed as only error-creating biases. Better yet, these same biases often give people a good enough answer to important questions in life— for readers, profilers, and people being profiled.

What follows are some classic heuristic examples from *Judgment Under Uncertainty: Heuristics and Biases* (Kahneman, Slovic, & Tversky, 1982) related to profiling. (The more recent Kahneman, 2011—a gloss on the 1982 work—already cited in this book may be more easily available and accessible for readers.) The first involves *representativeness*, a way toward judgment as to what seems typical for a person, place, or thing. It turns out that small samples of data about someone or something may lead one to make significant errors about what is typical. This may be because small samples—that have not been carefully managed to be randomly drawn—may contain more extreme values than what would better be characteristic of a much larger sample. (This is also termed the *regression effect* as initial and rarer extreme values will drop off in frequency the greater the sampling of some characteristic for some population.) And these extreme values would be less likely to be viewed as extreme for the person, place, or thing being judged.

In any case, people tend to use small samples to judge typicality—often because larger samples are too time-consuming, logistically formidable, or costly to develop. For an individual decision like whether someone is worthy of being labeled as a spy suspect, readers and profilers might ponder whether in these cases it's better to go with what you have; randomly, if possible, pick a value for typicality; or deem the whole exercise unethical or deemed to failure. But then again, the small sample approach to judging representativeness may work often enough, at least fairly well.

The second involves judgments about *causality and attribution*. I've already mentioned the work of Ross (1977) on the *fundamental attribution error* earlier in the chapter. Another attribution-related heuristic is the combination of *distinctiveness, consistency,* and *consensus* in making attributions about whether an individual's behavior is largely caused by something about that individual or about the situation in which the act occurs—even if the two are also interacting in some way, as when a situation need something to act on and that *something* has some characteristics (Kelley, 1967). An example of *distinctiveness* would be whether an individual acts a certain way in all situations, all or some situations of a certain type, or just a specific situation. In high distinctiveness, the act would occur only in a specific situation. An example of *consistency* would be whether the individual always or sometimes acts a certain way all the time, some of the time, or in a specific manner. So a highly distinctive act would be low in consistency, because it does not occur across situations, even if the individual is consistent in acting a specific way in a specific situation. An example of *consensus* would be whether most other people or just some or no people act the same way as the individual. If all people act in the same manner, there is high consensus.

Significant research first seemed to indicate that if distinctiveness, consistency, and consensus are all perceived as high, then causality of some event would be more likely attributed to the situation than the individual. If consistency is high and consensus and distinctiveness are low, then the individual would be more likely perceived as the cause of some event as opposed to the situation. For other variations of high and low for distinctiveness, consistency, and consensus, there'd more likely be ambiguity about the cause of an event. However, it has turns out that more recent data suggest that the *consensus* heuristic has not been well supported by research.

What does this mean for profilers? If one knows that an individual's behavior is unique or rare for that individual, the attribution that the case may well be something about the individual and not the situation will *not* occur. And if one knows that all or most people engage in the same behavior, the attribution that the case may well be something about the situation in which the behavior occurs also will *not* be made. Of course, in the former case, the individual may just be displaying an expression of something about them that others or even the individual were not aware of. And in the latter case, the situation may be irrelevant and some common aspect of human nature is being expressed. An unknown area meriting further research would be how often the impervious of social judgment to consensus information and the effect on it by distinctiveness and consistency information contribute to accurate or inaccurate profiling. Again, readers must note that this approach to judging the locus of causality (person or situation) may work often enough— when it's working may not be that obvious.

The third heuristic example relates to the role that information is *available* in making judgments about the social environment. Certain categories and constructs are more likely to come to mind—are more available—to the degree that they have been conditioned through experience, are intrinsic to how our inner psychologies develop, and various combinations of the two. So we're more likely to use them in making social judgments sometimes for our good, sometimes not. I still often remember the advice of the professor who first trained me on formal psychological assessment—an example of high availability in that it affects my thinking about assessment and about profiling. The advice was that the assessment report often contains more accurate information about the assessor than the assessee. At times, the report is almost totally about the assessor. This is the case to the extent that the assessor uses the same grouping of categories in describing people regardless of the people being assessed—the grouping being a signature of the assesse, or better yet the streetlight allowing visibility for one corner of one street but applied to all streets and street corners. So, the assessor may provide comments about how people stack up on the same categories regardless of the relevance of those categories for those people.

Here I think of a paraphrase from Heidegger (see Chapter 3) that a depressed person sees a depressed world and one from Freud (also see Chapter 3) that sometimes a cigar is only a cigar (and not a phallic symbol). The Freudian paraphrase is probably apocryphal, although someone I highly respect—the American historian and public intellectual Peter Gay (1961)—wrote, "After all, as Sigmund Freud once said, there are times when a man craves a cigar simply because he wants a good smoke." Whether profilers smoke or not, they need to be on guard for smoke and mirrors and the blowing of smoke produced by their own and others' availability heuristic.

Yet another heuristic example involves how people perceive the *covariation* of events and apply meaning to this covariation. Out of the infinite events continuously occurring both within and outside of one's perception, there seems to be a very uneven record of success and failure in making the right calls. This encompasses not noticing that two or more events occur or don't occur concurrently or have some sort of temporal relationship—even if by definition all would have some relationship even if seemingly random, chaotic, or beyond linguistic description. It also encompasses *not* just what event may have some sort of causal relationship with some other event. Following Aristotle's *Physics* and his *Metaphysics*, these causal relationships would be *material* (i.e., what something or someone is made of affecting that something or someone), *formal* (i.e., the shape or structure of the material having causal properties), *efficient* (i.e., some sort of force from something or someone affecting some other something or someone), and *final* (i.e., some desired or inevitable end state). Instead, the covariation also would encompass what events have semiotic value, i.e., are signs, symbols, or some other indication or designation for another event.

The *covariation* heuristics comprise many variations. For example, one's prior expectations of what events covary or not as well as other related preconceptions about the interaction of social life and epistemology significantly affect present and future estimates of covariation. This may lead to what the American psychologists Loren Chapman and Jean Chapman (1975) termed *illusory correlation* and what American psychologist Ellen Langer (1975) termed *illusion of control*—an expectancy of success in understanding and influencing an event higher than what some objective probability would suggest even as the latter may be knowable in situations for high stakes out of an experimental laboratory. And even judgments characterized as illusory may *work* and, for good or for bad, accurately characterize profilers and those they profile.

The heuristic example of *confidence* may easily induce a sense of familiarity with readers and profilers alike. As one amasses information about someone or something, thinks more about the implications, and then commits on a perspective by sharing an opinion, one's confidence in being correct tends to increase. The problem, however, is even if one's accuracy improves as confidence increases, the accuracy may be significantly lower than confidence would suggest, for example, being 90% confident of being right in a series of ratings but being right only 60% of the time. And accuracy seems to reach a ceiling level even as confidence continues to increase.

Finally, the lack of a heuristic—the *counterfactual* approach to social judgment. One example comprises decision makers including profilers who may be too quick to assume that (1) a desired consequence occurring after implementation of a technique intended to cause that consequence or (2) some other event seemingly operative in causing that consequence is, indeed, the case. What often does not happen is estimating how often the desired consequence occurs without the intended or unintended technique being viewed as the causal agent or at least associated with the consequence.

Heuristics often enough impact judgments of risk—a calculation of the threat matched against various vulnerabilities facing an individual, group, organization, or larger entities. An example relates to explicit and implicit preferences for identical options differentially described as resulting in positive or negative consequences. In a very simple case, selecting an individual as the most likely perpetrator might be stated as having a 70% chance of being correct or a 30% chance of being wrong. Each contains the same risk of being incorrect, but the former is chosen significantly more often than the latter. Apparently, even as the objective consequences—for good or for bad—are identical, there are implicit subjective differences bearing on choice of risk-related option.

Now here's some work suggestive of other heuristics—with the potential of bringing more negative than positive consequences—from Villejoubert, Almond, and Alison (2011) bearing directly on profiling. They studied how people interpreted profiling information based on how the probability that the information was accurate was expressed by the profilers. As one example, they found that *verbal* probability expressions have a higher potential for misinterpretation than *quantitative* ones. Yet, profilers may not have accomplished appropriate analysis for providing quantitative expressions of probability. As another example, the phrase *it suggests* was interpreted as suggesting very low probabilities for *some* people and very high probabilities for *others*. (Profilers might want to avoid the phrase, given the ambiguity of how it may be interpreted by a specific individual.) As a third example, verbal expressions of high probability for dangerousness were interpreted as more likely to be true than verbal expressions of a low probability for dangerousness. And here people in general seemed more ready to believe that characteristics inferred as associated with greater dangerousness would actually have such an effect than characteristics inferred as associated with lesser dangerousness having *this* effect.

Is this third example of being primed to believe the worst in people why horror films and scary stories continue to have a loyal following? If this *ready to believe in more dangerousness* is actually the case among potential consumers of profiling, then profilers might need to modulate their language about dangerousness accordingly so their actual conclusions are properly understood. I also wonder, given that human profilers are, well, human, how they guard against being hoisted on this socially cognitive petard.

As a fourth example, consumers of profiles seemed to be significantly less uncertain when a profile had a statement about the presence of a human characteristic than its absence—and when the identical meaning was more positively than negatively expressed, for example, it is likely that an individual lied versus it is unlikely that the individual did not lie. The good news here is that encouraging interpreters of profiles to think about profiling claims in both their positive and negative equivalents may attenuate, at least a bit, interpretive biases. The bad news is that, again, profilers are people, too, and may be as susceptible to this cognitive phenomenon. Good and bad news is that this heuristic example may *work* in some situations—thus its staying power across human generations.

But even though heuristics have positive and negative features, the latest on attenuating the negative in high-stakes, real world situations is mostly disheartening. Unfortunately, there does not appear to be an easy fix. Just informing people that there is a potential for bias, that is, the negative aspects of heuristics, seems to have little practical effect (maybe because people intuitively, even unconsciously, grasp that the potential for bias may still *work*). If one ups the information to include the likely negative effects of a heuristic, again little of practical change in decision making may ensue. If people undergo training including illustrations of how heuristics operate, there still may be little of practical consequence. The same seems to be the case, if people undergo extensive and elaborate education and training including the ministrations of a social cognition coach. It's as if adages like *knowledge is power* may not be the case here. (A contrarian opinion is based on the work of American psychologist Harry Levinson, who employed the psychodynamic languages to changing leadership and management techniques with positive consequences for many people within work environments [Levinson, 1972]).

I believe that the main culprits were described by the American psychologist Baruch Fischhoff 30 years ago in Kahneman et al. (1982). As alluded to several times already in this book, researchers and practitioners cannot escape the present in judging the past and future. They cannot easily break the bonds of what constitutes acceptable processes and methodologies—and if they did, they would face the *Daubert* problem (see Chapter 2). There are many psychological, political, cultural, and social impediments to constructing, maintaining, and using data on the accuracy of decisions, especially as these decisions become more important. And, finally, knowing whether the rationale for our decisions are linked to the decisions' accuracy may be unknowable. But as I advocate in Chapters 5–10, profilers should still march on. After all, there are positive features of heuristics as well, primarily increasing the probability of attaining rough, satisfactory answers by the human being still struggling to escape the baby's inner world described by the American physician, philosopher, and psychologist William James (1890) in *Principles of Psychology* as "… one great blooming, buzzing confusion" (p. 462).

I'd now like readers to engage with LO 4.4 and *dec* the various heuristics impacting social cognition in conditions of uncertainty applied to profiling. The context is a film fragment from *Pride of the Yankees* (Goldwyn & Wood, 1942). Star baseball player Lou Gehrig (played by Gary Cooper) has just been given bad news about his medical condition—what we now know as amyotrophic lateral sclerosis—but his wife (played by Teresa Wright) hasn't yet been told. She enters the room and is sensitive to verbal and nonverbal cues from her husband, the physician, and a team hack and friend. What heuristics lead her to the heartbreaking truth? Do heuristics *work* in this scenario?

4.5 STATISTICAL ISSUES

I maintain that there are two kinds of statistical issues facing profilers. The first comprises quantitative approaches to demonstrating the effectiveness of profiling in the real world. The second comprises quantitative approaches to constructing a profile. The first is product marketing, the second product development. Here are some relevant questions applied to both. Which statistics are best suited for various profiling tasks? What are the assumptions about the events that are analyzed with the use of various statistics? Now here's a very complicated one. Are profilers using analytic and interpretive strategies founded on assumptions about these events and the people behind them that are different from the actual characteristics of said events and people? And should this matter?

It's been my impression that not all profilers worry much about statistical issues. Some profilers use statistics much as some folks might use garlic or a cross to ward off vampires (at least in films)—with the hope of desired consequences without prying too deeply into the foundational beliefs and myths, that is, assumptions. Still other profilers look at common statistical approaches to profiling and related tasks and use them almost ritualistically without questioning the statistics' appropriateness or having many beliefs at all about them. (This last is the *I'm a profiler, not a statistician* approach.)

What's interesting to me is that even many profilers who don't worry much about statistics seem to be believe that statistically validated prediction, postdiction, peri-diction, understanding, and influencing yield significant incremental value to the profiling task (at least they quote statistics, use them in research, and look for research containing statistics). This should not be surprising in that there have been many statistical success stories in the private and public sectors with tasks similar to or compatible with profiling. As Seifert (2007) pointed out in a *Congressional Research Service (CRS) Report for Congress*, entities as diverse as banks, insurance, and retailing industries have employed data mining to reduce costs and enhance research, sales, and profits. Some of the main players developing related capabilities include the SAS Institute, IBM, Microsoft, and MicroStrategy (Lohr, 2012). And public sector entities have applied statistics to detect waste and fraud and improve program performance. Moreover, in academia, there are growing attempts to identify *themes* and *meaning* out of huge amounts of text, even when those themes and meanings are not explicitly communicated. For example, Princeton University's David Blei (2012) and his colleagues are developing something called *probabilistic topic modeling* to these ends. At Harvard University, a group called the *Cultural Observatory* (Culturomics, 2012) is focusing on identifying historical changes in language through time that might suggest concurrent social, cultural, and scientific changes.

Yet it is not clear how much *practical* success can be validly ascribed to statistics, as opposed to the vagaries of chance as Freud pointed out with the success rate of dream interpretation. For example, during the writing of this book, JPMorgan Chase (JPMC) disclosed a $2B trading loss (since moved to as much as $9B) based on implementing risk attenuation investments founded on statistically based models of risk measurement (Protess et al., 2012). Using only some financial jargon, I relate that it appears that a JPMC unit was created to minimize risk from investments in corporate debt—based largely on statistical analyses and modeling. The unit bought insurance against losses in that debt; that is, it hedged the investment. The unit then hedged against this first hedge by buying additional financial products that would go up if the first hedge went down—so not all eggs would be in one basket so to speak. But the two hedges contained asset-backed securities and various structured products often free of legal regulations applying to other types of investment. The latter included combinations of derivatives, that is, contracts to buy and sell instruments like single and multiple securities, options, indices, commodities, debt, currencies, swaps, yet other derivatives for certain values at certain times. The amount of money in these two hedges became so large, more than $100B, that other non-JPMC investors identified the two unusually large bets and came to believe that the bet was unsustainable. So, these latter investors bought financial products that would yield profit if the JPMC hedges lost value. And partly because of this, JPMC's hedges, especially the second hedge, lost quite a bit of value. A related part of the story is that during all of this, JPMC changed its overall model of risk management—to one that masked the degree to which it was exposed by the two hedges. When JPMC switched back to a more accurate estimate of risk, it was too late to do anything about selling the problematic hedges because the market to unload the hedges had dried up. And this was because the word was out on the vulnerability of the very hedges (the bets) that JPMC was trying to sell.

Now this happened to a JPMC led by Jamie Dimon, who had been publicly recognized as one of finance's best, if not *the* best, risk managers who had huge success through the global financial crisis of the last few years. And other huge risk failures based on statistical models for financial institutions just over the past few years included MF Global and UBS. So even in the rarified and intentionally opaque world of high finance and very high stakes—with much more on the line than the behavior of college sophomores in some artificial experiment or the acts of some natural born killer who will ultimately have a direct effect on only a very small number of people and the a larger number of viewers when the ensuing book and film come out appealing to prurient interests—statistical models created by humans about ultimately human decisions may be much *less* than appears at first blush. (I'll add here that there are ongoing profiling efforts to ascribe internal psychological characteristics, often negative ones, to people like Mr. Dimon *explaining* why such financial events of interest occur. In contrast, situational events—that investment banks can make risky trades because they are operating with federally insured deposits—often are discounted.)

Continuing with commentary on statistics, when it comes to profiling terrorism (and, I believe, espionage), Seifert (2007) noted that there are problems with statistical approaches—problems that are less technology related than personnel related. One still needs interpretive specialists to apply meaning to the data and work with technology specialists on structuring algorithms. Although statistics provide patterns and relationships, they don't provide their value or significance. Statistics are necessarily based on data collected from the past, but in prediction and peri-diction are applied to events not in the past—and the time of past collection does not correspond with the past of post-diction. Also, beyond the well-known observation that a relationship among variables does not prove or even support anything related to what causes what, events *not* collected on will *not* be identified as mediating or moderating events and events of interest. Moreover, the successes previously described in the private and public sectors are based on the collection and analyses of many millions of times the event of interest has occurred—like an upward or downward movement in the price of pork bellies. Terrorism and espionage do not seem to occur anywhere near that frequently (but deception does, which presents different problems that I cover in Chapter 9).

Another challenge relates to the various statistical assumptions. My contention is that many applied researchers in profiling are unaware of or largely discount the constraints of statistical methods applied to data. In other words, certain relationships that may be operative among events and events of interest will not ever show up for each statistical choice made. Other such relationships may be identified too easily, too quickly, and too strongly. What follows are some important statistical approaches to knowledge in profiling.

4.5.1 SIGNAL DETECTION THEORY (SDT)

This approach illustrates trade-offs in making decisions about events as to which may be more or less suggestive of some event of interest. In Figure 4.1, we see two curves. The one to the right is the distribution of some event, such as explosive residue (ER) on one's hands while attempting to go through an airport security checkpoint. The one to the left is the distribution of some other event, for example, carrying a *Batman* comic book (BC) while attempting to go through the checkpoint. The y-axis shows the probability distribution of each event. The x-axis shows the degree to which there's an intention to commit terrorism (IT)— the event of interest. (An even more important event of interest would be the degree to which there are terrorist behaviors.) In the real world, these distributions are largely unknown, but we are now engaged in a thought experiment.

In Figure 4.2, we see the results of applied profiling, if profilers make a decision that anyone displaying a specific value beyond a standardized unit (a criterion, C1) will be subject to special treatment like further screening at an airport, arrest, or what Jerry, a presumed CIA operative in the film *Apocalypse Now* (1979), directs "... terminat[ion] with extreme prejudice." The area of the (ER) curve to the right of the criterion represents the people with explosive residue who, indeed, will be specially treated. The area of the (ER) curve to the left of the criterion represents those who won't be specially treated. The same reasoning applies to people with a *Batman* comic book on the (BC) curve who are to the right and left of the criterion. Readers should note, then, that some people with explosive residue will be missed, and some comic book carrying people will be specially treated who shouldn't be. (This is based on the *assumption* that regardless of the relationship between corresponding

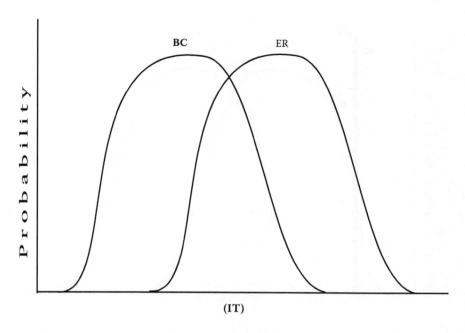

FIGURE 4.1   Explosive residue, comic book, and intention for terrorism.

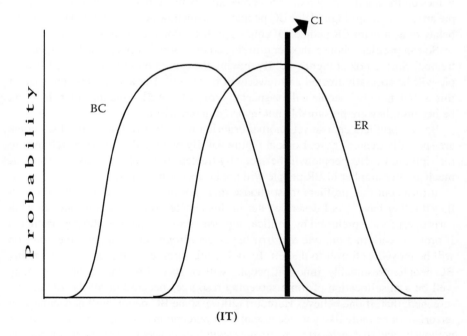

FIGURE 4.2   Explosive residue, comic book, and intention for terrorism.

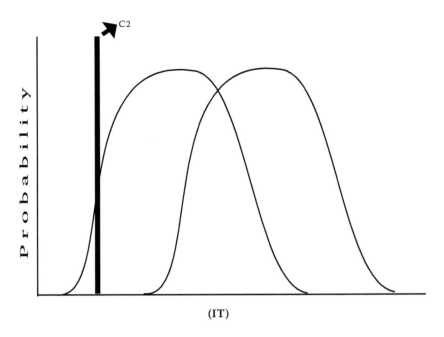

FIGURE 4.3 Explosive residue, comic book, and intention for terrorism.

values on the x-axis and y-axis, ER people are involved in terrorism, while BC people are not. Perhaps high IT for BC people are somehow not associated with terrorist behavior as it is for ER people. Of course, profilers don't know this for sure.)

So can profilers choose another criterion so that more ER people will be specially treated? Sure. Look at Figure 4.3. By moving the criterion to the left, more ER people will be specially treated and fewer will be missed. But another consequence of this is that more BC people will be specially treated as well—and the latter shouldn't be because they are presumably not involved in terrorism.

So can profilers choose yet another criterion to minimize how many BC people are specially treated? Sure. Look at Figure 4.4. By moving the criterion well over to the right, fewer BC people will be specially treated. But look what else happens. A much greater number of ER people will not be specially treated.

It turns out that profilers must choose their poison, that is, what sorts of errors they'd rather have. (As I describe later in this chapter, this often translates to what sorts of errors are preferred by political authorities and the people who pay profilers.) If profiles work in a *not one terrorist better get through* environment, the criterion will be moved well over to the left. By doing this, profilers are accepting that many BC people, presumably, innocent people, will be specially treated; that there may well be a misallocation of finite screening resources because of all the BC people screened; that, if one believes Harcourt (2007), some BC people will now engage in terrorism or be more likely to because of their perception of being treated unfairly or noxiously; and that terrorist planners may switch to attacks not dependent on contact with explosive material.

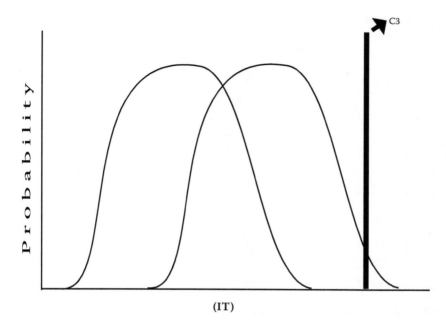

FIGURE 4.4 Explosive residue, comic book, and intention for terrorism.

If profilers work in a *not one person's rights and liberties better be violated* or a *daily air operations better not be negatively affected* environment, the criterion will be moved well over to the right. By doing this, profilers are accepting that many ER people will not be specially treated so that more terrorists will get through; that the resulting terrorism may lead to a more severe crackdown on rights and liberties beyond what was initially viewed as too severe; that the resulting terrorism also will endanger the economic viability of air operations; and that a public security crisis may ensue that often brings out the worst in many political leaders and the general public—in the latter often enough a conspiracy oriented ethnocentrism, vigilantism, and lynch mentality.

Figure 4.5 presents a conclusion to the previous analysis. Depending on the results of applied research and various other epistemological approaches described earlier, profilers may have access to distributions far apart or close together. The two distributions to the left in Figure 4.5 are the two we've been working with and are close together. The two distributions on the right are much farther apart. Let's look at the two on the right. Except for the most extreme choices of a criterion, it's more likely that most of the ER people will be specially treated and the BC people will not be. The same applies if the two distributions, respectively, represent people displaying all items on a list of events associated with terrorism and people who are not characterized by any of the events on the list.

A few last points. Continuing with Figure 4.5, the distance between distributions represents a concrete example of many such choices confronting profilers. Returning to the ER versus BC distinction, as the separation between their two respective curves

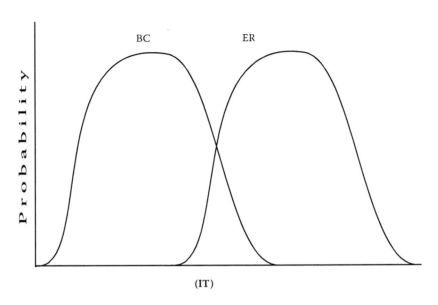

FIGURE 4.5   Explosive residue, comic book, and intention for terrorism.

increases, profilers may achieve a high true positive rate (specially treating people who should be specially treated) and a low false positive rate (specially treating people who shouldn't be so treated). The higher the d' index—often called a sensitivity or discriminability index—the more this will be the case. The lower the d' index the more true positives and false positives will concurrently rise. In fact, choices between distributions and also of what criteria to choose yield the d' for a specific set of distributions as can be seen in Figure 4.6. (I refer readers to Wickens [2011] for more details on d' and more quantitative examples. Note that I was an undergraduate engaged in SDT research with military applications under the guidance of graduate students within a psychology department that was receiving significant SDT grant money.)

But we've just been through several thought experiments, which model how profilers might wish to model their task. Perhaps someday, one might be able to empirically compare profilers or profiling organizations for the size of their discriminability indices for like and dissimilar sets of distributions, for which sets of distributions seem to be more commonly used. And now for another way of thinking about the profiling task via Bayesian analysis.

4.5.2   BAYESIAN ANALYSIS

Let's assume profilers are engaging in a peri-dictive task. They're trying to identify employees within an organization who are currently engaged in an event of interest (E)—espionage—against it. Let's also assume that profilers have developed and are using an *espionage detector* (ED)—actually a list of events each positively correlated with espionage with none of these events decreasing the correlation of any other with espionage, and with the contribution of each not overlapping with any other.

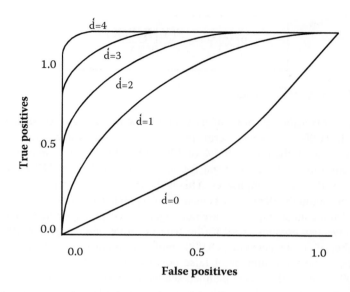

FIGURE 4.6 Discriminability index, true positives, and false positives.

Figure 4.7 provides an example. In the organization, 1% of the employees are engaged in espionage, so 99% are not. The ED will detect 80% of the E employees and miss 20% of them. A total of 10% of the non-E (NE) employees will be detected as E, so 90% will not. I believe that the 80% and 10% percentages are highly optimistic in the real world of profiling. The 1% espionage percentage may be high and today is likely unknowable.

Figure 4.8 illustrates the two accurate and two inaccurate estimates that together form the overall validity—perhaps, perhaps not, the utility—of the ED. Within the upper left frame of the 2 × 2 matrix of Figure 4.8, we find that 80% of the 1% of the E employees are accurately detected. This is called the *true positive*

	Espionage	No Espionage
Detect as E	80%	10%
Detect as NE	20%	90%

FIGURE 4.7 True and false positive and negative percentages for espionage detector.

	Espionage	No Espionage
Detect as E	800	9,900
Detect as NE	200	89,100

FIGURE 4.8 Absolute numbers of employees accurately and inaccurately identified by espionage detector.

$$P(X \mid Y) = \frac{P(Y \mid X)P(X)}{P(Y)}$$

FIGURE 4.9 Bayesian analysis.

percentage—even though most of us would view betrayers of trust negatively. If there are 100,000 employees overall in the organization (some sprawling government bureaucracy), then 80% of 1% of 100,000 yields 800 E employees correctly detected. So, too, in the upper right frame we see that 10% of NE employees are detected as if they are E employees. This is the *false positive* percentage pertaining to employees wrongly identified as engaged in espionage (E) who are not so engaged (NE). And since most employees are not engaged in espionage (NE), then 10% (the false positive percentage) of 99% (the true negative percentage) of 100,000 (the total number of employees) yields 9,900 employees incorrectly detected as engaged in espionage (the total number of false positives within the employee population of 100,000). (I hope they have planned second careers after their service with the organization is terminated or further progress is impeded.) In the lower left frame is the estimate of E employees who get away with it, because they are identified as non-E. This is 200, because there are 1,000 spies in total, 80% of them—800— are correctly detected, 20% are not, and that leaves 200. This is called the *false negative* percentage, because this corresponds to the number of E employees who weren't detected as such. In the lower right frame is the estimate for the number of non-E employees corrected identified as such. They're not engaged in espionage. The estimate is 89,100 because there are 99% of the 100,000 total employees or 99,000 who are non-E, 10% of them or 9,900 are wrongly detected as E, so that leaves 89,100. This is called the *true negative* percentage, even as many of us would view them quite positively.

So what are the chances that someone identified by the ED as being an E employee actually is engaged in espionage? Well, this chance should comprise all the separate ways this result could occur. First, we have the 80% accurate detection figure of the 1% of employees engaged in espionage, or .008. Second, we have the 10% inaccurate detection figure of the 99% of employees not engaged in espionage, or .099. So the chance of being detected accurately or inaccurately as an E employee is .008 + .099, or .107. Now we're ready to answer the question leading off the paragraph—what are the chances that someone identified by the ED as being an E employee actually is so engaged? It's .008/.107, or .0747, or about 7.47%.

A general statement of what we've just been through is depicted in Figure 4.9. If X refers to any event of interest that profilers are trying to predict, post-dict, peri-dict, understand, or influence, and Y refers to an event or list of events developed by profilers indicating that the event of interest, respectively, will be present, has been present, or is present, then the following holds. The probability of X occurring given Y will be equal to the probability of Y occurring given X times the probability of X divided by the probability of Y. In somewhat plainer English, the probability that the *event of interest* will be, has been, or is present given the *event* is the product of the probability of the *event of interest* times the probability of the *event given the event of interest* divided by the probability of the *event*.

Again, this is a thought experiment about the high stakes situations in the real world. We rarely if ever know the true probabilities of statistically deviant, if not all events of interest, especially for specific people in specific situations. The same is the case for the validity of the various profiling instruments like lists of events, even those differentially weighted when not all events contribute in the same way to the probability of the event of interest. But the thought experiment illustrates the main questions profilers should have answers to in making estimates and recommendations affecting human lives based on common descriptive and inferential statistics employed in the psychological, behavioral, and social sciences.

On the other hand, and interesting to me at least, the face validity of statistics does not seem to impress decision makers in certain high-stakes situations. For example, Krauss, McCabe, and Lieberman (2011) found that venire jurors (i.e., prospective jurors from which a jury is constituted) are less influenced by empirically based actuarial testimony than "less scientific" clinical expert testimony.

4.5.3 BINOMIAL EFFECT SIZE DISPLAY

Profilers familiar with research literature often discover various correlations—degrees of association—between events and events of interest. At one extreme, a value of +1 can denote that when the event occurs so will the event of interest, often as well that when the event of interest occurs so will the event. At another extreme, a value of –1 can denote that when the event occurs, the event of interest will never occur, often as well the converse. In the middle, a value of 0 can denote that there's just no association between the event and event of interest. So, a correlation between eye blinking and deception for certain types of people in certain situations for certain questions may be +.3. Or a correlation between people who have symmetrical and consensually pleasing facial features (often an operational definition of physical attractiveness) and staying home alone on Saturday night may be –.4 (at least for societies wherein physical attractiveness is very highly valued over other human characteristics). Or a correlation between enjoying the writings of St. Thomas Aquinas and enjoying a specific brand of tea or color of cloth may be 0.

After years of reading psychological, behavioral, and social research, I assert that very strong positive correlations between events (various human psychological and behavioral characteristics) and events of interest (e.g., criminal behaviors) are often in the +.4 range. (This statement assumes events that are both sensitive [associated with the event of interest] and specific [not also associated with just about anything else— *breathing* is sensitive but not specific as a characteristic for a murderer.] Is this good enough for profilers to hang their hats on? Undergraduate students are often taught and their faculty often parrot that one should square the quantitative value of the correlation to get the percent of *variance* explained by the correlation. So +.4 squared would be .16, or 16% of the variance explained, the rest, here 84%, to be explained otherwise. In other words, 84% of the event of interest to be explained by other events than the event currently doing the explaining—and to make it more complicated, some of these other events might decrease the correlation of the initial event with that event of interest even as they are themselves correlated *with* that event of interest.

In plainer or at least different English, what's happening here is that an assumption is being made about squaring the correlation between the event and the event of interest. The assumption is that squaring relates to a set of equations bearing on the difference of each value of the event of interest measured at various points in time and its mean value. The larger the squared correlation, the more it is presumed to be associated with these differences. And further, the more it is so associated, the more the event is associated with the event of interest. To go further with this analysis would take us into the philosophy of mathematics and maybe some embarrassing non sequiturs and leaps of faith within statistics, so I'll stop this explanation with the following brief example.

Imagine research on the correlation between an event (symmetrical and pleasing facial features) and an event of interest (staying home alone on Saturday night) carried out over a year. An assumption is that the higher the squared correlation, the more facial features explain the differences between each person's number of times spent alone on Saturday night and the mean value for all people. A follow-on assumption is that the more there's an association between facial features and staying home, the more the former can be used to help predict, post-dict, peri-dict, understand, or influence the latter. (Less so, perhaps, for the latter helping with the former. Again, further exploration would take us too far afield, but note that part of the issue here is *what* is identified as the *event* and *what* as the *event of interest*. Facial features, staying home, and anything else can serve as either event or event of interest depending on the needs of the profiler and the challenges at hand.)

But is there a better way and is a +.4 correlation and the 16% variance explained good enough for profilers? Here's where the *binomial effect size display* (BESD) comes in to offer another way of looking at how much of an impact, especially how much *utility,* research results may have. And Figures 4.10 and 4.11 will show this. (See Rosenthal & Rubin, 1982, for a seminal article popularizing the BESD.)

Let's assume there are 200 people who have been identified as hard-core terrorists based on all-source intelligence (and unlike the real world, they all have been correctly so identified). They are now residing in a well-protected prison compound controlled by security authorities of the U.S. government. Half, or 100, of them go through a special education and rehabilitation program (R) that allegedly turns terrorists inspired by disparate and renegade interpretations of Islam into nonterrorist, Republican Rotarians inspired by disparate and renegade interpretations of the

T	NT
80%	10%
20%	90%

FIGURE 4.10 Terrorists continuing to terrorize when rehabilitation is uncorrelated with further terrorism.

	T	NT
R	30	70
NR	70	30

FIGURE 4.11 Terrorists continuing to terrorize when rehabilitation is correlated with further terrorism (r = 4).

Christianity. The other 100 don't go through anything else but the day-to-day hell of being exposed to daytime American television game and reality shows. Four years after all have been released prison, 100 of the 200 terrorists have since reengaged in terrorism (T), and 100 have not (NT). So did the education and rehabilitation program make a difference, hopefully the right one?

Let's say there's a +.4 correlation between going through rehabilitation and no longer engaging in terrorism. As readers now know, 16% of the variance of no longer engaging in terrorism can be explained by going through rehabilitation. But now, let's continue. If the correlation were instead 0, then all four frames in Figure 4.10 would contain 50, because there'll be equal numbers of terrorists continuing to engage in terrorism or not, whether they go through rehabilitation or not, because rehabilitation has no effect. In essence, the probability of reengaging in terrorism is 50%. But because we have a correlation of +.4, we can move the decimal point two places to the right to get 40, divide by 2 to get 20, and add to the 50 in the upper right-hand frame to get 70. Then we can modify the other three frames accordingly given that we still have the original 200 people who had initially engaged in terrorism. So, we end up with Figure 4.11.

Explaining 16% out of 100% of the variance of some event of interest may not strike profilers as much of an advantage. But at least the face validity of a 70–30 split as opposed to a 50–50 one may well strike profilers and those who pay them much differently—as if there's some sort of intuitive understanding of a strong relationship. Again, there are many ways to show how strong a relationship may be between two events, among many of them, or associating them with an event of interest. This all depends on various assumptions, and, thus, there may be much more subjectivity to *objective* quantitative analysis than appears at first blush.

For example, in the illustration just covered, we have equally sized groups for those who went through rehabilitation and those who didn't. There's also an assumption that there's equal variance for the two groups around their respective mean values. As well, the previous BESD assumes a 50% base rate for both the rehabilitation and nonrehabilitation groups—an artificial situation that often is unknowable in the real world. Moreover, I specifically chose the numbers in the previous BESD illustration to avoid explaining that most BESD examples represent standardized percentages not actual raw data in each frame. There are many different opinions on what the consequences are when these assumptions are significantly violated. There *is* consensus that using the BESD (or working with a statistician to develop a BESD) is advantageous when deciding on the significance of meta-evaluations bearing on profiling (see Chapter 2).

4.5.4 Logistic Regression

This set of techniques is most often used to help identify events that will help predict events of interest—especially when the latter are dichotomous, that is, they happen or don't as in a person does or does not engage in terrorism, spy, or deceive. More recently, logistic regression is being used for events of interest that can be conceived by multiple categories as in degrees of severity or frequency, such as how bad the consequences of espionage might have been. And a very similar approach, *linear regression*, is commonly used when the events of interest are continuous and the events used for prediction are either dichotomous or continuous. (By *continuous* one assumes there can be additional values between any two values observed for a variable. Loyalty, aggressive intent, approximation to some truth often are assumed to be phenomena that can be characterized as continuous variables.) Finally, with the more generic and overarching approach, *multivariate analysis of variance*, while the *events* are dichotomous or characterized by multiple categories and attributed to two or more different groups of people, the *events of interest* are continuous. Also, of significant interest to the profiler is group membership within some event is predictive of the events of interest.

For all generic versions of logistic regression, the events useful in prediction each may partially contribute toward this prediction. Also, statements can be made about increments and decrements in prediction validity and utility based on the addition and subtraction of events to some existing set of them. A significant problem is that a specific event may look significantly contributive to prediction or not based on the profiler's choice of what other events are collected on and analyzed. Multiple repetitions of how various sets of events in various combinations contribute to prediction allow profilers to arrive at what will be termed the most valid and useful set of such events facilitating prediction of some event of interest.

Two common approaches supporting estimates of the predictive validity of an event for some event of interest are the *Wald statistic* and the *odds ratio*. The former, named for the Transylvanian statistician Abraham Wald, helps identify how statistically significant or probable an event's relationship may be with an event of interest. The latter helps identify how changes of the probability of some event of interest's occurrence may be dependent on changes of the value of an event assumed to help predict it. As Groscup (2011) reported, odds ratios are being used more commonly in at least one significant research journal bearing on relationships of psychological variables and aspects of legal decisions.

Given that people and situations change with time as do specific profiling predictive tasks, logistic regression should be an ongoing enterprise that is mined by profilers working cases. Logistic regression continues to comprise a very common set of procedures employed in commercial profiling—viz., differentiating people who do and don't buy specific products or service, spotting changes in the profile based on ongoing purchasing preferences. This time sensitivity to possible change in the validity and utility of a profile should be but often isn't emulated in criminal profiling when prototypical example of specific kinds of criminals or crimes are the issue.

4.6 EFFECT SIZE AND STRUCTURAL EQUATION MODELING

Two other statistical concepts of relevance to profilers are *effect size* and *structural equation modeling*. The *effect size* is the measure of the magnitude or strength of a relationship between variables that goes beyond what most readers are familiar with—that is, *statistical significance* suggesting how likely a relationship between and among events and these with an event of interest in a sample might also be the case in an entire population. The main problem with statistical significance is that even weak relationships between events may appear significant, the greater the number of events in the sample being analyzed, while even strong ones may not, the smaller the sample. In contrast, *effect size* is *not* dependent on sample size and thus facilitates meta-evaluations among profiling-relevant studies when each, as likely, contains different sample sizes.

Most simply, *structural equation modeling* encompass techniques used in an attempt to produce patterns and types of organization among events either collected through observation or then systematically manipulated through experimentation or created in a simulation of what events could be observed and then manipulated. The latter are often called Monte Carlo simulations—named as such by the Polish mathematician Stanislaw Ulam and the Greek physicist Nicholas Metropolis after popular games of chance in Monte Carlo—and are handy when resources for actual event observation and experimentation are not available or inadequate. Partial Monte Carlo simulations would add events to collected and manipulated ones through interpolations (adding additional events and their values within an interval already sampled) and extrapolations (adding events and their values beyond sampled intervals).

One would then develop estimates of how closely, with what levels of significance, and with what strengths and weaknesses a model fits the data. Then these patterns and organizational types are presumed to have meaning that may have relevance for prediction, post-diction or peri-diction, understanding, and influence. I remember many creative moments in a graduate class on factor analysis when topical themes or labels were applied to various patterns and organizational types—presumably reinforcing their psychological meaning. Whether such meaning represented or corresponded to human psychology of those profiled or the human psychology of the profiler could not easily be differentiated. This is especially the case—as popularized by the American policy and management consultant Jim Manzi (2012), in a recent book *Uncontrolled*—because minor modification of technical assumptions in many models can have significant impact on the models' meaning; models developed to assess government policies and programs often show that what is assessed aren't effective or worse, thus impeding the quest and priority for assessing other policies and programs; and as I've already alluded to, the world seems to be changing so fast that the validity and utility of models may be lost before results are published—underlining the need for profilers and others to be in a continuous modeling mode. Yet again, Helen Gurley Brown of *Cosmopolitan* fame is donating $30M to the Brown Institute for purposes including improving journalism through "…developing computer programs to help reporters spot patterns in huge data sets

… [and] … new types of interactive charts and graphs to display statistics … in more compelling way" (Legendary, 2012).

Chapter 5 will present a way of thinking about events associated with an event of interest analogously based on the statistical perspectives described in this section. That is, *as if* these perspectives were actually being employed. This approach by analogy is essential, because the collection of events on large numbers of people to measures differences among them, viz., a *nomothetic or normative approach*, often is tangential at best to profiling in an individual case. For example, they measure *how different an individual is to some central tendency* based on measuring people in general on some characteristic and, thus, doesn't really measure any one individual on that characteristic or others that might be more meaningful.

The approach by analogy is also essential because measuring some individual across time on some characteristic and between and among characteristics, viz., an *idiographic or ipsative* approach—from the Latin *ipse* denoting *himself or less sexist the self—often* is unknowable or has not yet been on matters of relevance to profilers. In fact, the comparative advantages and disadvantages of the two previous approaches need to be empirically validated for profiling usage (cf. Rogers & Widiger, 1989). Returning to the advocacy of Meehl (1954), Dawes (1994), and Faust (2012) for simple statistical algorithms applied to profiling-like tasks, going from the *as if* to the *is* research of the type just described would be *idiographic* in that it would involve the study of single individuals over time and *nomothetic* in that it would study many individuals across time. The term for this is *idiothetic* (Lamiell, 1981) and was alluded to in Chapter 3. Eventually, profilers would have their algorithms and usually perform better than through their experience, judgment, and intuition in developing statements about terrorists, spies, liars, and whomever and whatever else might be of interest.

I'd now like readers to engage with LO 4.5 and *dec* the statistical approaches and assumptions bearing on data employed by profilers. I'm hoping for conceptual understanding, not quantitative manipulation. The context is a film fragment from *The Deer Hunter* (Spikings et al., 1978) directed by Michael Cimino. The fragment portrays a Vietnamese version of Russian roulette with U.S. prisoners of war (POWs) as participants. Based on the verbal and nonverbal behavior of the two POWs playing the game (played by Robert de Niro and Christopher Walken), what events might the POWs have perceived, what inferences might they have arrived at, De Niro's character especially, based on the previous statistical approaches that might be associated with the event of interest—the bloody climax to the roulette?

4.7   DECEPTION ANALYSIS

As with the heuristics described earlier in this chapter, deception has positive and negative consequences. I'll define it as the intentional misrepresentation of events to influence the internal and external events associated with some target (including some relevant situation) in a manner advantageous to the misrepresenter. This might involve presenting the truth when one expects the target to perceive it as false. Deceptive seeds may be planted so that the misrepresentation may become significant only much later in time. As opposed to Winston Churchill's statement at the Tehran Conference in 1943 that "… in wartime, truth is so precious that she should always be attended by a bodyguard of lies ...," deception may be quite effective when the right falsehood is attended by a bodyguard of truths.

The relevance for profilers is threefold. Insofar as there are competing psychological phenomena intrapsychically, profilers may engage in self-deception as to their own motives, how stringently data are being analyzed, the impact of heuristics, and so on. Second, people being profiled may know or suspect this (that they are being profiled) and act accordingly. Or they may be deceptive as a common personal, social, or professional lifestyle or—borrowing from trait language—deceptive by disposition. This could apply to profilers aware of the likelihood they're being observed by personnel from internal affairs and counterintelligence entities and even by similar personnel or by friends and associates related to people whom they (the profilers) are profiling. Third, all of this could apply to other sources, informants, and observers of profilers' activities.

Deception may be somewhat adaptive for all of us, regardless of Golden Rules highly valuating truth telling and living in truth. I truthfully confess—even as this phrase may appear ironic or strain the credulity of readers—that I have speculated to colleagues and students that living a life of truth may most likely lead to prison, a psychiatric hospital, or an early demise, more charitably to social ostracism. (This is elaborated upon in Chapter 9.)

With this as an introduction, what sorts of issues bearing on deception should be considered by profilers as they engage in predictive, post-dictive, peri-dictive, understanding, and influence challenges? The key here should be not the *if,* but the who, what, where, when, why, and how of deception. Unfortunately, there's much heat but little light, to my mind at least, in common deception recommendations for analysts including profilers as can be seen in the following adapted from Heuer and Pherson (2011)—in many ways a fine example of the genre.

The potential deceiver has a history of conducting deception. Well, we all are deceivers and potential deceivers, and we all have our histories. A better issue might be frequency, consistency, types, and purposes of deception for each deceiver.

The profiler receives information at a moment or interlude of critical time pressure (so deception may be more likely)—a report deadline, the beginning of a trial, significant competing priorities. I offer that all times are the right times for deception, because we live in a world of competing priorities. (Also, a potential deceiver reading this paragraph may then decide to slip the deception into some less critical interlude.) Moreover, at moments of less or more time pressure, profilers still may develop the rationale and motivation to discount, ignore, properly analyze, or obsess over the information and its relationship with all other relevant events. (Here self-deception and quasi-paranoid trends may work for or against the profiler primed or sensitized for deception.)

Information is received from a questionable source. But an *unquestionable* source is the most lucrative source from which a deception can be launched. As to questionable sources, those with sterling truth telling have been with us before the Trojan princess Cassandra and, I suspect, will continue to be. My reading of *Agamemnon* by the Greek tragedian Aeschylus is that she speaks the truth but is never believed after going through a psychotic-like episode induced by the god Apollo for not agreeing to his sexual desires. In the *Trojan Women* of the Greek tragedian Euripides, her own mother does seem to be comforted by Cassandra's tales of the impending deaths of Greek heroes and Cassandra's own coming murder. In today's world, instead, women who refuse sexual ministrations of their husbands and owners, are sometimes killed, mutilated, raped, otherwise abused, and not always believed. And when they are it's too late. Case in point is Lee Marvin playing Nick Acropolis in a 1961 episode of the television series *The Untouchables* who realizes almost too late that his wife has *made* one of his gunmen as out to get him from the very beginning—"Stella was right. Stella is always right."

Believing new information would lead to expending significantly more resources in the profiling task, in the adjudication of the profiling issues, or the consequences for the political authority controlling the process and aftermath. I think this is relevant to deception, but even more so and more typical to organizational self-deception leading less to finding the truth than constructing a satisfactory case given organizational dynamics and various political concerns.

The possibility of deception cannot be rejected simply because there seem to be no events associated with it. Whether there seem to be events associated with deception or not, there is no necessary connection with whether deception is occurring or especially what kind for what purpose. As I write this, there's public discourse on a recent military parade in North Korea concerning what appear to be fake missiles on display (Choe, 2012). Does the fakeness associate with an intention on the part of deception planners to engender truth in observers or some false perception? Similarly, if the missiles were not fake, are deception planners intending to engender truth or falsehood? Also, *no events associated with deception* is just another name for the event of no events being employed for deception.

Be suspicious of human sources whom you don't meet and about whom you're unclear how or from whom they received information. As will become clear in Chapter 9, direct contact with sources can increase the probability of successful deception as well as decrease it or have no effect—whether from sources or subsources. Also, given that people differ in the consistency of their displayed and hidden psychologies, it may be a fair statement that we may never meet all human sources even *within* the human with whom we interact.

Does information from one source conflict with that from another source? A better question is when would conflicts be expected and when wouldn't they be—especially given common empirical findings about the many times eyewitness testimony seems to be unreliable. Take a typical U.S. presidential election when a blowout might be a 60/40 split of the popular vote between the two major candidates. Is that 40% of the electorate who were just wrong?

Does a potential deceiver have a way to monitor the impact of a deception? In other words, is there some human or technical penetration of one's profiling work? This takes us into the areas of security (operations, communications, physical, and personnel) and of counterintelligence and is a significant issue even depicted in the film *The Verdict* (Brown, Zanuck, & Lumet, 1982). Here the law team defending the Archdiocese of Boston penetrates the adversarial lawyer's operations in a medical malpractice case. The team does through the latter's seemingly accidental meeting with a woman at a local saloon that leads to what he thinks is romance but what she knows is a setup. (As someone born in Boston, I object that the lawyer, even the alcoholic one played in the film, wouldn't have *been wise* to her from the very beginning.)

Most of this section relates to the risk of profilers being deceived by others. I submit that rigidly held beliefs about what events lead to what events of both interest and aversion to suspending both belief and disbelief are main culprits in profilers' self-deception and ease of exploitation by others. And now it's time for readers to *dec* LO 4.6 as applied to profiling. What deception tactics and strategies are illustrated in the film fragment from *Betrayal* (Spiegel & Jones, 1983), based on an adaptation of a Harold Pinter play. In this short interlude in a woman's bedroom, who is trying to seduce whom? Does the deception-rich environment obscure what's happening? Are meanings changed by the time flow of the film in which the beginning of the tryst/ affair is shown at the end, the end at the beginning traveling back throughout the film to that beginning? (I'm wondering whether I've deceived readers up to this point who may have believed that *Betrayal* is on that list of the 100 greatest films according to the American Film Institute [See the preface]. It's actually the only one used in this book's *dec* LO exercises that isn't.)

4.8 CLOSE READING THROUGH INTERDISCIPLINARY SOURCES

Close reading is a construct from literary criticism. Here are some of the components based on common usage as described by the OED (2012) and my own discussions with professors specializing in literary criticism. The essence of close reading is critical and detailed analysis of text where *text* may refer not only to what is written and what is spoken but also to various cultural products as described in the preface (film, dance, painting, novels, essays, poetry, and music). In addition, text may refer to any event and event of interest—that is, anything or anyone can be *read* including events associated with some event of interest, person, and or situation.

As Abrams (1953) described, one might read text through inferred meanings based on events associated with the text's author or creator; events presumed to be effects from the text onto the text's reader; presumed representations and reflections of or correspondences to events in the world outside the text, such as a woman's physical mutilation by a male religious leader corresponding to the mutilation of feminine souls by a patriarchal world in the perspective of feminists; and presumed meanings, structures, and dynamics among components of the text itself. As I mentioned in Chapter 2, this last is a dicey proposition in that readers might accomplish it only with the aid of combinations of the first three approaches to reading text. It is for this reason I so appreciate the comment of the American literary critic Leslie Fiedler (1952) from the *Sewanee Review* that close reading is a "cant phrase of the antibiographist"—that is, something favored by those who reject that events associated with the author or creator of text are significant in inferring meaning and who have not critically thought through their position on this.

Yet it's this last approach that most often is associated with close reading. So where does this leave us? Readers might figuratively immerse themselves in the text and through this immersion, correct or adaptive meanings, structures, and dynamics may become apparent without the need for *dérangement* and the like described earlier. This may not seem that different from a group of investigators and analysts closed off in some smoke-filled room with interminable cups of foul tasting coffee enveloped by just the facts and waiting for eureka moments of discovery or, sadly, *groupthink*. But applied to interdisciplinary sources, profilers might get a better feel for the opportunities and threats related to finding the right meaning from text.

From the abstract to the concrete, here's a case in point—part of a close reading of Herman Melville's (1967/1855) story *Benito Cereno*. Much like a profiler, an American sea captain, Amaso Delano, boards a Spanish ship, meets its captain. The eponymous protagonist begins to feel that something is not right but until the very end of the story gets it all wrong. Delano senses that Cereno is not displaying appropriate authority, tasks are not being carried out efficiently, and assumes the problems stem from Cereno who—because he's Spanish—probably was given the captaincy as a sinecure without appropriate training or experience. Delano has a sense that, perhaps, something evil is afoot, but his degree of innocence about the real world and his penchant to think the best of people and things prevent him from following this line of thought along. Most of the crew is what we would now call African American but with the racism prevalent at the time, the *best* Delano can think of them is that they may be going along with Cereno in whatever may be not right. After all, from his perspective, they're barely fit to be servants and slaves; as a real-world successor to Delano, Al Campanis, the general manager of the Los Angeles Dodgers, stated on a *Nightline* interview with Ted Koppel in 1987, "They may not have some of the necessities to be, let's say, a field manager, or, perhaps, a general manager [or a leader or manager in general]."

It turns out that there's been a slave revolt and mutiny. It's been in plain view the entire time, but Delano in post-9/11 lingo *doesn't connect the dots*. Even when Delano's in the process of returning to his own ship and Cereno jumps overboard and into Delano's rowboat with Cereno's servant (in Delano's eyes) right behind him, he (Delano) still doesn't *get it*. Only when the servant tries to kill Cereno is the fog of incomprehension lifted. The many, many events before this point are now radically reinterpreted by Cereno (and readers). This includes a startling, earlier moment when the servant cuts Cereno while shaving him and then intentionally cuts himself—the servant is *playing at* being subservient, but he's not.

I maintain that a close reading of this story affords profilers a unique immersion in the challenge of opportunities and threats they face. I share the results of my own close reading of events and events of interest bearing on terrorism, espionage, and deception in Chapters 7–9. But for now, I also add that the moment of total reinterpretation may be a false *eureka*—from the classical Greek, I have found it, but the *it* is something even further from what the profilers needs or seeks whether through self-deception, deception, ignorance, or bad luck.

I'd now like readers to engage with LO 4.7 and *dec* the construct of interdisciplinary close reading as applied to profiling. The context is a film fragment from *Sunset Boulevard* (Brackett & Wilder, 1950), that's right, Billy Wilder again. Can readers immerse themselves in the fragment deeply enough to experience the world as the aging, and probably insane, actress Norma Desmond (played by Gloria Swanson) does? Does Norma really believe she's on a movie set? What does the quote, "All right, Mr. DeMille [a famous film director and producer]. I'm ready for my close-up" mean and how does it relate to an event of interest—her murder of a paramour much earlier on?

4.9 PROFILERS AND POLITICS

I described in Chapter 1 some of the political phenomena associated with profiling. The main focus of that section was profiling as it relates to (1) how people are controlled in a society, (2) how people with formal and de facto power in a society can maintain or even increase their power through a profiling industry and the nature of what constitutes profiling, and (3) how cognizant or not profilers may be of these politics. What follows are other political phenomena that focus less on the society as a whole and more on what I'll term *profiling cultures* that apply more generally to knowledge cultures and the sociology of knowledge.

I'll begin by referring to research by Bickman (1996, 1997) on mental health services for children and adolescents. It's not the results but the consequences of the results that to me are extraordinary. The research explored the consequences of implementing the best possible mental health services based on the wisdom of highly respected textbooks and refereed journal publications. These services were all combined into a comprehensive capability and intended to optimize assessment validity and utility, therapeutic progress, and other desired goals like access to care, continuity of care, consumer satisfaction, and providing treatment to consumers in least restrictive environments. As well, the research was accomplished only after there was a general consensus among informed professionals that a *gold-standard* study was in the making. (In other words, experts with different empirical and theoretical orientations largely agreed ahead of time that the study should deliver significant positive consequences—because the best services were being offered and the best ways of measuring them were being used.)

Suffice it to say that the results were grossly *underwhelming*. On one hand, there were all the good things that therapists aspire to approach and use and bemoan when these things are absent because of an austere budget—for example, continuity of care, least restrictive environments, what we now call evidence-based services. On the other hand, these things seemed *not* to yield huge positive increments in functioning but pretty much the across-the-board combinations of successes and failures with which therapists are quite familiar.

But here's the kicker. Did such momentous results—momentous because of their underwhelming nature—induce providers of mental health services to seek totally new avenues of assessment and intervention? Or new theoretical analyses leading to new assessment and intervention techniques that would then be subject to empirical and experimental estimates of validity and utility? No. Instead, it was business as usual. Why? I believe this was largely due to the culture of mental health services constituted by many vested interests including those who train therapists; those who believe they are properly trained; professional, interest group, and government stances on accepted practice and what is not accepted; the proprietary entities marketing assessment instruments and therapeutic products; the values, research paradigms, and varying distances with the real world of academic departments enmeshed in scientific and professional traditions; and the hopes, desires, and the reactance or lack thereof of the general public and of those embracing various urban mythologies who are seeking services for their children and adolescents. In other words, in the face of underwhelming results, too much had to change for change to occur. And the quest for truth, still a survivor even in an age-old conflict between skepticism and belief, was the victim.

Profiling cultures are similar. Without mentioning names—itself a political choice as well as one of due diligence in the context of potential litigation, calumny, and character assassination among parties—I offer the following. Professional and scientific journals each have their own preferences for what research topics and findings are most desirable and what theoretical rationales and quantitative or qualitative procedures are most credible and appropriate. Mass media venues, especially cable news, and social network channels seem to favor the sensationalistic and what is not complex. There are personal and ideological vendettas including those over issues I've already described such as the importance or lack thereof of what cannot be easily measured—as if what's easy is or will be *prima facie* more valuable than what is not; whether there's an *unconscious* and, if so, what its relevance might be (see Chapter 3); and whether a law enforcement background is crucial to profiling knowledge (see Chapter 2). Profilers may come up with recommendations consonant with a story they think will sell to a consumer—such as a law enforcement organization, lawyers, various nongovernmental funding entities, broadcast journalists—than one based on honest attempts at a truth-based analysis regardless of what the *truth* construct denotes and connotes. (Profilers are profiling consumers about what will sell as profiling.) There also are the self-politics of the quest for fame and acting out psychological conflicts including those based on overcompensations for feelings of inferiority (see the preface). And then there's profiling's version of *Wheel of Fortune* where at issue are book sales and well-remunerated presentations and specialized continuing education curricula. To conclude this section, while the politics in Chapter 1 relate to profilers in the service of the power of others, this section relates to profilers seeking their own power.

4.10   CONCLUSION

So what are readers to make of Chapter 4? Most importantly, how optimistic can we be that the various intrapsychic processes of profilers can be modified toward more valid and useful contributions toward prediction, post-diction, peri-diction, understanding, and influence? Besides the rather pessimistic opinion provided herein, a recent review of research on working memory (Shipstead, Redick, & Engle, 2012) supports this pessimism. Working memory (WM) is here defined as a cognitive system that strongly relates to a person's ability to reason with novel information and direct attention to goal-relevant information. (This seems congruent with what profilers attempt to do.) Although there are studies supporting the significant and long-term improvement of such cognitive functioning, Shipstead et al. find that these studies have four problematic components: (1) the people who allegedly show improvement are assessed on a constrained breadth of relevant tasks; (2) the WM tasks analyzed often are used and interpreted inconsistently; (3) the control groups either go through no credible experimental manipulation (like some sort of placebo improvement session) or something that defies credibility of possibly being effective; and (4) many measurements of purported positive change in WM are subjectively based, that is, come from a person's own opinion as opposed to other kinds of subjectivism like from (a) raters in a double-blind study whose judgments are assessed at least for reliability or (b) empirically validated objective and standardized measures of WM. An overall conclusion about *what* the *who doing the profiling* brings to the task is that profilers are playing with a deck of cards containing some aces on the one hand and jokers on the other. (Germane for profilers consulting and engaging in relevant research is the site *PsychFileDrawer.org*. This site not only is an archive for failed replication attempts—which for most of the history of scientific psychology would not be published in refereed journals—but also maintains a list of the studies that its users would most like to see what replicated. A study that purports to demonstrate how aspects of WM, viz., fluid intelligence—variously defined as innate intelligence or intelligence not yet tapped or actualized—can be significantly changed in the long-term has been rated at the top during early May 2012. Rated at number 20 was whether there are really gender differences in the accuracy of parking automobiles.)

I'd now like readers to engage with LO 4.8 and *dec* the profiling politics involving profilers' quests for power. The context is a film fragment from *Citizen Kane* (Welles, 1941)—the film recognized by the American Film Institute as the *best (American?) film* of all time, maybe because it's largely about how to get, keep, use, and lose power. The fragment is the very end of the film. Kane has died; all his physical possessions remain; many of them are being intentionally destroyed; and then there's the mystery around his last dying word—"rosebud"—and what it means. I'm hoping readers can match up examples of profilers' power quests with those presumed to be of Kane himself and identify what profilers' rosebud might be.

5 The Profiling Matrix

After the first four chapters, some readers might wish to give up. Why go any further? They may be thinking of something so well described by W. B. Yeats in "The Second Coming" (1919):

> Turning and turning in the widening gyre
> The falcon cannot hear the falconer;
> Things fall apart; the centre cannot hold; ...
> The best lack all conviction, while the worst
> Are full of passionate intensity...
> And what rough beast, its hour come round at last,
> Slouches towards Bethlehem to be born?

But this chapter and the one that follows are intended to strip the application of science to profiling down to its essence. I assume in these chapters that the observation, collection, analysis, and then communication of data are the most appropriate means to attempt to know the world and the events within it. However, I also assume—following the work of philosophers like P. Kyle Stanford (2006) in *Exceeding Our Grasp: Science, History, and the Problem of Unconceived Alternatives*—that even with something called amply collected data scientists may not be able to conceive of those data's best explanation, let alone identifying the data as the best among competing data sets. Stanford calls this *contrastive underdeterminism,* perhaps because scientists have not identified or just do not identify the best event to explain an event of interest, but only the best in contrast with a finite number of other events.

As well, I assume that when an explanation for an event of interest, that is, the identification of events as most closely associated with an event of interest, is unsupported or disconfirmed by data, scientists cannot immediately discount the event as unworthy. This is because an explanation cannot be completely evaluated in isolation but only with other related explanations with which it derives meaning. Stanford (2006) calls this *holistic underdeterminism,* perhaps because scientists can evaluate explanations only within the whole welter of other explanations—and this can be only approximated. One implication of contrastive and holistic undeterminisms is that whenever readers and I come up with what seems to be the events best associated with an event of interest, we cannot be sure of at least two things: (1) how closely we approach a literally accurate description; and (2) what will be the most valid and useful association of events and an event of interest in allowing us to interact with the world, that is, have our predictions, post-dictions, and peri-dictions *work* for us as we seek understanding and influence.

Now from theory to more concrete examples. As described by Bumiller and Cushman (2012), U.S. infantryman Robert Bales has been accused of massacring

16 or 17 Afghan citizens in the Panjwai district of Kandahar Province—the event of interest. But what are the associated events? In public discourse, these seem to include (1) general war and combat experience including four deployments in Iraq and Afghanistan; (2) war injuries resulting in (a) the necessity of the removal of part of a foot arch through surgery and (b) cognitive problems and loss of some impulse control from traumatic brain injury (TBI) after a Humvee flipped over reactive to an improvised explosive device (IED) detonation; (3) alleged financial pressures; (4) being passed over for promotion to E-7 (Sergeant First class); (5) so-called brushes with law enforcement including dropped charges for crashing into a parked car and then leaving the season and, maybe, for assault; (6) worries about leaving his wife pregnant and with the responsibility of parenting alone; (7) possible posttraumatic stress disorder (PTSD); (8) alleged alcohol abuse near the time of the alleged massacre (and later allegations of ongoing use of an anabolic steroid); and (9) witnessing a buddy lose a leg in a land mine explosion the day before the massacre. How do we address this information as to associations among events and between them and the event of interest?

Or Turvey (2011, pp. 311–329) provides a chapter on interpreting motive for an event of interest. He provides a listing of a number of possible motives and differentiates motive from intent—so both instances of *motive* and *intent* might be associated together and with an event of interest. However, he does not provide examples of how one actually chose among possibilities in a specific case. He also does not show how other types of internal and external events might have been associated together and with the event of interest. However, he much more closely demonstrates how to develop such associations in his description of an introduction to crime reconstruction, that is, what might have happened based on physical information at a specific location, based on his elaboration of Locard's exchange principle. (A good example is Turvey's treatment of three murders on pp. 261–262.)

My very broad interpretation of Locard is as follows. I agree with most criminal investigators that Locard directs us to generate hypotheses necessary to understand how physical events came into contact with a crime scene, but I also add the who, what, where, when, why, and how concerning physical events becoming (1) positioned and located at the scene; (2) absent from a specific location; (3) changed or maintained due to weather; (4) decomposed and at what rate; and (5) in contact with other living organisms and the consequences of this. *Foundations of Psychological Profiling* is primarily focused on answering questions about how such questions can be most validly and usefully answered. What questions? Questions that apply to studying the person or persons who may be associated with situations, situation or situations that may be associated with people, and the interaction of the two.

What profilers need to do is create a unique mapping of the events assumed to be associated with the event of interest. They need to show the judgments associating the various events with each other and with the event of interest—and how strong these associations are at the moment the event of interest has occurred. And they need to be changing the who, what, where, when, why, and how concerning the events and event of interest based on the continuous collection, analysis, and reanalysis of information. They need, in other words, to create and maintain a *profiling matrix*.

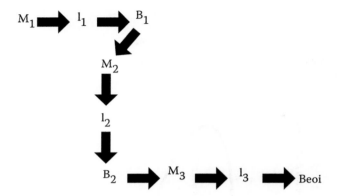

FIGURE 5.1   Simplified profiling matrix.

To illustrate, let's begin with some material from Turvey (2011). He asserts that *motives* are significant in understanding events of interest and defines motives as emotional, psychological, and material needs that drive and are satisfied by behavior—and here I add my opinion that *psychological* may subsume *emotional,* that *cognitive* may be included as a type of motive, that the individual may or may not be aware of a motive. He also asserts that *intentions* are significant in understanding events of interest—and here I'll note that intentions in the vast corpus of scientific psychological literature most often refer to (1) a behavior an individual desires and anticipates engaging in or (2) the motive the individual desires and anticipates satisfying.

Figure 5.1 depicts a simplistic profiling matrix showing how various motives (M1...Mn) and intentions (I1...In) might be related to each other, to resulting behaviors (B1...Bn), and to some behavioral event of interest (Beoi). Why is this matrix simplistic? It assumes that there is no interdependence or reciprocal influence among the various motives, intentions, and behaviors. For example, surely a motive may directly affect the kind or strength of other motives without having to influence only through some intermediary intention and behavior. Moreover, behaviors may influence the strength of the very motive and intention that are assumed to lead to it. As well, the same behavior may be arrived at through various motives and intentions. In addition, Figure 5.1 implies that only linear as opposed to curvilinear and nonlinear relationships are operative, and there is no time dependence between and among the motives, intentions, and behaviors—that is, when the various relationships hold and when they don't. Finally, Figure 5.1 does not indicate the strength of the various relationships and whether this changes with time or not. And just an obvious point: I'm sure Turvey (2011) would be the first to point out that many other events besides motives and intentions might be associated with the Beoi. These other events comprise the many constructs of the five profiling languages described in Chapter 3.

Figure 5.2 contains a more complex profiling matrix involving the Robert Bales case. The first main point depicted by the matrix is that there may be an overdetermination of the massacre, that is, multiple, strong pathways to leading to it. One pathway goes from two domestic events and one professional event converging on anger and then to the massacre. A second pathway goes from an IED detonation

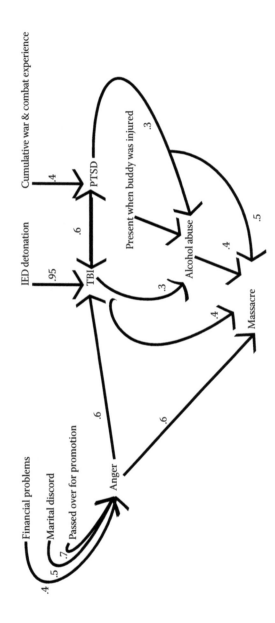

FIGURE 5.2 Less simplified profiling matrix.

to a TBI to alcohol abuse and then the massacre. The third goes from cumulative war and combat experience to the development of PTSD to alcohol abuse and then the massacre. A fourth from TBI to the massacre. A fifth from PTSD to the massacre—also a continuation of the third. (And as readers can see, I'm not describing all possible pathways.)

A second main point is that the strength of each association between and among events is quantitatively estimated with possible values from +1.0 through 0 to –1.0 with the meanings and implications identical to what was described in Chapter 4. The numbers are not intended to add up. For example, the .6 final pathway from anger, the .4 from TBI, the .4 from alcohol abuse, and the .5 from PTSD could add up to 1.9, but with +1.0 as the highest possible value, such adding up can lead us only to some estimate of overdetermination closer to this +1.0 figure. In fact, the interactive effects among the various events might lead to one pathway being partially increased or decreased by another—although not depicted this led to much less overdetermination, for example, the .6 from anger to massacre partially canceling out the .4 from alcohol abuse.

A third main point, already alluded to, is that some interactions and contingencies are depicted. TBI and anger affect each other, as do TBI and PTSD. Alcohol abuse is affected by TBI, PTSD, and being present when a buddy was injured.

A fourth main point: The events used in the matrix must be somewhat incorrect and definitely incomplete, as they are based solely on newspaper articles, that is, just one source of information. And contrary to many profiling languages, little seems to be relevant before war experience begins—for example, psychosexual events of childhood, traits, early conditioning experiences, putative biological precursors of aggression, and already strong beliefs about the meaning of life and what constitutes self-identity.

A fifth main point: How much of this can actually be known so that profilers might develop such a matrix depicting the very moment when the massacre occurred? And given that the massacre allegedly went on over at least two separate periods of time on the same night, an accurate matrix might well be needed moment by moment, not only in the time leading up to the event of interest but also during it. A significant challenge to identifying changes in a matrix through time are the internal deliberations and dialogues within the individual being profiled, especially as they impact on various self-images, elements of fantasy, and interpretation of external text including that contained on jihadi websites as seems to have been the case with Mohammed Merah (see Chapter 2). Finally, as with the profiling schematics in Chapter 3, the ideal depicted through computer graphic design would be an ever-changing matrix theoretically beginning at birth if not before and leading to the end of the event of interest and even after if later events can help shed light on what came before.

In any case, the quantitative estimates indicating strength of associations between and among events within a matrix are subjective—based on what *might* be the case for this specific individual, even as massive data collection subject to sophisticated quantitative manipulation is, ultimately subjective as well. Where do these estimates come from? Maybe from research knowledge bearing on alcohol abuse, TBI, and PTSD. Maybe from intuition, some higher military authority, and the rest of the basic epistemological approaches. Maybe they're affected by some of the examples of social cognitions under uncertainty, logic, formal argumentation, empiricism, experimentalism, deception analysis, interdisciplinary close reading, and politics described in Chapter 4. Maybe they're affected by confusion related to collected data going against common expectations or seeming to be partially conflicting. For example, there are findings that single tours in combat zones may be more strongly associated with alcohol abuse and emotional and mental disorders than multiple tours (Associations, 2011), even as the greater the number of traumatic events, the more morale can be lowered and emotional and mental problems increase (Joint Mental Health Advisory Team, 2011). (A further complication is delineating actual combat experience in a war without traditional frontlines and a uniformed enemy.)

To be blunt, I am advocating for the profiling matrix, even as it will often be a blatantly subjective simulation of a quantitative, objective methodology that itself is ultimately subjective. Students using the matrix in specific cases are often uncomfortable in taking responsibility for their own judgments as to (1) what events are associated with other events and the event of interest and (2) the quantitative indicators of the strength of these associations. They become more comfortable once they realize that appropriate data bases for much of what is profiled are just not available and that their (students') engagement in a proto-systematic knowledge process at least reinforces accountability for profiling judgments and can lead to a systematic accumulation of knowledge over time as to what linkages may have more validity and utility. Students also become more comfortable with the limitations of traditional science applied to human psychology and the potential benefits of the arts and humanities coupled with the sciences in developing knowledge about people.

So getting back to the term *maybe*. The profiling matrix is based on many *maybes*. This may infuriate some readers including some who are profilers, but maybe that's all we can do.

As a more detailed illustration, I offer an intermediary draft matrix (Figure 5.3) from a project (Anderson-Cutright-Cisneros et al., 2012) developed by a group of upper-level undergraduate students in a course on personality and profiling. Their task was to develop a matrix and, later, a narrative (see Chapter 6) containing events and their relationships bearing on an event of interest—Jim Jones's inducement of his followers to commit suicide at the communal settlement of Jonestown (PBS, 2012). This is a task of post-dictive profiling.

The events depicted are in a chronological sequence from left to right from earlier to last events. It doesn't have to be this way, just as films such as *Pulp Fiction* (Bender & Tarantino, 1990) and the previously discussed *Betrayal* (see Chapter 4) meaningfully relate events without a beginning to end. Time is actually a tool of profilers in conveying why something may have happened.

There are multiple pathways of events leading to the event of interest: a .8 from paranoid personality disorder, a .4 from the formation of the settlement, a .6 from a combination of fear of a U.S. government intervention (investigation and follow-up action) of the settlement and an actual site investigation.

Many of the events are interdependent. The paranoid personality disorder affects fear of government intervention and the actual event of interest. Growing up in poverty leads to support for a political ideology (socialism) and specific political positions (equal rights and racial integration). Multiple events lead to the formation of

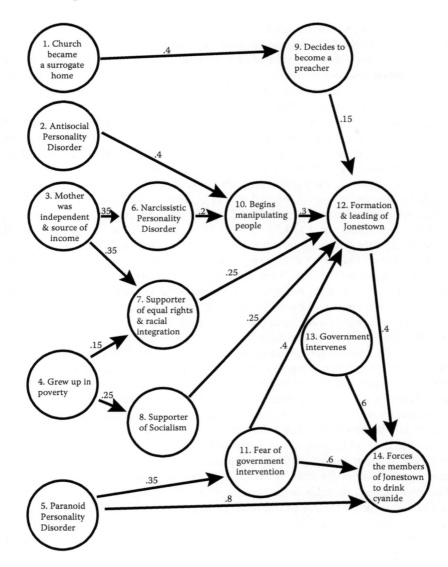

FIGURE 5.3   Jones matrix.

the settlement including the decision to become a preacher, beginning to manipulate people (more to follow on this one), his support for socialism and support for equal rights and racial integration, and fear of government intervention (investigation and follow-up action).

The events reflect the use of different profiling languages. The use of the construct of a personality disorder (based on matching criteria to the *Diagnostic and Statistical Manual of Mental Disorders IV-Text Revision* [DSM]) comprises the use of all five languages depending on how one interprets the DSM criteria's text. The citing of growing up in poverty might bring with it some highly probable conditioning experiences. An environment within which psychodynamic conflicts and evolutionarily based behavioral repertoires were expressed might lead to specific consequences including the nurturance of identification with or introjection of political ideologies and positions bearing on matters of existence. (I apologize for my use but not for the students' use of some common psychological terms that too easily elicit the reaction of the American-born author Henry James in his preface to *The Tragic Muse* for the novel *War and Peace* by the Russian author Leo Tolstoy—a loose and baggy monster with queer elements of the accidental and the arbitrary. Only some of these events might actually be consciously experienced or experienced at all by Jones, and none may have some ultimate ontological substance.)

Now let's look at some problems with the students' draft matrix. The biggest might be the sparse use of internal events to help post-dictively understand the inducement to collective suicide. Based on my own reading of multiple sources on Jones and Jonestown, I feel the absence of *hot* events—that is, those that impel extreme behavior or drive it forward—like believing one is god or god-like; unconscious and conscious urges to express sexuality and violence with little to modulate or impede them; and beliefs in what death is, what it holds out, what may come next, and whether there actually is a difference between life and death. Is there some sort of extreme overcompensation for being at the mercy of others while in poverty so that one must control totally, hold the power of life and death over others, and, ultimately, show no mercy or compassion through no mercy?

Although common clinical lore on personality disorders dictates that these cannot be *cured* but only better or worse managed, perhaps there are fluctuations in the frequency, intensity, and content of the criteria constituting the diagnose. Perhaps there are interludes where for all intents and purposes there is no disorder—especially given that the disorders are identified through observable and inferred psychological and social phenomena that themselves may vary in social acceptability and utility.

A case in point bearing not on personality disorders but being "power hungry" is an op-ed piece on Robert Caro's multivolume biography of the late U.S. president Lyndon Baines Johnson (Nocera, 2012). Nocera quotes Caro from the latter's first two volumes on Johnson as being a man with "hunger for power in its most naked form, for power not to improve the lives of others, but to manipulate and dominate them." Nocera then wonders how Caro can focus within the fourth volume on Johnson being such a success in getting legislation passed with a significantly "liberal agenda" including the Civil Rights Act. Nocera concludes that Caro "can't countenance Johnson being both ruthless and compassionate in the same volume. He has to be one or the other." A challenge in developing a profiling matrix is that no one has to be anything and anyone can be anyone or *anyones* even harboring everchanging contradictions.

Two minor, one major, and then one concluding point with the students' matrix. One minor point is that neither Jim Jones nor anyone else began manipulating people (and attempting to) so late in life concurrently with the impetus from two different personality disorders. Perhaps, the students are referring to a specific kind of manipulation? The other minor point is that the wording and phrasing of each event might be more specific and closer to its essence. To be fair to the students who developed this matrix, they also prepared an appendix containing more details on each of the events in the matrix and even color-coded the events in the matrix by type such as internal psychological event, external social event, and so on.

The major point is that the matrix in static form (Figure 5.3) is a prisoner of its own medium. A more realistic depiction would be one that is continuously changing with each event changing shape, getting bigger and smaller, linkages between events increasing and decreasing, some events and linkages even disappearing to reappear or appear nevermore.

The concluding point and one that leads into the next chapter is that the students' matrix needs further development about a struggle between—or what Nietzsche might have termed *beyond*—good and evil. According to the matrix on Jones, the same sorts of events that may lead to a life of selfless dedication to others and a renunciation of material well-being and advancement instead become associated with yet other events leading to an endpoint of horror. Perhaps the matrix and the scaffolding of argumentation that can be abstracted from it need further buttressing by a rhetorical product as timeless as it may be powerful in conveying meaning and influencing meaning's recipients. This is the *profiling narrative* to which we turn in Chapter 6.

But first, it's time for readers to engage with LO 5.1 and *dec* the profiling matrix. The context is a film fragment from *Lawrence of Arabia* (Spiegel & Lean, 1962). What profiling matrix can be constructed leading to leading to the great achievements of Lawrence's past, present, and future—events leading to the events of interest—based on this dialogue between him (played by Peter O'Toole) and Sherif Ali (played by Omar Sharif). Of great interest is how much is fated, how much is determined or overdetermined, how much is free will or accident. (And by now, some readers have grasped my strong acceptance of *the auteur theory* of film through my citations of the *director* with each film and film fragment mentioned in this book— that the *director* is most responsible for the profile or profiles crafted by the film.) Thus, it's with a sense of irony and the bittersweet that as I write these words, I think of the death just a day or so ago of Andrew Sarris, the American film critic, who many years ago introduced me and many other students at Columbia University to the auteur theory (Sarris, 1996/1968). His profiles of film's profiles through the director as profiler will live on.

6 The Profiling Narrative

I maintain that when confronted with most if not all events, individuals ineluctably construct a *narrative* as part of generating the events' meaning—and this meaning is almost always imbued by and within a social context. What is a narrative? For our purpose, not a *story* but a *plot*.

A story is usually just a chronicle of events with the events ordered in a temporal sequence from the past forward. Even here, individuals usually generate at least some meaning as to how the events relate to each other—the who, what, where, when, why, and how. On the other hand, a plot, much more than a story, generates meaning about the events' relationships. Unlike a story, the plot will almost always *not* include everything that happened concerning the events and *not* every event, but only those events and details that bear on the important aspects of their relationships. And even among the events described, some will be emphasized, some discounted or barely mentioned. Also, unlike the story, the plot may not be described in a temporal sequence from past to the present and beyond but will convey meaning of the very temporal sequence it may not literally follow.

For example, in the plot for *Double Indemnity* described in Chapter 1, Walter Neff is the narrator of the plot and begins near its end and then goes back to its beginning, then to the present where he has begun through to the end. For profiling, the *plot* is key, and it is based on the profiling matrix. As the latter changes, so should the former. All details in the narrative must be traced back to some event or events in the matrix. In fact, there should be nothing in the narrative that does not relate to predicting, post-dicting, peri-dicting, understanding, and influencing the event of interest.

Here's an example of a narrative's power. Following Dwyer (2012,) a police officer took the role of a whistleblower and reported the wrongdoings of his superiors. His report of wrongdoings forms one narrative. He allegedly—as a result—was brought in cuffs by these superiors to a psychiatric emergency room. Based on their accounts of his behavior, he spent three days in the emergency room and then three more days in a locked psychiatric ward before his father tracked him down and brought him home. His superiors' accounts of his behavior form another narrative. In fact, one might speculate on how easy it would be to take the police officer's own narrative about wrongdoing and use it to support his superiors' narrative about his being paranoid, conspiracy oriented, and agitated. (Might one not be agitated, if one's well-meaning reports of wrongdoing led to a psychiatric admission instigated by superiors in whom one formally should trust and until then did trust?)

As well, what do readers make of the apparent fact that psychiatric authorities relied much more on information from the whistle-blower's superiors than on documented clinical observations of the whistleblower as "coherent, relevant with goal-directed speech and good eye contact." (Of course, they apparently did not view him as a whistle-blower.) There were yet other contradictory notations (still based on

Dwyer, 2012) such as impaired "insight and judgment" and "irritable with appropriate affect" that might suggest to a profiler profiling the profilers in the psychiatric service that—as Marcellus says to Horatio in *Hamlet*—something [was] rotten in the state of Denmark.

Beyond the alleged corruption on the part of the superiors, the two narratives might be reminiscent of a famous article published in *Science* (Rosenhan, 1973). In Rosenhan's research, women and men briefly *feigned* experiencing auditory hallucinations to try to gain admission to psychiatric hospitals. All were successful in this endeavor and were admitted and diagnosed with psychiatric disorders. After admission, they attempted to act *normally*—(presumably, how they usually behaved, although I'm not sure what this would be like in a psychiatric hospital for most people). They also told doctors and staff that they had not experienced any "more" hallucinations and were feeling fine. Not one of these research subjects was detected as a bogus patient, and some were confined for months. One of the aforementioned hospitals challenged Rosenhan to send more bogus patients who would be accurately detected by doctors and staff. Rosenhan agreed, and the doctors and staff did identify people presumed to be bogus patients. But Rosenhan had lied. He had sent no one to the hospital. Lucky for him there was no controlling narrative wherein such lying qualified as psychopathological and warranting of involuntary psychiatric admission as it has in both totalitarian and quasi-democratic political cultures.

Above and beyond (1) the ethics of lying and deception in the service of science and the greater public good and (2) various methodological issues such as the differential diagnostic validities of self-admitted hallucinations, readers should now appreciate the power of narratives. What remains to be explored is material pertinent to the types of common narratives and narrative components. Not only are these relevant in the seeking of events to help understand events of interest, but also they can be handy rhetorical devices to help other people understand why something might well occur, has occurred, or is occurring. Of course, a narrative is itself an event in larger narratives, for example, on profiling, and changes through time just as the profiling matrix on which it's founded, just as other people, situations, and other narratives change. Again, the need for computer graphic design to illustrate continuous change in a plot through time, through more data collection, through more analysis.

Narratives contain *actants*—a term popularized by the Lithuanian linguist Algirdas Greimas (1987) borrowed from the French linguist Lucien Tesnière. The presumption is that narratives contain action, people, and things—some of the last endowed with person-like qualities. People and things act, are acted upon, or merely observe or are aware of action. Common classes of actants include entities that desire or are desired, send or receive, or help or impede. The respective examples might be a man desiring to rape a woman, sending a gift to an authority figure like a political official that is intended to explode upon opening, and making a bomb for a bomber. In attempting to predict, post-dict, peri-dict, understand, and influence, profilers may attempt to identify who and what the actants might be for the narratives of suspects or for convicted bad actors—even narratives encompassing the meaning of salient situations like crime scenes. (Sometimes, people or situations seem so initially bizarre that a state of *defamiliarization* or what the Russian literary critic

Victor Schlovsky termed *ostranenie* [Crawford, 1984] ensues. It may take the collection of more information and repeated attempts at using multiple epistemological approaches to break free to narrative development.)

Narratives contain different types of plots. Both the Canadian literary critic Northrop Frye (1957) and the American historiographer Hayden White (1973) concur on at least four different styles—*romance, satire, comedy,* and *tragedy. Romance* is not necessarily a love or lust story. Its essence is a combination of some magnificent triumph over challenge, some transcendence over trials and tribulation, some liberation from the world of everyday events—even from the material world (preferably with angelic hosannas). Individuals coming to the attention of profilers may be acting, are acting, or have acted based on such a plot type. In fact, horrible events of interest from the profilers' perspective are often the most cherished and highly cherished from the perspective of some suspect or bad actor—the very thing that will lead to triumph, transcendence, or liberation. An obvious example is the religiously motivated suicide terrorist.

Satire is not necessarily comedy, although it can be in a dark way. Its essence is that things get in our way; what we're told is often not what's true; and as cited in common English translations of the title of a play by the French existentialist philosopher Jean Paul Sartre, there's *no way out* (*Huis Clos*, 1944) until death, and maybe not even then. From the perspective of profilers', individuals may feel entitled to act in any way they wish, even those ways that hurt others or that violate law, ethics, and morals. From an absurdist perspective, why not kill, commit espionage, or deceive gratuitously? After all, don't we live in an absurd universe? The Joker of *Batman* lore might come to mind. Another implication for profilers, such people may not have a strong motivation to avoid death, at times may even seek it, especially if important people or large numbers of people die as well. (I admit to some trepidation using the phrase *at times*—sounding too much like the rhetorical styles described in Rowland [2008] and wittingly or unwittingly emulated by some profilers from time immemorial, at times.)

Not only satire but also *comedy* may not be comedy. The essence here is that although life often has successes and failures, opportunities and threats, and various conflicts, most, if not all, are not the transcendent variety expressed in romance narratives. Instead, they are mundane, and, in the end, we overcome most of them and can celebrate. In the contemporary era, situation comedies have put comedy into comedy. This tradition, however, goes back at least to the time of the French playwright Molière (17th century), if not further back and more controversially to the times of the Greek playwright Aristophanes (5th century BCE). A closer-to-home example for profilers might be the rogue as lady's man who often cheats well-deserved jail time or even the hangman's noose because of what the American blues musicians Willie Dixon (writer) and Howlin' Wolf (vocalist) called being a *backdoor man*—with the judge's wife pleading with the judge for mercy so she won't lose *the good thing*. From the profilers' perspective, misbehavior should continue, because somehow and some way things will turn out fine in the end. That Molière has the Sun King himself, Louis XIV, intercede to make everything alright for the husband Orgon in *Tartuffe* (1664) might suggest a gender-bending irony beyond the scope of this book but is essential for the knowledge of profilers.

A *tragedy* is just that: a mixture of the good and bad with the *bad* coming out on top. If there's any comedy here, it's like that of the fool in Shakespeare's *King Lear* who may speak the truth but with the laughter of whistling by the graveyard. While often ending in the death of victims or of the perpetrators, at other times the protagonist may end up after falling from the heights, living and working within more limitations including limited hopes. Profilers should note that the fall can occur from the greatest heights, often facilitated by some trigger event or crisis in conjunction with problematic dispositions (feelings of inferiority, sexual and violent instincts) that in other circumstances might yield benign consequences. (This last observation about tragedy will be picked up again in Chapter 8 on espionage.)

Hayden White (1973) also noted that a narrative suggests how its possessor (profilers or those being profiled) views basic components of the world and their interaction. My reading of White suggests four main views. Is the world constituted by objects including people, each with independent properties with independent effects on others, a *formist* approach? How about if these objects are integrated and can aggregate into larger or smaller wholes—for example, competing properties within an individual or competing groups of people against other groups, an *organicist* approach? Or the world functions according to some natural or supernatural laws or principles, a *mechanistic* approach suggesting that some events cannot be forestalled whether seeming to derive from within or without? Or yet again things happen because of their specific contexts and would happen differently in other contexts, a *contextualist* approach? Although this material might seem too abstract, even esoteric, the profiling implications pertain to mental phenomena—constituting components of an inner narrative—seeming to determine what will happen, has happened, is happening.

White (1973) also suggests that narratives contain tropes (i.e., figurative language), with a bearing on human motivation. Examples include metaphors (e.g., believing certain types of people can be labeled as a Great Satan or a dog) and synedoche/metonymy (e.g., self-usages like someone believing she's an iron fist within a velvet glove or he's one big pimple); to this last, some of my students believe this was integral to the self-image and motivation of American mass murderer Robert Hansen. Maybe mass murder was the way to pop, lance, or exfoliate it.

American psychologist Dan McAdams has amassed a significant body of work on the significance of narratives for understanding people. His 1988 book is still highly relevant for profilers in emphasizing two prime needs—for *power* and for *intimacy*—as a foundation of human internal and external events and in some ways different from the sex and violence of Freudian instinct theory described in Chapter 3. These themes often crop up in post-dicting some of the low-frequency but highly unusual events of interest such as necrophiliac cannibalism—that is, a sure fire way to get close to people at least until decomposition may put an end to the affair.

Nietzsche (1980/1874), again, asserted that there were three main narratives—even as he termed them histories instead. *Monumental* ones inspire or influence the possessor to excel, maybe even to overreach. *Antiquarian* ones influence the possessor to be conservative in the sense of maintaining or returning to a status quo even if the meaning of the status quo is lost in the effort and only ritual remains. *Critical* ones often lead to breakdown or self-fragmentation in the quest for accurate self-analysis. (And insufficient work has been done on whether the possessor needs to be aware of the narrative for it to affect behavior. The same applies for whether the narrative exists in any *ontological* sense—that is, it's real in that who it describes is aware of it, as opposed to being just some language fragment that's useful in profiling.) The key profiling point here is that in looking for an event that has had a historical impact on an event of interest, an individual's understanding of history may be that event.

Two other giants of philosophy are relevant here. Kant (1963/1784) posited that narratives contain paradoxes including the conflict between *being social* and *wanting isolation* and between *freedom* and the *coercive political authority* that best could offer it. The German philosopher Hegel (1953/1837) posited that all narratives—at least in the history of mankind if not the life history of an individual—eventually constitute freedom and is characterized by reason even if the passions are the media for this to occur. (And if the passions are the media, pure reason needs to be uncontaminated from these passions.) To profilers, the implications are that events of interest are—to borrow from the psychodynamic language of profiling—compromise formations or tools in the service of conflict resolution of the quest for freedom through one's capacities, limited though they may be, for reason. Other people may or may not get in the way of this conflict resolution, with consequences that may bring a call for the services of profilers.

Another approach to narratives is common to many contemporary historiographical commenters—viz., on what constitutes historical narratives. I'll cite from memory material from several lectures I have heard delivered by the American historian Alan Guelzo. In historical narrative, one finds all or some of the following: inversions wherein what has been happening goes from one extreme to the other; annals and chronicles that are contemplative observations of what has occurred so far; celebration that exhibits pride for accomplishment; declension wherein the fat years become lean either literally or figuratively; the imitations of others or other times; escapism through fantasy or behavior bordering the mindless or irresponsible; and reappropriation taking back what one once had. The translation for profilers? Regardless of what may be occurring in the objective world around an individual, that individual's inner world of narrative construction is crucial to understanding and influencing that individual's outer world. Each of Guelzo's examples may constitute a motive force bearing on that outer world.

Before we turn to a concrete example of the narrative contribution to profiling, I feel impelled to add three caveats. First, as previously mentioned in Chapter 1, Canter and Youngs (2009) also employ narratives as part of profiling, but their empirical correlates of types of plot such as tragedy and their linkages of roles constituting self-identity to plots, such as the revenger to tragedy, seem quite different from the narrative development of White and of Frye. (So as with *sex*, when someone says they've had it, the best question might be what they mean.) Second, Lyotard (1984) described the breakdown of what he calls metanarratives—ongoing plots containing large-scale meanings and operative principles in life—in contemporary life. In other words, narratives are becoming so fragmented and are losing so much of *our* faith in them that they may be losing their coherence and value for helping us understand and influence human internal and external events—and the situations they may create or interact with. My reading of Lyotard is that this may be the case for the much simpler narratives of our everyday lives as well, so profilers now might be confronted with the challenge of multiple, fast-changing narratives or ones defying description. Third, a simpler version of narrative is to include the basics of all lives—as opposed to the psychosexual milestones of Freud and the developmental challenges of Erikson—that might characterize a biography if the individual lives long enough. As the British-born biographer Nigel Hamilton asserts via the table of contents of *How to Do Biography: A Primer* (2008), these often include (1) a starting point, (2) situating a person of interest by birth situation and then childhood and youth, (3) love, (4) work, and depending on age, (5) the twilight years, and (6) then some meaningful ending. Something similar seems to apply in how the sequences of many films are constructed or how we construct them—even if the sequences are out of order or implicit.

As a concrete example of narrative in the profiling context, I offer an intermediary draft narrative (Figure 6.1) from a project developed by a group of upper-level undergraduate students in a course on personality and profiling (Berryhill et al., 2012). Their task was to develop a narrative (and a matrix) containing events and their relationships bearing on an event of interest: Anders Behring Breivik's attacks on July 22, 2011, that left 77 people dead, 8 with a car bomb in central Oslo, Norway, and then shooting 69 on the nearby wooded island of Utoya, most of them teenagers attending a Labor Party summer camp (Lewis & Jolly, 2012). This is a task of postdictive profiling.

Before I comment on the students' narrative, I wish to consider a comment made on Breivik by a significant researcher on profiling already cited in this book—David Canter. Professor Canter was interviewed about how well Breivik might tolerate the "strain" of a trial: "... But I think he has built such an heroic narrative for himself that he has convinced himself he is on a mission that will carry him through ..." (Lewis & Jolly, 2012). This quote relates to several issues.

First, a narrative can have significant enough psychological impact to protect from the strain of a trial. Readers might extrapolate—once they escape from the faulty assumption that whatever *stress* might be is always something to avoid, attenuate, or modulate—that Breivik's stress protection, if indeed the case, might generalize to all the events leading up to and including the attacks, thereby facilitating the deaths. They also might ponder that an often positively valued phenomenon, *stress protection*, might be associated with positive or negative consequences. When associated with negative consequences, stress protection might involve the removal of inhibitors to antisocial or other statistically deviant behavior.

As well, a specific type of narrative, the *heroic*, might be associated with positive or negative consequences. (As previously mentioned in this chapter, I believe that Canter labels and interprets the content of narratives somewhat different from me—and Frye and White.) In addition, although heroes may be most frequently associated by the general public with *romance* and, less so, *tragedy* narratives, they also may be the significant figure in or the possessor of *comedies* and *satires* as well. Something we might want to encourage in an individual—to believe one is a hero, at least as defined by the striving and evaluating associated desired social goals supported by political authorities—can still be associated with horrible consequences. Finally,

NARRATIVE

There are three main paths that led Breivik to mass murder. First, he was emotionally isolated at a young age. Second, he believed he was a member of the Knights Templar. Third, he harbored desire for revenge after expulsion from a Muslim oriented gang.

Anders Breivik's parents split up at an early age. Soon after this event, and possibly a reaction to the emotional trauma of the divorce, Breivik became involved with a Muslim–Pakistani gang known as GSV at the age of 12. At age 16 Breivik was caught vandalizing walls. This incident caused him to be not only expelled from his gang, but also his father stopped all contact with him. After the vandalism incident Breivik was very isolated; during his isolated period he began scheming for revenge.

Anders Breivik believed that he was a member of a reincarnated Knights Templar, a group in Medieval Europe that would carry out missions for the Catholic Church. The group played an infamous role in the Crusades in their mission to eradicate Muslims from Jerusalem. This belief helps explain his hatred for Muslims.

Breivik was openly against the influx of Muslims migrating into Western Europe. This and the fact that he was very isolated and looking for a group to associate with led him to take part in much of the formation of the English Defense League. Breivik described himself as an active participant in their meetings, possibly the most active member of the meetings, or so he said in his manifesto. The truth, described by the EDL leadership, was that Breivik attended one or two meetings and rarely spoke. Narcissistic personality disorder could easily account for his clear delusion toward the group and his perception of progress in the formation of his own organization, the Norway Defense League. Nevertheless, his perception of participation with the EDL, even if it was a manifestation of his mind, illustrates his feelings toward ethnic diversity in Europe and increases the possibility that an attack would occur.

In the early 2000s, after his first business went bankrupt, Breivik decided he would carry out an attack to initiate a campaign against ethnic diversity. The loss of his company may have brought back the desires for revenge against his former friends.

Breivik was openly against the influx of Muslims migrating into Western Europe. This and the fact that he was very isolated and looking for a group to associate with led him to take part in much of the formation of the English Defense League. Breivik described himself as an active participant in their meetings, possibly the most active member of the meetings, or so he said in his manifesto. The truth, described by the EDL leadership, was that Breivik attended one or two meetings and rarely spoke. Narcissistic personality disorder could easily account for his clear delusion toward the group and his perception of progress in the formation of his own organization, the Norway Defense League. Nevertheless, his perception of participation with the EDL, even if it was a manifestation of his mind, illustrates his feelings toward ethnic diversity in Europe and increases the possibility that an attack would occur.

In the early 2000s, after his first business went bankrupt, Breivik decided he would carry out an attack to initiate a campaign against ethnic diversity. The loss of his company may have brought back the desires for revenge against his former friends.

FIGURE 6.1   Breivik narrative.

while Canter is quoted that Breivik has constructed his own narrative, readers could better consider that the narrative may be an ongoing product of conscious and unconscious events *constituting* Breivik as well as social and other external events.

In any case, the students studying Breivik developed three interrelated narratives associated with the murders. One involves living in a world that has mistreated him early in life and deserves to be the target of revenge. Some of the events here include the divorce of his parents before he reached 10 years of age, his expulsion by his peers from a youth gang (one largely populated by youth of Pakistani and Islamic origins), and his father cutting off all communication with him. However, these same events might be associated with very different events of interest for other people or the same people in other situations. A much more positive event of interest—except for most anarchists—might be to seek revenge by achieving success, respect, and love through excelling at socially approved activities. So *why* the events and others in the first narrative would be relevant in Breivik's attacks is left unclear. As with many students in my experience, these students so far have constructed a narrative with a *formist* approach, that is, independent factors each with a presumed effect on an individual. In addition, these students are employing the Kantian emphasis on the conflict of *isolation* versus *socialization*, as the very attempts to seek social solace lead to aversive consequences, more isolation, and more attempts at being embraced socially. The narrative appears to be one of *tragedy* with either a *satire* or *romance* as unlikely intermediaries or endpoints. Already there are several *inversions* and *declensions* from belonging to no longer belonging with the father and the youth gang. Finally, there are *intimacy* issues and a lack of *power* to satisfy them that interface with then conflict of *isolation* versus *socialization*.

A second narrative features being a hero through believing he's a member in some reappearance of a group extant in medieval Europe—the Knights Templar. (This is Breivik's claim, as others consider this founded on a psychotic belief, some more common wish fulfillment, or Machiavellian manipulation.) He has stated that the group's purpose during some of what we now call the Crusades was to take Jerusalem back from Islamic forces and eradicate these forces at the bidding of the Roman Catholic Church. Now he can claim victory if his murders lead to a change in Norwegian policy—way too accepting toward Islamic immigrants and, perhaps, other foreigners.

This second narrative is based on the conflict of *freedom* and *coercion* in that the freedom to eradicate Islamic immigration is up against the coercive powers of the Norwegian government and of Islamic forces. Breivik may be viewing his attacks foreshadowed by the history of the Knights Templar as constituting events within *annals* and *chronicles*. The narrative affords its possessor a sense of *power*. It certainly suggests a *romance* with ultimate salvation thus avoiding some future *tragedy* or approaching a tragedy with an endpoint of romance through resurrection and eternal life. It embraces the *monumental* through the high impact of his activities and the *antiquarian* through *reappropriating* a former state that is *highly* desired. And this narrative is compatible with either *formist* or *mechanistic* views of the world and how it operates—the former through the effects of independent factors and their associated consequences, the latter through some natural or even supernatural laws characterizing the world. Breivik is constituting the actant of *helping* even as other forces attempt to *impede* him. His self may be tropically described through his weapons. He may be the weapon.

Taking some liberties with the students' work, I'll interpret the third narrative as an interpretation of the world and its events through the prism of a narcissistic personality disorder. The students claim that the requisite number of criteria as described in the DSM pertaining to the disorder are met for Breivik. And it seems to be the case that some of the criteria as events might be especially germane to the murderous attacks as the event of interest. For example, a grandiose sense of self-importance might magnify the motivational properties toward changing the world by any means necessary, if it is not exactly the way one desires or expects. Believing oneself to be special or unique with a sense of entitlement might free one from the bonds of what is deemed acceptable for most other people and allow one to dare to transgress. This line of thought was an extremely common one in the 19th century within European intellectual traditions. There is Hegel's conception of transgression via acting on the passions by someone who is a great historical actor, such as Napoleon, as mandatory for history to dialectically progress toward the optimal endpoint of pure reason. Another is Dostoyevsky's Raskolnikov, by no means a great historical actor but just a student down on his luck and, perhaps, mad, who kills both the pawnbroker and her sister partially based on a crude ideology of greatness defined by gratuitous murder.

One point of contention between the students and clinical authorities who have evaluated Breivik is that some of the latter believe that personality disorder (actually two, narcissistic and antisocial) is not especially salient for the profiling of mass murder nor even a valid ascription of Breivik. Instead, he is *psychotic,* a clinical term, at least for the time immediately before and during the attacks and *insane* as well, a legal term (Lewis, 2012). One definition of *psychotic* supported by the U.S. National Library of Medicine within the U.S. National Institute of Health (Psychosis, 2012) is "… a loss of contact with reality, usually including false beliefs about what is taking place or who one is [delusions] and seeing or hearing things that aren't there [hallucinations].…" As well, when it comes to *psychotic* being associated with personality disorders, not the narcissistic or antisocial but others—the "… schizotypal, schizoid, paranoid, and sometimes borderline …" are most often cited.

Why such a difference among groups of clinicians, for now leaving the students out of matters? One possibility for both formal psychological assessment or profiling is that some practitioners tend to conflate ideological and other likes and dislikes with labels of psychopathology. This can be the case regardless of professional credentials and the use of various psychometric clinical and personality instruments. And the more dislike, the more severe the psychopathology (see also Chapter 8 for a discussion involving conflation and pedophilia).

Here's a quote attributed to Breivik (Lewis, 2012) that bears on the conflation of likes and dislikes with psychopathology: "This case, is very simply that I am not a psychotic case and I am sane.… I understand that when you see something too extreme, you might think it is irrational and insane. But you must separate political extremism from insanity." And even as labeling someone as psychopathological may or may conflate with social likes and dislikes, its use may well affect the various events within a narrative as well as how they relate to some event of interest. For example, the presumption of an intense psychotic fantasy may *preclude* violent behavior because of the former's self-reinforcing properties obviating the need for violent behavior or *impel* such behavior through overriding various inhibitory mechanisms.

But the students who studied Breivik did not establish the interrelationships of events and these with the event of interest with the use of *personality disorder* for the *first two narratives* previously described. For example, with the disorder, Breivik might have perceived and experienced the first narrative as a mere example of many severe wounds to the psyche. Also, with the disorder, all the seeming grandiosity of the second narrative might still be deemed insufficient for what would be an acceptable state of psychological and social affairs for Breivik.

In any case, this third narrative based on personality disorder seems to be largely infused with the need for *power* popularized by McAdams (1988); is suggestive of a *romance* or *tragedy* as defined by White and by Frye—perhaps depending on profilers' political ideology; may be infused with Nietzsche's *monumental* (the magnitude of Breivik's acts as self-perceived), *antiquarian* (returning to the pure essence of a Christian world), and *critical* (the contemporary world as base, corrupt, and defiled) constructs; and *mechanistic* (complying with and even constituting natural and sacred laws) and *contexualist* (the current political dangers to white Christians and extremist violence in contemporary Norwegian history coming mostly form the far right) takes on the world and how it operates as defined by White.

A final comment on the students' profiling of Breivik: Of the five profiling languages described in Chapter 3, the psychodynamic and biological are not used. Conditioning languages may be inferred based on the alleged effects of early events, and the existential and humanistic based on political statements and involvement. The most significant language used by the students in studying Breivik is that of traits. I have found this to be common among individuals being introduced to the challenges of profiling. In fact, this recapitulates the history of contemporary research on the psychology of statistically deviant behavior from the 1960s largely focused on sex, illicit drug use, pop culture, and collective political behavior conflated with sex, drugs, and pop culture. For example, a *Time* magazine article (Youth, 1967) described the so-called *Freudian proletariat* as altruistic, honest, gentle, quiet, joyous, mystical, and nonviolent—a red warning light for the American way of life according to historian Arnold Toynbee of the 12-volume *A Study of History* fame. And a few observers *did* revert to biological languages. For example, a term paper I wrote in the late 1960s on action potentials of the brain purportedly differentiating college students supporting the New Left Movement in the United States from those who didn't was unfit for prime time then and has retained this status to the present day. The case may well be that the most valid and useful profiling languages of this time were nonpsychological in nature embracing the political, social, and cultural (cf. Fraser, 1988, for a more international perspective on such matters). I'll end here by emphasizing that for each case of profiling one must enter the case willing to believe that any language might best illustrate events and events of interest and that any language may best illustrate itself or some others.

Now it's time for readers to engage with LO 6.1 and *dec* the profiling narrative. The context is a film fragment from *The Last Picture Show* (Friedman & Bogdanovich, 1971) directed by Peter Bogdanovich. What narrative might one construct to embrace the narratives of the adolescent Sonny Crawford *still trying to figure it all out* (played by Timothy Bottoms) and the middle-age, lonely wife, Ruth Popper (played by Cloris Leachman), of an *always away* high school athletic coach as they prepare to reengage the residua of their sexual relationship? (As an illustration of the difficulties facing profilers, imagine a reality—which the same Leachman playing the heart-rendering Popper also played the head nurse, Nurse Diesel, in Mel Brooks's *High Anxiety* [1977]. She's heart-rendering in a much more literal sense, especially if one is into discipline and bondage. How varied are the characters we play in life?)

7 Profiling Applications
Terrorism

So through a close reading of interdisciplinary sources, how does one prepare to develop a profiling matrix and narrative on some terrorist event of interest? And, what is terrorism, this event of interest? Without an easy-to-apply definition that also seems to comply with readers' construction of reality, the prediction, post-diction, peri-diction, understanding, and influence of terrorism may become both problematic and a fool's errand. To arrive at a definition, readers might wish to immerse themselves in data.

I most often use the following sources. The first is managed at the University of Maryland and is titled the *National Consortium for the Study of Terrorism and Responses to Terrorism* (START, 2012). START was established in 2005 funded as a Center of Excellence by the U.S. Department of Homeland Security. I most value its *Global Terrorism Database* (GTD). For each GTD event, readers can find its date and location, the weapons used and nature of the target, the number of casualties, and, when possible, the identity of the perpetrator. The GTD continues to be updated and contains both global and domestic terrorist events going back to the 1970s—close to 100,000 in all.

START also contains other databases that bear on the types of events profilers might choose in analyzing a specific terrorist event of interest. (I will ask readers to consider whether these data bear on anything that is or should be termed terrorism further along in this chapter.) A *Minorities at Risk Organizational Behavior* (MAROB) database seems founded on the premise that ethnic minority status might be significantly related to terrorism. (Readers might consider that there are many minority classifications beyond *ethnic* and wonder what's so special about ethnic as a something that is more likely to be associated with terrorism.)

A *Profiles of Perpetrators of Terrorism in the United States* (PPT-US) database contains information on internal and external events related to organizations identified as having engaged in terrorism. These events include professed and assumed ideology and goals; history of relevant behaviors including how financial resources are secured, maintained, and used; and structural features of organizations and networks. My biggest concern here is that the language often used in textbooks on organizations and organizational behavior may not optimally correspond to the revolution and evolution of human interpersonal behavior facilitated both by processes (1) of how societies and cultures transform and (2) still-to-be-discovered and understood mediated by changes in telecommunications—technologies, social networking options, and burgeoning applications (see Chapter 3).

The Big Allied and Dangerous (BAAD) Lethality database contains information bearing on events putatively leading to organizations committing *more lethal* terrorist events of interest. Internal and external events include ideology, location, size, structure, and funding. I find it important that this database also includes information on organizations' allies, rivals, targets, and state sponsors. This helps profilers avoid the tunnel vision of looking for events associated with a terrorist event of interest only within some terrorist entity. It also facilitates looking at various interactive possibilities from local, regional, international, and global perspectives. The same applies to two other START databases—*Muslim Public Opinion on U.S. Policy, Attacks on Civilians, and al Qaeda* and *Public Opinion in the Islamic World on Terrorism, al Qaeda, and U.S. Policies.* The premise here seems to be that attitudes of others who interact with and observe terrorists may influence and have influenced past, present, and future terrorist behavior—with the constraint of being focused on variations of a specific religious tradition. (Note that the very collection, development, and maintenance of such a database—along with public knowledge about its existence—may have various effects on terrorism perpetrated by and against people from the religious tradition.)

Although seemingly without face validity for terrorism, the START's *Public Warnings and Evacuations: California Station Fire* database is relevant because it bears on the impact of public warnings on people's behaviors and on inferred internal and on external events—terrorism at times being constituted as a warning. The same is the case for the *Experimental Study of the Effects of Government Terror Warnings on Political Attitudes* that explores the effect of warnings on political attitudes and behavior. START's database on *Predictors of Activism and Radicalism: Past Activism, Past Radicalism and Grievance Against the Government* would seem to have face validity, but the leap from activism and radicalism to terrorism may be so uncommon as to create a huge false positive error for profilers attempting to predict the next attack. (A huge false positive error as described in Chapter 4 may be tolerated depending on the political needs of decision makers or the panic they experience.) The *Predictors* database includes demographics, examples of radicalism and activism, grievances with the U.S. government (USG) and attitudes toward U.S. law enforcement. (As with the U.S. Department of State's [DOS] *Country Reports on Terrorism* that I describe in this chapter, the implicit notion that there's a war against terrorism and that terrorism is not practiced by the USG are both problematic and controversial to some state actors and nonstate actors including some U.S. citizens.)

The second major source, the DOS's *Country Reports on Terrorism* (from 2004 through 2010 at the time of this writing)—replacing DOS's earlier *Pattern of Global Terrorism* (from 2003 back to 1995 is easily accessible)—is developed in compliance with Title 22 of U.S. Code, Section 2656f that requires DOS to provide the U.S. Congress an annual report on terrorism (U.S. Department of State, 2012). For example, the 2010 report that came out in August 2011 contains chapters on terrorist activities by global region, a list of state sponsors of terrorism, and terrorist safe havens. It also is intended to contain complete statistical information on the number of noncombatants, including U.S. citizens and dual nationals, killed, injured, or kidnapped by each terrorist group during the preceding calendar year. This requirement is satisfied through the inclusion of a statistical annex based on information provided by the U.S. National Counterterrorism Center (NCTC). What makes it into the report may be colored by various political issues. Ongoing public discourse on whether the Mujahadeen Khalq has or still is engaged in terrorism illustrates the sorts of issues that may occur (Shane, 2012b) with various *experts* and public officials coming down on both sides of what may be a multisided question.

The University of Chicago's *Chicago Project on Security and Terrorism* (2012) maintains a searchable database on all terrorism-related suicide attacks from 1981 to 2011, with additional updates to be added. The database includes the location of attacks, target type, weapon used, and demographic and general biographical characteristics of suicide attackers. An important feature of the database is that it expands the breadth of data available in English to native language sources (e.g., Arabic, Hebrew, Russian, Tamil) that are likely to have the most extensive relevant information. (Readers should note that I published a review of a textbook by the researcher who has led the Chicago effort, Robert A. Pape, for the American Psychological Association's *PsycCRITIQUES* and reviewed it very favorably [Bloom, 2005]. The book is discussed further in this chapter.)

The fourth major source is *PsycNET* developed and maintained by the American Psychological Association (2012). Unlike the previous databases, this collection must be paid for. I believe it's well worth the access for anyone interested in research on biopsychosocial events affecting any of life's issues. For the keyword *terrorism*, readers might launch a search for all books, journals, articles, and other formats containing it by title or mentioned anywhere through a text search. One can then make the search more specific through the use of additional keywords.

And I recommend a few other proprietary collections. *LexisNexis* provides full-text documents of many news, business, legal, medical, and reference publications with many search options. *ProQuest* (2012) provides citations, abstracts, and some full-text items from magazines, journals, and newspapers covering many subject areas. It also contains full-text articles from journals in psychology and computing—with obvious relevance to profiling, screening, data mining, and so on. *LexisNexis* is usually a better bet for global newspaper articles, *ProQuest* for academic resources. The *CQ Homeland Security News* (2012) provides policy, program, and legislative trends. The *Digital National Security Archives* (2012) hosted online by George Washington University contains declassified government documents. *Stratfor* (2012) provides open-source intelligence collection and analysis as well as intelligence from a network of human sources. (Some readers may remember that *Stratfor* has been the focus of public discourse for allegedly being hacked into by *Anonymous* [self-titled activist computer hackers] resulting in the compromise of subscriber names, credit card numbers, and email content; Sengupta, 2012.) The SITE Institute (2012) bills itself as a monitoring service focusing primarily on what are termed the jihadist threat (including translations from non-English languages) and the White Supremacist threat. (Given its posted kudos from the Federal Bureau of Investigation, readers might well assume this source is at least partially funded by the USG.)

Another nonproprietary source, this one dependent on donations and grants, *Secrecy News* (2012)—a project of the *Federation of the American Scientists* and supported by grants from the Open Society Foundations, the CS Fund, the Mauman Foundations, the William B. Wiener Jr. Foundation, and the Stewart R. Mott Foundation—contains unclassified and declassified documents that can be accessed through terrorism-related keyword searches. (Of special note are archives of various security and intelligence related reports from the U.S. Congressional Research Service, not easily available, even though they are unclassified.) In addition, I have developed an online source, the *International Bulletin of Political Psychology* (2012), with many articles on terrorism from 1996 accessible through keyword searches and free—thus allowing me to feel ethically comfortable in citing it.

All these databases are controlled by U.S. individuals, groups, and organizations; are primarily in the English language; and come with obvious caveats in how one might interpret such information in contrast with information controlling by non-U.S. sources. This is a constraint based on my reading fluency in only a very few languages. I suppose terrorist sponsorship of English-speaking propagandists is a boon to some researchers, even as it is a bane to the safety and security of some populations because of the nurturing of English-speaking terrorists (and it has also been a bane to English-speaking terrorists like the late Anwar al-Awlaki).

But is it now time for our long awaited definition of terrorism based on my study of such sources and my discussions through the years with people interested and involved in the phenomenon? It turns out that readers will still have to wait. I don't have a definition with which I'm satisfied. In the context of one common defini-tion—from Title 22 of *the United States Code* (USC), Section 2656f(d)—here's why.

In the USC definition, *terrorism* denotes premeditated, politically motivated vio-lence perpetrated against noncombatant targets by subnational groups or clandestine agents. As part of this definition, *noncombatant* denotes not only civilians but also military personnel (whether or not armed or on duty) who are not deployed in a war zone or a war-like setting. The problem with *premeditated* is that people vary both within themselves and between and among themselves about how aware they may be about their intentions. They also vary as to how significantly intentions as events may be associated with events of interest based on whether they believe they (1) are largely in control of their behaviors or not, (2) are largely being controlled by other internal or external events or not, (3) have free will or not, (4) believe the experience of free will has a controlling factor on their behavior or not, (5) are aware of control-ling events impacting their behavior or yet other internal and external events or not, and (6) are, indeed, controlled by internal or external events regardless of intentions including those bearing on *premeditation*. These complexities have forensic implica-tions for personal responsibility, for what philosophers call *agency* (being a control-ling factor in some event), for innocence and guilt related to investigations and civil and criminal adjudication, and for actual profiling.

The problem with *politically motivated* is that we might easily term all motiva-tions as *political*, especially if all motivations bear on living in a social context with infinite need and finite resources—a definition of *political* more expansive than that just pertaining to the form, organization, and administration of a state and with the regulation of its relations with other states (OED, 2012). In addition, a common strategic postulate of military science is that all military activity is a tool to achieve political goals, *politically motivated* becomes militarily motivated. Moreover, inso-far as terrorism involves violence or the threat of violence, it becomes compatible with the essence of military capability. In fact, for many people the whole point of terrorism is engaging in something that's *not* military, so that when the military engages in terrorism, something inviolate has been violated.

Yet again, *political* might seem a constraining choice if motivations of people alleged to have engaged in terrorism are better characterized by religion or personal conflicts or perceived slights or reversals. As well, *motivated* is a hypothetical construct reputed to denote something psychological that actually exists but (as readers have already been appraised) may be a common language application only among members of that language's users often yielding desired consequences but having no bearing on whether that psychological something exists.

Moreover, people in power—in total or partial control of a polis, that is, a political population, be it people controlling a government, state, nation, organization, or group—may legally or in some other socially approved manner engage in the very behaviors with *political motivations* proscribed to people labeled as terrorists. At other times, these same people in power *cannot* engage in such behavior legally or social approved. Is the issue, then, one of motivation, or merely who's allowed to act on motivation, and, if the latter, why should this be allowed to some and not others? Are we back again to definitions, research, and profiling supporting those in power or those who want it? (Readers might consult the British political philosopher Isaiah Berlin [1969/1959] on the violent atrocities committed in the name of abstract principles such as democracy, freedom, the Word, a New or Old World, terrorism or antiterrorism.) Those people who connote terrorism with evil and evildoers have some serious explaining to do on this point.

Now, just a bit more on the USC definition. *Violent* most often denotes behavior or the threat of such behavior that injures or kills people, damages or destroys things, or engenders fear or some other aversive cognitive and emotional nexus. But again, proscriptions on violence may relate to who uses, manages, and protects power—a power game—as opposed to either contributing to some greater good for the greater number of people or preventing behavior that is somehow inherently bad regardless of consequence.

The proscription of violence against *noncombatants* with an inference they somehow are innocent or not part of a conflict often can be logically and ethically challenged. Noncombatants often pay taxes supporting military activities. They often support socially, culturally, emotionally, and politically one side of the goals of military activity, military tactics and strategy, and military personnel. They may engage at work supporting one side of a military conflict. Noncombatants—men, women, and children—can become military personnel now or in the future. Some terrorists and terrorist analysts assert that noncombatants are all combatants differing only in distance from the finger that pulls the trigger from chow hall cooks, voters, to being on a photograph supporting some other combatant's morale. Why should there necessarily be distinctions—psychological or otherwise—between and among people who target noncombatants and those who don't. That there are legal distinctions takes us again to rules related to power and those who seek it and seek to keep as much as possible. Identifying others as terrorists thereby authorizing violence against them may truly be the pot calling the kettle black.

That the previous definitional problems have practical consequences for profiling becomes clear in reading terrorism-related research. The different combinations of internal and external events allegedly associated with terrorist events of interest for similar individuals and situations vary significantly. So profilers immersed in terrorism databases to find likely hypotheses between and among events and events of interest for a specific case at hand may have much from which to choose but less than desired guidance about what to choose. The real challenge here is attempting to understand a phenomenon that may be more artifact of power politics than some natural anomaly, a constructed deviancy more than some natural threat.

What follows are commentaries on terrorism that may be used in choosing profiling languages and developing profiling matrices and narratives. The commentaries will be based on what I consider the most significant profiling contributions on terrorism from the 1960s to the present. One focus of these contributions has been on what are commonly called left-wing and right-wing terrorisms. (The left-right distinction, as the term terrorism itself, takes us back to the late 18th-century French Revolution. In 1789, members of the National Assembly sat by self-segregation—the supporters of the king to the president of the Assembly's right and supporters of the revolution to his left. This later generalized [at least in France] to the *left* denoting the party of movement and change and the *right* the party of order and status quo.)

The other focus is on what is often called Islamic or Islamicist terrorism at times stretched to include terrorisms of fundamentalist and fanatic religions of any stripe. Regardless of the appropriateness, that is, how accurate it might be to link terrorism to interpretations of variations of a religion and the residues of ethnocentrism and sectarianism that may be associated with this second focus, it's worthy of study because of the global common usage. And readers should note that I *am* aware of many other ascriptions of terrorism that are specific to various national governments, corporate entities, interpretations of religions, cultures, societies, sects, tribes, criminal organizations and groups, families, and allegedly unaffiliated or at times uncohesive—what U.S. slang would term being *not fully wrapped*—individuals. For purposes of exposition, I'll bring these other ascriptions up as appropriate.

I start with the American psychiatrist Jerrold Post, who's been and remains a long-time leader in applied research on the psychology of terrorism. He's currently a professor of psychiatry, political psychology, and international affairs at George Washington University; has founded or cofounded several unique capabilities including the Central Intelligence Agency's Center for the Analysis of Personality and Behavior; and developed profiles of Israeli prime minister Menachem Begin and Egyptian president Anwar Sadat for use by U.S. president Jimmy Carter in what became known as the 1978 Camp David Accords—and other profiles for use by various national political leaders. I will now elaborate on two of his many profiling contributions.

Post (1990) developed a 2 × 2 matrix comparing youths' loyal or disloyal attitudes toward their parents with parents' loyal or disloyal attitudes toward their government. When parents and youths are both loyal, presumably no terrorism by youths occurs or the expectation would be very low. When parents and youths are both disloyal—don't forget that the youths' disloyalty is toward the parents, not necessarily to the regimes—youths might engage in rightist terrorism if their parents are against the regime in a leftist way, leftist terrorism if the parents are against the regime in a rightist way. These youths might transcend terrorism by exiting as much as possible from the political world, perhaps through creating a hippie commune or better yet making a lot of money through developing the next Facebook. (These last two examples are mine, not Post's.)

The key comparisons involve the two pairings of loyal youths and disloyal parents and then disloyal youths and loyal parents. In the first, Post posits that the youths will engage in what he terms *nationalist-separatist terrorism*, carrying on the causes of their parents. (I might broaden this to include supporting the parents' cause and even taking further whatever the cause—nationalist, separatist, or anything else. I believe that Post focused on *nationalist-separatist* based on the data sets with which he was working.) In the second, Post posits that the youths will engage in what he terms *anarchic-ideologue terrorism*, attempting to resolve inner conflicts and intrapsychic wounds through attacking and attempting to destroy the world order or their piece of it. (I might broaden this again to include leaving the political world in a more pacific manner or staying in it in a more ironic but nonviolent one, such as Baudelaire's *flâneur*—an idler strolling through and fascinated with urban crowds.)

Post's 2 × 2 matrix based on attitudes between youths and their parents or parent substitutes and between parents and government or political authority is consonant with several of the five profiling languages in this book. It may relate to an external expression of psychodynamic issues, the product of conditioning histories, traits as far as attitudes are related to traits, and the big issues of existential and humanistic languages founded on youth–parent interactions.

Depending on the events collected on each youth–parent pairing, any of the four narrative themes from *romance* through *comedy* and *satire* to *tragedy* may be germane. Youth–parent relationships often are constituted by needs for *power* and *intimacy*, and how the attitudes match or don't match may have direct implications for how conflicts between and among *socialization* and *isolation, freedom* and *coercion,* and *reason* versus *passion* are resolved. My reading of Post suggests that Nietzsche's *antiquarian* historical approach would be more related to nationalist-separatists and the *critical* to anarchists-ideologues. As actants, *helping* and *impeding* might best help to describe the parent–student dynamics. For variants of historical narrative, *inversion, declension,* and *celebration* seem most relevant.

The pairing of youth–parent attitude would necessitate that the attitude construct be an important component of a profiling matrix and a key aspect of a profiling narrative. However, several qualifications are necessary. First, scientific research in social psychology contains many studies on when attitudes will lead to congruent or incongruent behavior or to no behavior at all (cf. Fabrigar et al., 2006). To my knowledge, this research has not been applied to Post's matrix. Second, when will behaviors congruent with attitudes be activated not toward a government regime or other political authority but merely toward the actors in the attitude pairing, that is, the youth and parent? In extreme cases, violence would remain all in the family not so much as (1) the Oedipus—unknowingly killing his father and causing the suicide of his mother—so analyzed by Freud and popularized by the Greek tragedian Sophocles, but more as (2) the Kronos of Greek mythology castrating, killing, and deposing his father Uranus. (Kronos then kills and eats each of his children, in turn, fearing that one of them may do to him what he did to Uranus.) Third, in our contemporary world seemingly so transitional courtesy of cyber technology, globalization, and the remnants of postmodernist philosophies, how compelling and impelling is the youth–parent attitude pairing? As young people say often enough today, *what*ever. What may have been the case for most of history and still in the time of Post may not be the case today and into the future.

Another contribution popularized by Post in the context of terrorism is the construct of *malignant narcissism*. This construct goes back at least as far as the American psychoanalyst (by way of Austria, Germany, and Chile) Otto Kernberg (1970). The essence of this construct is a combination of intense narcissism, antisocial features, paranoid traits, and very aggressive fantasies and intentions constituting and leading to rage and then destructive aggression.

According to Kernberg, malignant narcissism is most associated with several psychopathological conditions. One combines severe personality disorders. (I've already used this construct in Chapters 3, 5, and 6, but I believe that it's appropriate now to provide further details. If a *personality* constitutes what makes a person that *specific* person—enduring patterns of inner experience and external behaviors—the *disorder* might be characterized by varying significantly from cultural expectations, taking up quite a bit of the overall personality, being little open to change, and leading to psychological or physical pain and impediments to personal, social, and professional achievement.)

A second psychopathological condition combines what Kernberg called *perversions*. During Kernberg's clinical training and much of his professional life, certain experiences and behaviors leading to sexual gratification were often deemed intrinsically abnormal in a manner similar to Kant's categorical imperatives—those concerning what *not* to do. Today, perversions—if the term is used at all—are usually associated with gratification leading to pain and impediments to various appropriate personal and social achievements.

A third psychopathological condition covers the *functional psychoses*. (See Chapter 6 for a definition of psychosis and note that *functional* just implies that there's no significant evidence of brain phenomena being the cause—even as there's no evidence that brain phenomena are not the cause.)

There's long been public discourse on the psychological normality or abnormality of terrorists. When contemporary research on terrorism began to explode in the 1960s courtesy of something called *Palestinian terrorism*—the use of which is much more diagnostic of the user than some representation or correspondence to or reflection of a putatively objective world—the early returns often implicated some sorts of psychopathology as causally blameworthy. After all, terrorism was deemed bad, so it must be associated with bad actors with bad psychological components. Supporters of terrorisms objected to this, of course, but so did some behavioral scientists employing deductive and abductive logics. After all, if psychopathology was partially defined by pain and impediments to successful social achievement—even if the *social* could refer to *terrorist* societies—how could psychopathological individuals be successful terrorists except at the hands of luck and serendipity? (The counter to this is that they would have been even better terrorists without the psychopathology. One counter to this counter is that psychopathology may be correlated with successful and unsuccessful terrorism for different people in different situations.) So although one may make much of the *malignant narcissism* construct not only with barely and almost famous terrorists but also with Saddam Hussein and Muammar Qaddhafi as well, *the mother of all counters* might demand an answer to how Qaddhafi was able to take power and then rule a country of very diverse peoples for over 40 years and Hussein for well over 20.

Be that as it may, *malignant narcissism* is compatible with several languages of profiling, especially the trait and psychodynamic. (Both Kernberg and, to a lesser extent, Post have received psychodynamic training.) It can be used as a key component of a profiling matrix and narrative and color the expression of many of the constructs offered by Frye, White, Kant, Nietzsche, and Guelzo. I do believe it unfortunately may lead inexperienced profilers to discount the possibility that terrorism may be seen as good not bad and to overemphasize inner psychological as opposed to external social and cultural events in matrix and narrative development.

Now I turn to the American psychologist Albert Bandura, long of Stanford University, who has made a name for himself in languages based on conditioning theories, especially in social learning theory and vicarious conditioning (see Chapter 3 for further discussion). This last is quite germane to profilers, because it illustrates how individuals do not have to come into direct contact with reinforcement, omission training, and punishment but can still be conditioned by observing others coming into such direct contact. (As commented on in the preface, this is why many parents are concerned about who their children associate with and what they watch on small and big screens—whether the wish is for children growing up to be antiterrorists, terrorists proterrorism, or like most people largely uninformed and oblivious.)

And, perhaps, a caveat here. I was on a panel with Professor Bandura at the Woodrow Wilson Institute for Scholars back in the late 1980s at which another one of his major conceptual contributions, self-efficacy (or the belief and to some degree capability that one can adequately affect one's world), was discussed in the context of terrorist profiling. My job was to be the commenter on his presentation, a task that led me to seriously question my own self-efficacy.

But I'd like to concentrate on several constructs from a diagram Bandura has used in several papers (see Bandura, 2004). These constructs describe how someone might engage in terrorism based on *moral disengagement*—how someone defines terrorism's associated behaviors, consequences, and human targets. And one might then presume the sorts of conditioning histories and even traits and psychodynamics that might lead one to develop and maintain these definitions.

As to the behaviors of terrorism, Bandura has used a more general construct *reprehensible conduct,* even as this word choice may say more about him than the behaviors—not by any means that he's reprehensible but that he's the kind of person who so views terrorist behaviors. Examples of the construct include *moral justification, palliative comparison,* and *euphemistic labeling.* The idea is that terrorist behaviors are so terrible and that most or all "normal" people believe this or should believe this. So, the perpetrator's *mind* must employ language to make what is to transpire, has transpired, or is transpiring acceptable (to the perpetrator). So they think or approach thinking that the terrorist behaviors can be suitably explained as good not bad (moral justification), aren't that bad compared with *badder* behaviors (palliative comparison), or are really something different from what others might think or do think. (This may not be that far away from former President Bill Clinton's various opinions during the *grand scandal* about whether he had sex with Monica Lewinsky—except for one big difference. While many of us presume that Clinton was knowingly trying to best play the bad hand he held, Bandura's terrorists are closer to being true believers, as they are their own psychological targets even as terrorism ultimately has other psychological consequences for survivors and observers.)

As to the consequences of terrorism—what Bandura calls *detrimental effects*, again with Bandura presuming that the consequences are detrimental—the associated constructs are *minimizing, ignoring,* or *misconstruing.* Since no one in his *right mind* could wish to wreak such havoc, an *unright* mind must be made right. Is this the "... termina[tion] with extreme prejudice ..." of Chapter 4's discussion of the film *Apocalypse Now*? Is it the *mopping up operations* or the *Peace Is Our Profession* (motto of the former U.S. Strategic Air Command) of military lingo? The *I'm going to clean this town up* of the film genre known as the Western? My conclusion is that one may minimize, ignore, and misconstrue *directly* through attenuating or even reversing noxious effects on some target (cf. *sent him to his Maker*) or *indirectly* through maximizing alleged positive consequences for others and attenuating preexisting noxious consequences for others through one's acts on the target.

As to the target or what Bandura calls the *victim,* he employs the constructs *dehumanization* and *attribution of blame.* The victim is viewed as *not* human, so unless one is a pure *Jainist* attempting to lead a life path of nonviolence toward all living things, one can do things to *it,* that's right, *it,* that would not be appropriate if done to humans. (However, Isaiah Berlin's take on most proponents of better living through mass murder is that keeping the soon-to-be-victims human somehow makes the abstract idea allegedly benefiting from death even more right and pure.) Or the victim is human but deserves what they get because the victim *had it coming.* Here we may hear the bitter and ironic quotes from the film *The Unforgiven* (Eastwood, 1992), "... Well, I guess he had it coming ... We all have it coming kid ..." even if Bandura wrote of these matters before the film came out.

I believe that Bandura's choice of *moral disengagement* to encompass these constructs is itself ironic, because I don't think any disengagement is going on. Instead, movements from universal to specific judgments may be occurring, or what Nietzsche termed reevaluations and transevaluations based on perspectivism—trying on, wittingly or otherwise, different viewpoints on the data at hand including how to weigh and interpret these data. By implying if not boldly stating that morals are being disengaged, Bandura again may be exhibiting a compassionate, humane, and decent take on the *shoulds* of humanity. Yet terrorism may cry out for dealing with the world as it *is,* not how it should be. Profilers should take note of this as they contemplate using Bandura's ideas in the development of a profiling matrix and narrative.

Next, I briefly present some ideas from Iranian-born psychologist Fathali Moghaddam, who has been working out of the Department of Psychology and Department of Government at Georgetown University. Of special note to me and, hopefully, to readers is an ongoing effort to identify what may be psychological universals among diverse peoples as defined by cultures. If there are such universals, they may be significant in the development of profiling matrices and narratives for otherwise very different people in very different situations who are being studied to understand some event of interest. As well, he has worked in relevant areas such as (1) how a country's global power may underlie the global power of its theories of psychology and motivation (used by profilers explicitly or otherwise) regardless of those theories' validity or cultural breadth, (2) the impact of narratives on human social behavior—Moghaddam calling the study of this *positioning theory*—and (3) the value of integrating what he calls mixed methodologies such as scientific psychology and the literature of the humanities (something highly valued by me).

I want to emphasize, however, his contribution of a trope—a metaphor—of "… a narrowing staircase leading to the terrorist act …" (Moghaddam, 2005). Each floor of the staircase on the way up has fewer and fewer doors and spaces that might lead someone *not* to climb even higher. Finally, one arrives at a floor on which the only possible outcome is to engage in some terrorist act. I find it ironic and enlightening that Moghaddam attributes this trope to two American social psychologists, Bibb Latané and John Darley. A full 35 years earlier, they were attempting to engage in prediction via post-diction for at least at first blush a very different event of interest—whether an individual will or won't help others in an emergency. I write at first blush because I believe that some terrorists believe they are helping others in an emergency by engaging in terrorism. These terrorists also may believe that those who are not supporting or engaging in terrorism are *not* helping people in crisis.

Now to the narrowing staircase metaphor. On the ground floor of the staircase one interprets material conditions from the perspective of fairness and justice. I read Moghaddam to emphasize interpretation by three *whethers*—whether the process of asset distribution and maintenance is fair, whether the resulting differences or lack thereof are fair, and whether each person gets what they deserve. From calculations and perceptions of these whethers come thoughts and feelings about who is deprived and why. Where many profilers go wrong is assuming that having little implies unfairness, injustice, and growing resentment. However, these last three conclusions may arise whether one or others have a lot or almost nothing. (When I heard from an associate on May 18, 2012, that Mark Zuckerberg of Facebook might now be the 29th richest person in the world, I wondered how much unfairness, injustice, and resentment the former 29th richest person might have been thinking. I then wondered in the converse direction about someone in the darkest, dankest slum who finds an extra morsel of urine-saturated bread to eat.)

If things on the ground floor are fine, one may go no farther. If not, one moves from the ground floor to the first floor of the staircase on which one perceives the number and viability of options to fight what may be unfair and not just. Moghaddam rightly points out that at least as far back as Plato, the threat from people to political authority can be significant if they believe that there are insufficient and inadequate venues to change what is unfair and not just. Thus, Karl Marx posited religion as an opiate of the masses, false consciousness as its consequence—for example, that one should accept this world's unfairness by belief in an eternal fair world to come. (Actual opium may cause one not to care, at least when high. Religion may cause one to view unfairness as an actual ticket to eternal fairness, while the unfair are on track for damnation or that the material world is but an illusion, thus suffering from it unwarranted.) A final *first-floor* point—some political theorists believe political authorities can more easily keep order when there's no hope. So only when there' even a ray of potential, some sufficient or adequate light at the end of the tunnel does one leave the first floor for the second floor.

What awaits on the second floor is *displacement of aggression*. Moghaddam seems to assume that aggression (as a need or motive that may be neither necessary nor sufficient for violent behavior) is at least at times a component of terrorism; that it can be directed at primary, secondary, and even more remote targets; and that the type of aggression can be overt or covert, active or passive. So walking farther up to the third floor depends on whether there are options to express aggression on the second floor in a manner deemed more appropriate by political authorities—athletics or rooting for teams or sports heroes, healing the ill through surgery (the sublimation of Chapter 3), focusing anger and violence toward outgroups like foreigners or domestic enemies differentiated by religion or race. In essence, staying on this floor means one has been bought off with the chump change of violence—a version of this makes up the first chapter of the American author Ralph Ellison's *Invisible Man* (1952). From the perspective of political authorities, the only thing better than this would be sating one's violence and walking back down the staircase.

But the second floor does not suffice, so on to the third floor. Here one finds or develops a new explanatory vehicle based on some moral structure and dynamic—why there's unfairness and how to confront it through violence. Moghaddam uses the term *moral engagement*. He more clearly than Bandura (at least to me) notes that one is not disengaging from morality but is instead leaving one morality for another or engaging in some change process on a moral, multidimensional continuum. On the third floor, terrorism-compatible morality is instilled, maintained, and malignantly nurtured through frequently isolating the floor's inhabitants; carefully controlling available information; modulating types and frequency of positive social interaction; and shaping a fluctuating but omnipresent fear. I've been in such situations and can testify that the above is no psychological hokum but is perceived and felt as extremely tangible and powerful. One can experience a huge pressure when one contemplates even acting on something that is not proscribed because it's not prescribed either. One looks around and realizes that the inhabitants of this floor (as one perceives them) ineluctably fluctuate from alien others to bosom compatriots. It feels like an all-or-nothing environment. In essence, one is controlling oneself and others more efficiently than any external control mechanism could (see the discussion of Foucault in Chapter 1). If one leaves the third floor, going back *down* may seem like the figurative destruction of a world or of one's self. So one may feel impelled to go *up*, even if what awaits may be physical destruction.

According to Moghaddam, once climbing to the fourth floor of the staircase, leaving the floor/staircase alive may not even be possible. There are severe distinctions between one's ingroup and the larger outgroup, a hugely salient *us versus them* mentality. There's a hugely strengthened categorical imperative—quite different from what Kant may have meant in the service of God's creation—that certain things viewed as anathema by the larger society are now highly valued among inhabitants on the floor (although some profilers might argue for a moral equivalence between competing anathemas of ingroup and outgroup).

The only movement available now is up to the fifth floor to walk the walk, not just talk the talk. It's showtime—and the end of material time for successful suicide terrorists and their human targets. Failure occurs only through ineptitude, a last-minute failure of will, technical problems, and serendipity. It may be facetious to ascribe the label of a Led Zeppelin song *Stairway to Heaven* (1971) to Moghaddam's metaphor. It's maybe more worthwhile noting that all the social aspects of the metaphor don't necessarily require other people, that one carries around one's own staircase and one's own self-enablers, self-enforcers, and so on.

Post, Bandura, and Moghaddam may all be contributing valuable constructs for specific individuals at specific points of a timeline for profiling matrices and narratives. And I should apologize to and for the many significant contributors on the psychology of terrorism left out of this chapter—including but definitely not limited to Randy Borum, Martha Crenshaw, John Horgan, Arie Kruglanski, Clark McCauley, Jessica Stein, and Jeff Victoroff. Readers would find it quite profitable to access materials written by these authors for additional constructs and processes that also might be valuable for profiling matrices and narratives. (This can be easily done by identifying relevant work through visiting their websites, *PsycNet*, or common search engines.)

Now I'll add some comments about the most current research on profiling and terrorism—having already mentioned Monahan's (2012) work in Chapter 2. Campana and Lapointe (2012) analyzed much of the last decade's writings on terrorism and admit that there seem to be no structural root causes, that no universal or extremely basic and common causes have been identified. They attribute these conclusions to the extant body of research being fragmented as to information collected; to there being no common paradigm leading toward knowledge; to differences in how terrorism and other related constructs are defined; and to a dependence on sources of information (terrorists, terrorist supporters, counterterrorist personnel) of questionable and problematic credibility and accuracy. I believe another possibility is that there truly are no structural root causes—and thinking there would be brings us back yet again to the problematic notion that what works in physical science must in psychological, behavioral, and social ones as well.

A paraphrase of research posted on *Science Daily* for a future issue of *Law and Human Behavior* finds differences and similarities between male and female terrorists (Jacques & Taylor, 2012): "… Compared with [male terrorists], female terrorists were equivalent in age, immigration profile, and role played in terrorism, but were more likely to have higher education attainment, less likely to be employed, and less likely to have prior activist connections" (p. 1). These findings would seem to present little of value in profiling an individual case and to illustrate Lamiell's point (see Chapter 3) that group averages may have little to do with the characteristics of any individual in any group.

As a brief introduction to the next study, please consider the tale of "Silver Blaze" from *The Memoirs of Sherlock Holmes*. In it, the fictional detective attempts to solve the apparent disappearance of a famous racehorse (Doyle, 1995). The key dialogue centers upon Inspector Gregory and Holmes in an exercise of post-dictive profiling. Gregory asks, "Is there any other point to which you would wish to draw my attention?" Holmes responds, "To the curious incident of the dog in the night-time." Gregory then responds, "The dog did *nothing* in the night-time." Holmes retorts, "*That* was the curious incident."

Dutter (2012) follows Holmes's lead and attends to situations wherein people who seem to be on the road to terrorism step back before they get close to committing it;

that is, they end up doing nothing *terrorist*. His case study involves Quebec separatists who seemed on the verge of a comprehensive terrorist campaign in the 1960s and 1970s. Dutter finds that *reversing* denial of access to the political arena, lack of economic opportunity for members of groups seeming to be moving toward terrorism, and a direct or immediate physical threat to the group or its members may lead to terrorism *not* occurring. (This reads as if political authorities unwittingly or otherwise have influenced would-be terrorists to go back down Moghaddam's staircase.) As important is deterring or attenuating what Dutter calls "... an ethos of political violence or armed struggle ...."

Also, Dutter rightly notes that many other events *will* be significantly associated with terrorism—helping it wax or wane. These include what contributes to the viability of a government or nation-state; individual group, and organizational characteristics—structure, function, and process; the historical context of politics and political violence; and basic social and cultural practices relevant to political expectations and the acceptability of violence. I list these rather abstract notions just to emphasize the need for multiple profiling languages from the most internally biological and psychological to the most externally social, cultural, and political—these last encompassing the situational.

In a doctoral dissertation, Hsu (2012) studies the possibility of *terrorism displacement* that is quite relevant to work I do in the area of aviation security and terrorism. Here displacement is not a psychodynamic defense mechanism but instead refers to whether incipient terrorists just change method or mode of attack, if a preferred method or mode of attack is sufficiently stymied through counterterrorism techniques. If displacement occurs, one might conclude that ineluctable, internal psychological events largely impel terrorist behavior. Or perhaps these events are mediated or precipitated by some situational event—one of long or short duration—that necessitates terrorist behavior even if one variant has been stymied through counterterrorism. It may be that in developing a profiling matrix and narrative, one needs to be on the lookout both for terrorism that (1) is overdetermined or highly determined and (2) may occur only when the stars align in some relatively unique and rare fashion. Hsu concludes that displacement often does not occur. This may support option (2) not (1). On the other hand, Hsu's collection of information may be insufficient to support or rule out either or any option.

Finally, Cottee and Hayward (2011) studied motivational elements of terrorism using the existential and humanistic languages of profiling. They identified the three most significant elements as desire for excitement, for some ultimate meaning, and for glory. Related to profiling matrices and narratives, Cottee and Hayward posit that terrorists are motivated as much by self-dramas and ongoing efforts to modulate and reconstruct self-structure and self-process. The implication is that, as with Dutter (2012), psychological profiling may lead to psychological counterterrorism based on social, cultural, and political interventions. (I prefer the term antiterrorism here as it often denotes the intent to decrease terrorism's probability, while counterterrorism often applies to managing some ongoing terrorist activity.)

I conclude this chapter with three last comments. The first is that the psychological constructs and processes advanced by most terrorism researchers to explain terrorism seem to me to be too logical, rational, and coherent. One does not have to be a heavy user of the psychodynamic languages to appreciate that people engage in behaviors—especially extreme behaviors—that seem to be beyond understanding including their own. Also, people may be in the throes of cognitive, emotional, and motivational morass that seem to defy logical rhyme and reason. This does not necessarily imply that valid profiling is unachievable and that the whole matter is unknowable. It does suggest that an approach based on narrative founded on a matrix should be malleable for logical, illogical, and nonlogical phenomena as appropriate.

Second, the focus on psychological constructs should not obviate the import of ideology. That is, while some experts might see ideology as just a psychological surface almost bearding more vital and significant psychological events, others are careful not to discount that true beliefs may be just that—one's truth without the need to explain it otherwise in a psychological manner. For example, Bjelopera (2012) identifies "… animal rights, environmental rights, anarchism, white supremacy, anti-governmental ideals, black separatism, and anti-abortion beliefs …" (p. 2) as legitimate pathways (in the eyes of the possessor) toward domestic terrorism. He then adds other events that might facilitate the pathway to terrorism such as prison radicalization and the trope of being a lone wolf as a way of being. Finally, he considers other events of interest that might or might not be considered nonviolent but still might be terrorism—for example, live liberations, economic sabotage, monkey wrenching, tax schemes, and frivolous litigation. I would add to these the many political change activities popularized by Gene Sharp (2010) of the Albert Einstein Institution intended to "… prevent and destroy dictatorships …" (p. 6) such as "pressures on Individuals"—methods of social, economic, and political noncooperation and methods of nonviolent intervention. *All* of these are, presumably, based on ideologies mitigating against the value of dictatorship and toward democracy more than an individual personality.

Third, there are examples of terrorism that may be directly associated much, much more with the support of or resistance to specific policies than with a welter of psychological constructs or with ideologies. A case in point is the work of Robert A. Pape (2005), who studied what is often called *Mideast terrorism* targeting U.S. personnel and matériel. He posits that the key events associated with terrorist events of interest have to do with the implementation of policy decisions to deploy and employ foreign military and civilian personnel. Their very presence can be perceived as a festering sore that must be treated by any effective means necessary. So the event of U.S. policy perceived as malignant by some people living where U. S. personnel and matériel are placed leads to events of interest perceived as malignant by those who are attacked. Foreign policy, not psychology, becomes the issue. I might counter this by pointing out that majorities of populations do not take the step of terrorism towards foreign personnel and matériel—thus clearing the way for psychological explanation of those who do. In fact, another psychological entry point may be one of *boundaries*—where one's sense of self ends and that of others begin, especially when it's perceived that an alien self is growing within one's own. This is the premise of Don Siegel's film *Invasion of the Body Snatchers* (1956) and its less nightmarish film sequels by Philip Kaufman (1978) and Abel Ferarra (1993), all based on the novel *The Body Snatchers* (1955) by Jack Finney. The anxiety and even terror of attempting to vanquish or do away with what grows within oneself seems compatible with terrorist acts perpetrated by those who view one's own territory as a motherland, fatherland, homeland, and, ultimately, the territory of one's self as being infiltrated with some horrible disease.

Now it's time for readers to engage with LO 7.1 and *dec* the various constructs and theories advanced to profile terrorism. The context is a film fragment from *Casablanca* (Wallis & Curtiz, 1942). One difficulty is identifying where the terrorism is. The very Nazi presence? The order of Major Strasser (played by Conrad Veidt) to stop the plane carrying Victor Laszlo (played by Paul Henreid). Rick (played by Humphrey Bogart) shooting Major Strasser? Ilsa (played by Ingrid Bergman) trying to manipulate Rick through sex and emotion?

8 Profiling Applications
Espionage

A Canadian naval officer may have provided Russian intelligence officers with sensitive information related to an intelligence alliance among the United States, the United Kingdom, Canada, Australia, and New Zealand (Schmitt & Austen, 2012). If, indeed, this was done in an unauthorized manner and constitutes espionage or something related to it, what events may be associated with this event of interest? Initial candidates have included being a "very, very quiet guy," "flew under the radar" in school, divorced, and financial problems (in 1998 "liabilities of $18,587 and assets of $1,000"; in 2010 debts on three credit cards and an outstanding loan), and slow progress for promotion in his military career. Are these even relevant in profiling espionage post-dictively? This chapter provides information to help answer this question.

Just as one can't handicap the horses without a racing form, one can't profile espionage without a workable definition. So, let's begin with what is espionage? Public intellectuals have weighed in. For example, Jacques Barzun (1965) wrote, "The advantage of being a spy ... is that there is always a larger reason ... for making any little scruple or nastiness shrink into insignificance" and "In the end, espionage ... is like advertising: the participants deploy their gimmicks and make their shifty eyes at one another exclusively."

To facilitate the development of a less negative definition, I suggest immersion within the works of the Defense Personnel Security Research Center (PERSEREC, 2012). Case histories can be accessed through *Espionage and Other Compromises to National* Security from 1975 to 2008. Herbig and Wiskoff (2005) and Herbig (2008) present and analyze elements of cases of what they call espionage perpetrated by U.S. citizens based on data from PERSEREC. As well, PERSEREC has issued data-based reports such as *Identifying Personality Disorders That Are Security Risks: Field Test Results; Evolution of Adjudicative Guidelines in the Department of Defense; Insider Risk Evaluation and Audit; Allegiance in a Time of Globalization;* and *Ten Tales of Betrayal: The Threat to Corporate Infrastructures by Information Technology Insiders Analysis and Observations*. These reports are based on assumptions that internal and external events can be identified that validly and usefully associated with events of interest—here, espionage.

Profilers should also immerse within the databases of the Office of the National Counterintelligence Executive (NCIX, 2012). (As I will soon suggest to readers, *counterintelligence* usually subsumes and otherwise conceptually interfaces with *espionage*. The two are not identical.) On the NCIX site, I recommend *True Psychology of the Insider Spy* written by psychiatrist David Charney and *The Insider Threat: An Introduction to Detecting and Deterring an Insider Spy* hyperlinked from the site of the Federal Bureau of Investigation (FBI). The FBI site (2012c) also contains information on some but not all espionage cases going back to 1938. As well, the NCIX site provides linkages to Carnegie Mellon University's Computer Emergency Response Team (CERT) Insider Threat site (2012) that readers should use along with the *Security Publications* and *Related Resources* options on the US-CERT site (2012) controlled by the U.S. Department of Homeland Security. Both of these combine information on the psychosocial element of espionage with the potential for compromising information technology activity. (Here I note that *insider threat* may be best construed as the potential of various misbehaviors by people hired by the organization at risk and by other people who are able and willing to get inside the organization—although it usually refers to the former. Espionage is only part of the insider threat.)

Based on the previous, I would recommend that *espionage* denote (1) obtaining and transmitting sensitive information (2) without official approval or authorization and (3) with the intent/foreknowledge of it hurting the security of the organization controlling the information. But as with *terrorism* in Chapter 7, there are definitional problems. The problem with need for *official approval or authorization* and *intent/foreknowledge* is that many observers would vouch that leaking information to the mass media is not espionage, especially when the leaker believes that some injury to the organization or what it represents will *not* occur. (As I write, this is an extremely sensitive and public issue. The U.S. Attorney General Eric Holder has just appointed two U.S. attorneys to investigate leaks bearing on the infiltration of a terrorist group, drone attacks on purported terrorists and terrorist supporters, and cyberattacks on Iranian activities purportedly related to nuclear weapons development; Savage, 2012a).

And the case has been made that some people convicted of espionage or some illegal variant had neither intent nor foreknowledge of organizational injury. For example, William Kampiles, often referred to as a former, low-level clerk employed by the Central Intelligence Agency (CIA), sold a classified technical manual to the Soviet intelligence officers. He may have believed he was making himself more attractive to work as a double agent and may have been surprised when he was charged with espionage by the USG (Sullivan, 2005). Larry Wu-tai Chin, often referred to as a Chinese translator employed by CIA's Foreign Broadcast Information Service, provided intelligence officers of the People's Republic of China with significant classified information. He claimed that he was trying to improve relations and avoid war between the United States and the People's Republic of China (Ragavan, 2003) even as there is extensive information that (1) he wanted money to live beyond his government salary and support what may have been a gambling problem and (2) engaged in sensitive compromises years earlier while translating for the U.S. Army that directly resulted in people being tortured and killed. (Both the Kampiles and Chin cases illustrate the complexities of developing profiling matrixes and narratives.)

With a problematic definition, profilers have more difficulty developing linkages between and among internal and external events and the event of interest. It's as if they are given the task of shooting without knowing exactly what they are shooting at. Nevertheless, profiling-related documents are and have been used for many years to guide personnel security decisions bearing on how who should be granted security clearances and special access to sensitive information as well as who should retain clearances and access through time. (These documents presumably help weed out people who may be more likely to engage in espionage.) As one example, I recommend study of *Annex C Adjudication Guidelines for Determining Eligibility for Access to Classified Information* within *DCI Directive 6/4 Personnel Security Standards and Procedures Governing Eligibility for Access to Sensitive Compartmented Information (SCI)* (2012).

This document is based on assumptions about what profilers call *select-in* and *select-out* criteria. The former are internal and external events presumably associated with the kinds of people government authorities wish to entrust with clearances and access. The latter are presumably associated with events that should not warrant such trust. A problem with *select-in* events is that authorities end up trusting people who look like they can be trusted based on guidelines such as one has *strong allegiance to the United States*, one's *personal conduct is exemplary*, and one *handles protected information well*. Looking this way, of course, is exactly what someone committing espionage frequently aspires to look like. And differentiating *looking like* from *being*, when we often judge *being* through *looking like* is a personnel security and counterespionage vulnerability.

A problem with *select-out* events is that authorities don't entrust people who look like they can't be trusted based on guidelines such as one has *financial problems*, one engages in certain *illegal behaviors* like *illicit substance abuse*, or one *advocated, threatened, or used force or violence to influence, federal, state, or local government*. However, having significant financial problems and having a significant disparity between how much money one has and how much money one desires are two very different things—and characterizes many government employees of many countries. Opportunity for significant enrichment through espionage also may not be a motivator depending on other events such as ongoing loyalty to one's government and country and the importance of loyalty to one's self-image and self-worth. (USG authorities publicly embrace a whole-person perspective on giving and taking away trust to and from people, but as described herein, often enough seems to perseverate on a piece of the person to the exclusion of the whole.)

While *illicit drug usage* may suggest at least transient impairment to carry out one's responsibilities or problems in compliance with law, profilers need to consider other possibilities. In specific cases, responsibility-related impairment may not be an issue. Also, legal compliance may pose the sort of issue it did during the Prohibition era in the United States, wherein many otherwise law-abiding citizens drank alcoholic beverages. That is, the problem may be the law not the people. And to insist on a global legal compliance to support trustworthiness might rule out large numbers of talented and loyal individuals who violate traffic and speeding laws, cheat on their taxes, and embrace idiosyncratic senses of entitlement impinging on the law. (In more extreme situations, practitioners of war crimes, crimes against humanity, and genocide often are protected by their own national law at the times these acts are committed. What, if anything, does this say about trust and the law?)

Regarding *advocating, threatening, or using force or violence to influence, federal, state, or local government*, is this not at times the American Way? Regardless of my own political beliefs, consider a former U.S. presidential candidate who frequently campaigned with the statement, "I would remind you that extremism in the defense of liberty is no vice! And let me remind you also that moderation in the pursuit of justice is no virtue!" (Goldwater, 1964). Many interpretations of this would embrace violence and the threat of violence to defend liberty and seek justice, if the U.S. government were perceived as what many in the intelligence and security communities would call a *bad actor* by its own citizens. In this context, Turvey (2011, pp. 571–576) correctly rejects a nomothetic profile that might apply to all or most bad actors even of a specific genre—including, presumably, violators of trust who commit espionage. I'd like to think most of us are fanatic about something important in our lives without necessarily increasing our potentiality for engagement in illegal, unethical, and immoral behavior.

A further problem with espionage-related profiling involves morality, personal taste, even ideology. How does this occur? It turns out that identical events (complying or not complying with personnel security criteria) presumed to be associated with the event of interest (espionage) may or may not have differing impacts on decisions about whom can or cannot be trusted. The positive side of this is that this is how wit should be. Any piece of information can have the same or different meaning in the same or different situations for the same or different people. This is why idiographic as opposed to nomothetic approaches to profiling have their place (see Chapter 3).

The flip side, however, is that profilers and also users of profiles tend to attribute negative consequences—that a person can't be trusted with a clearance or access— to events within a profile for reasons beyond the purposes for which the profile has been created. Here's an example. I had a heated discussion years ago with a profiler about what might go into an espionage-related profile. (I like to think the heat was coming from one side and that that side was not mine.) The profiler's position was that pedophiles should not be given a clearance and access to sensitive information, because there's a greater probability the pedophiles will compromise the information in some way including through espionage. My position was that the profiler should attempt to make this case for *each* pedophile who applies for a position requiring a clearance or access. If the case were to be satisfactorily made, the pedophile would *not* be hired or otherwise awarded a clearance or access. Moreover, an organization could also stipulate that *no* pedophile could be hired as a human resource choice, but not one based on nomothetic profiling between sexual behavior and espionage— even if the pedophile could be shown to have this disposition but not act on it. This is more than a Talmudic argument, because espionage-related profiling validity should not be contaminated with personal moral and ethical concerns as well as legal ones that might not be relevant.

Unfortunately, *Annex C* of *DCI Directive 6/4* contains wording that might make the conflation of the personally moral and ethical with profiling more likely. It stipulates that although adverse information based on a specific event within a profile may not be sufficient to deny a clearance or access, denial may still occur if available information is associated with a recent or recurring pattern of questionable judgment, irresponsibility, or emotionally unstable behavior. (What should be stipulated here, but is not, is the relevance of the pattern of questionable judgment, irresponsibility, and instability to engaging in a sensitive position in a manner worthy of trust.) *6/4* goes on to stipulate that notwithstanding the whole-person concept, an individual may still be denied a clearance or access because of "reliable, significant, disqualifying, adverse information." I read this as suggesting that even if a profile does not suggest denial, one can deny anyway.

We may agree that acceptance and denial of profilers' recommendations are the purview of decision makers. However, once decision makers' profiles as to what profiles are accepted or not are known, profiling validity may become suspect as profilers knowingly or unknowingly craft what will be accepted (cf. Alison & Rainbow, 2011). This analysis also illustrates how problematic a recent document from the U.S. Department of Defense (2012) is by leaving so ambiguous what "anomaly-based detection" is—the comparison of "... activities that are deemed normal against other observed events to identify significant deviations and anomalous behavior ...." (This definition is associated with others in the same and earlier documents aggregating to "... irregular and unusual deviations from what is usual, normal, or expected ....") Do we even want the usual, normal, and expected making decision about matters that are anything but?

Now for some useful constructs and theories bearing on espionage-related profiling. Given the common association of espionage against one's own people and organizations with betrayal of trust, the work of the American social psychologist Lawrence Kohlberg (1984) is very relevant for developing profiling matrices and narratives. Kohlberg furthered a research tradition bearing on the psychology of moral judgment and based on *how* people explained *how* they arrived at determinations of right and wrong for various social behaviors—like robbing a store of costly medicine that one can't afford and that will save the life of one's spouse. (He was building on the research of the Swiss psychologist Jean Piaget earlier in the 20th century.) He also sought to influence researchers to apply the work to life, to engage life by making it more moral. With a sense of respectful irony, I'll share that he died within a scenario that could have been used in his research tradition. After experiencing significant depression and physical pain for over 15 years at least partially related to what has been called *tropical disease involving parasites*, he committed suicide at age 59. His body was found washed ashore at Boston Harbor.

According to Kohlberg, betrayers of trust may be construed as making the same kinds of decisions on what is right and wrong as other people do in all areas of social life. There are six basic types of decisions on what is right or wrong and whether to act accordingly—each decision corresponding to one or more of six moral judgment stages.

In stage 1, *Obedience and Punishment Orientation*, an individual believes that there are fixed set of rules, that these rules have been handed down by powerful sacred or secular authorizes, and that these rules must be obeyed. Fear of inevitable and external punishment for external rule violation is key here. For betrayal of trust to occur, an individual might believe that the betrayal somehow is consonant with these rules, engage in the kind of cognitive gymnastics described previously by Bandura and Moghaddam for terrorism, magically believe that the inevitable punishment won't occur, or as with all moral judgments not internalize or not behaviorally comply on account of pathology dysfunction, accident, or the unknowable.

In stage 2, *Individualism and Exchange*, an individual believes that there may be different points of view, and people may act on their desires consonant with these points of view. Fear of punishment is still significant but more as a risk of transgression with less inevitability. An individual may betray trust as if immoral or amoral, but there may be an *honor among thieves mentality* as in developing a social contract to steal classified information for an agreed-upon financial reward. One also may transgress for some hope for benefit with or without reciprocity in the future.

In stage 3, *Good Interpersonal Relationships*, an individual believes that people should live up to social expectations to be good—based on members of the family and of the larger community. One's behavior should be based on good social motives. What is good can be construed differently by different people, but they should share the same intent to be good. Betraying trust, then, must somehow be construed as good as well. The other main possibility is to knowingly violate social expectations and to live with the sense of being a traitor, a noxious point within some interpersonal tapestry.

In stage 4, *Maintaining the Social Order*, the good is again social but broadened to include one's society in general, not just interpersonal relationships. At issue is how one's behavior may support or undermine the very social fabric. A typical issue would be how would society function if everyone transgressed? This might actually be used to excuse a betrayal of trust if one believes that everyone else won't transgress, so one can be free to receive and enjoy whatever fruits may come of the betrayal—a social freeloading effect.

In stage 5, *Social Contract and Individual Rights*, what's good is social, but what currently is social may not be good. So, perhaps, the social can be violated, if one believes through this a new, better *social* will result. Here the individual may transgress through the rationale that common social values are being transcended for other, better ones. These better values usually comprise what are deemed beneficial for all people in an environment in which people freely enter and leave—at least for people who are deemed people (cf. Bandura on dehumanization). People are deemed to have inalienable rights or something close to them. Democratic processes are to be upheld or one can act in a transgressive manner to uphold them, if need be (cf. Goldwater's extremism in the defense of liberty as no vice).

In stage 6, *Universal Principles*, the individual decides on right and wrong based on a conception of universal justice beyond democratic values in that a majority can advocate for unjust actions. One example of this is making decisions and acting on them based on a philosophical veil of ignorance, that is, not knowing in an identical or similar situation which role or which protagonist one might play. Another is that the individual would be more likely to engage in socially disapproved behavior— like a betrayal of trust—based on some universal value like a transcendent brotherhood with all sentient beings.

I must elaborate on Kohlberg's approach and point out that he seemed to focus more on judgment as opposed to subsequent behavior. He did not focus much on when behavior would and would not be consistent with judgments on what is and is not moral. Moreover, there's still significant controversy among researchers on how cross-culturally valid the six moral judgment stages are. Kohlberg himself seemed least sure about whether the sixth stage should even be used in deliberations on how people engage in moral situations. On the other hand, I think he does a great job in showing some of the complexities in crafting personnel security and counterintelligence policies, plans, programs, and profiles that are valid and useful. For example, the same sanction of severe punishment that might deter a stage 1 individual from treason might increase the probability of treason for a stage 5 or 6 individual. The latter might actually be baited to transgress as a way to show that punishment should not stand in the way of doing what's right or just. As well, some individuals very high on Zuckerman's sensation seeking trait described in Chapter 3 might be tempted to transgress, the more security authorities publicize that they will up the punishment for transgressors who are apprehended. The win-win for these transgressors would be the high of not getting caught and the high of punishment if caught.

Another commentary useful for espionage-related profiling is by Shaw, Ruby, and Post (1998)—Post being the same researcher identified in Chapter 7. Among other activities, Dr. Shaw has been a consulting and clinical psychologist who has focused on threat assessment and management; the profiling of foreign leaders, organizations, cyber-hackers, and the insider threat; and technology-mediated remote assessment. Keven Pape collaborated with Shaw and Post on other security-related publications, has been associated with the Chicago Project on Security and Terrorism, and is PhD candidate in political science at the University of Chicago. Although their primary focus is on the insider threat to information systems, I view the betrayal of trust involved similar if not identical to that occurring in espionage against one's own people, organizations, society, and culture. Based on their analysis of case histories provided through the U.S. Office of the Assistant Secretary of Defense for Command, Control, Communications and Intelligence and on their reading of *Project SLAMMER* (1990)—a USG-funded study based on mental health professionals' interviews and psychological assessment of perpetrators—they present what they term a *critical pathway to insider espionage*. I would relabel this as a specific structure for a profiling matrix and narrative, especially as the steps on the critical pathway often interact.

The pathway begins with *predisposing personal traits*. These may be anything from the trait languages of profiling described in Chapter 3 and broadened to include any of the five profiling languages from psychodynamic through existential and humanistic. Shaw et al. focus on *introversion*—a trait popularized by the Swiss psychiatrist Carl Jung in the early 20th century; prevalent throughout human history based on historical and cultural archives; often described as being more aware of and more frequently utilizing internal psychological content and processes as opposed to external, environmental ones; and quite common to personnel in the information technology field. I thought it might be more useful to share what Jung (1924) wrote about it: "... a turning inwards ... [one's] interest does not move towards the object, but recedes towards the subject [oneself] .... The subject is the chief factor in motivation while the object at most receives only a secondary value..." (p. 567). I translate this as a trait describing someone who gets more of their pleasure and pain, lives more of life focused on inner thoughts and feelings than on the external world. It's not necessarily someone whose focus on the self is narcissistic in the sense used in everyday language.

Shaw et al. (1998) assert that although not grounds for exclusion from hiring, introversion complicates the search for disaffected people who may betray trust because external appearances of disaffection may be more difficulty to detect. (After all, introverted people are not largely controlled by external stimuli and do not often wear their hearts on their sleeves.) And other traits and dispositions may be involved as well in developing a matrix and narrative leading to the event of interest of espionage. Shaw et al. cite the following dispositions as problematic: social and personal frustrations; dependencies on technologies—I would add any dependencies including those on other people, activities, and psychoactive substance; flexible and permeable ethical judgmental processes; decreasing loyalties to organizations—I would add to personal and social relationships and to society and cultures as well; narcissism and a strong sense of entitlement leading to believing one is owed or due quite a bit, and feeling aggrieved if this bill is not paid; and a weak sense of empathy so that the sensed feelings of those who may be hurt by betrayal will serve less as a deterrent.

From predisposing personal traits, Shaw et al. (1998) move to some *acute situational stressors*. At issue here are often marital, family, or other personal relationship problems; intervals of extreme substance abuse or unusual kinds or intensities of such abuse; work problems such as being passed over for promotion, being fired, laid off, demoted, or threatened with any of these—I would add as well gender, racial, and ethnic harassment and discrimination; and I add idiosyncratic reactions to times of social, cultural, political, or economic upheaval.

I read Shaw et al. (1998) to posit the third step in the critical pathway to internal espionage to be some *emotional fallout* from the interaction of predisposing personal traits and acute situational stressors. And the emotional fallout can take several forms. It might be something that feels negative with much discomfort that needs to somehow be extinguished—maybe depression, anxiety, guilt, anger—by any means necessary. It might be something positive, so positive that it just sweeps one along in a barely controllable elation. It might feel like nothing, like feeling numb, as if there's nothing to gain and nothing to lose.

But somehow, someway, emotion is conceived as a contaminant leading to the fourth step in the pathway—*biased decision making or failures in judgment*. Here *the die is cast* as popularized by the Roman historian Suetonius in 121 CE describing Caesar's decision to cross the river Rubicon in 49 BCE initiating a civil war. This example is apt in two ways. First, the phrase *the die is cast* is an error. Suetonius mistranslated Caesar's statement, itself a quote from a 4th-century BCE play *Auletris* by the Greek Menander—the correct translation being more like *let the die be cast*. And the betrayer of trust also is making a mistake (from the organization's or other collective entity's perspective at least). Second, crossing the river, much like not being able to step into the same river twice (cf. the Greek, pre-Socratic philosopher Heraclitus in the early 5th century BCE) cannot be undone. This consequence often is unrecognized at the moment of ill decision.

And then we arrive at what in many ways is a very crucial and underappreciated fifth step—*failure of peers and supervisors to intervene effectively*. This step actually can be concurrent with other steps at least as far back as step two. Compassionate and caring ministering coupled with more objective and security-conscious measures before betrayal occurs may deter the die from being cast. The same coupling *after* the casting may at least minimize the damage and the frequency and intensity of betrayals and may even set the stage for counterattacks against one's adversaries through double and triple agent and other deception programs.

The profiling matrix and narrative in specific espionage cases based on Shaw et al. (1998) may contain combinations of the five profiling languages; of events internal and external to the individual in question including situations; elements of romance, comedy, satire, and tragedy; inversions, declensions, and other historiographical components; Kantian struggles between isolation and socialization; Nietzschean strivings towards greatness, protecting the status quo, and self- and other-criticism; efforts to fulfill McAdams's needs for intimacy and power; actants involving helping and impeding; and at least White's formist, organicist, mechanistic, and contexualist views of the world. Everything and anything may be in play.

One more contribution for espionage-related profiling from American psychiatrist David Charney (2010). As I write this and look back over what I have written, even with the caveats in Chapters 3 and 4, I fear that readers might conclude that experts on the psychology of espionage, terrorism, and deception are primarily American, or at least what is termed *Western*. This is not the case. One might make the case that Americans are more likely to attempt to generate revenue through writing about such matters—including through screenwriting. And although there are classical writings already cited in the text from non-Western sources, such as China (Duyvendak, 1928) and India (Shamasastry, 1909) and journalistic accounts of great understanding arising from many historical eras and cultures, one might also make the case that writing about such matters might be unrelated to or negatively related to authentic expertise. I'll leave it to readers to conclude what may apply my efforts.

But back to Charney. He writes that he's been a consultant and therapist to members of the U.S. Intelligence Community for many years; also that he's been a member of the defense teams of FBI special agents Earl Pitts and Robert Hanssen as well as U.S. Air Force master sergeant Brian Regan—all of whom have been convicted of espionage-related activities related to betrayals of trust against the United States. Interestingly to me, he advocates *against* significant resources being poured into profile development—whether for prediction, post-diction, peri-diction, understanding, or influence. Instead, his analysis of espionage and betrayals of trust suggests that personnel security and counterintelligence authorities should create and maintain conditions making it less likely that individuals would get involved in betrayals of trust to begin with. Readers might consider how this can get done *without* continuing to develop profiles of people and situations to best understand what events should and shouldn't be created and maintained.

In any case, Charney posited a *core psychological event* rendering an individual susceptible to engaging in betrayals of trust, then 10 life stages on how the susceptibility plays out. The core event is developing an "intolerable sense of personal failure, as privately defined by that person." This reads like the narrative of tragedy with deeply unsated needs for power or affiliation and a hypercritical take on one's self-history. What I favor about the significance of this event for betrayals of trust is the component of the *individual's private self-definition*. The individual may look wildly successful in the eyes of others, but this may prove to be irrelevant or even leading to the betrayal of trust not the converse.

Now for the 10 life stages. The first, the *sensitizing stage*, involves a narrative or episodes involving one's early development, childhood, and adolescence that can be strung together into a plot of failures. To a degree, we all experience something like this, and even extreme versions do not lead to some inevitable conclusion, good or bad. The key here is that it constitutes a potential for betrayal of trust that we all carry. According to this line of thinking, we may not all have it coming, but we are all born in sin.

The second, the *stress/spiral stage*, involves one's ensuing adulthood with more challenges and more failures or the threat of them in our personal, social, and professional lives. For some of us, a rendezvous with some moment of crisis or challenge is becoming more likely as we head toward some *psychological perfect storm*. Maybe the gods see it coming. But, again, although we all may experience this to some degree—save for the most narcissistic or lucky among us—there still may be no inevitability to go bad or rogue.

The third, the *crisis/climax/resolution stage*, involves a seemingly insurmountable problem, a breaking point, and what Charney called a *personal bubble psychology*. There's a narcissistic injury, something felt as intolerable that needs to be treated, even if by any means necessary. The individual latches onto something that will seem to solve everything—some miraculous cure. For some people, this will involve letting oneself be recruited or even actively seeking recruitment, actually a *self-recruitment*. Charney also used the term *epiphany* here and compared its intensity with falling in love or some frenzied infatuation related to buying something like a house or car. Because of what the individual is about to do, I think the espionage-related epiphany can be an even more all-encompassing love or infatuation like a *Sicilian thunderbolt on steroids*.

The fourth, the *post-recruitment stage*, is a honeymoon period, often more so than the real thing for many of us. (My wife and I never had a formal honeymoon, so I'm OK, I think, if she reads this.) There's tremendous relief that a huge problem has been handled extremely well, and, in many ways, a whole new life is beginning. A connotation of *honeymoon*, however, is that it doesn't last—again, for most of us, and definitely for the new trust betrayer.

Thus, the fifth stage, the *morning after.* I think here of the talk show host Jay Leno's question to the actor Hugh Grant on July 10, 1995, concerning the latter's arrest after picking up a street prostitute, one Divine Brown. "What the hell were you thinking?" A paraphrase of Grant's response was that in life one knows what a good thing to do is and what a bad thing to do is ... and he did a bad thing. For the spy as betrayer of trust, what one thought was good to do is now thought bad to do, but one already did it. (Actually, this fits Grant as well.) One is now a double failure—what led up to the decision to betray trust was failure, and one has now betrayed trust (and, thus, failed at keeping trust) and there now seems to be no way out. (See the citation for Sartre's *no way out* in Chapter 3 and contemplate implications from the 1987 film *No Way Out* starring Kevin Costner as a double agent—with the identities of Yuri and of Tom Farrell.) When he disobeys and leaves his KGB handler, the handler's final quote is, "He'll be back. Where else does he have to go?"

The sixth, the *active spy career stage*, involves continuation of trust betrayal with a very discomforting sense of uncertainty. One may be caught or turned in at any time. One may be treated well or not at any time by one's controllers. One might make a mistake at any time. Again, there seems to be no way to stop. (See Beckett's *I Can't Go On, I'll Go On* citation in Chapter 2.)

But the seventh stage, *dormancy*, does involve stopping or diminishing continuing acts of betrayal, at least for awhile. As Charney implies, there may be magical thinking involved. Maybe they'll forget about me. Maybe I can make up for things. Maybe no *further* doing can *undo* what I've done. But then, one's controllers may threaten to turn him in. Or stressors involved with his initial prespying failures impel the continuation of spying or further betrayals of trust.

The eighth stage, *prearrest*, involves the individual actually engaging in behaviors increasing the probability of being caught by those who have been betrayed. This may be due to fatigue, cumulative stressors related to trying not to get caught, and conscious and unconscious guilt related to believing that one should be caught. Often enough it may be a relief to be caught. Finally, one thinks, it's over.

Charney labels the ninth stage as *arrest and postarrest*. It turns out, it's not over. Instead there's now a third failure—the arrest—along with the prespying failure and the honeymoon not lasting. Charney wrote that often the individual at this point will show little remorse, act arrogantly, and speak insolently to those whom he betrayed and their representatives. He's back at the beginning mired in failure, again seemingly with no way out.

The tenth stage, *brooding*, involves coming to terms with the current situation and the past. Often enough there are reparation attempts because the individual is rarely against who and what was betrayed, that is, there often has not been an ideological conversion. Often, the individual wants to share information about the psychology and the profiling of espionage to minimize the threat from others.

I have discussed Charney's ideas and some possible implications with some law enforcement and intelligence authorities about constructing work environments and expectations to minimize the fallout once a betrayal has occurred. For example, should there be explicit opportunities to continue one's career after some rehabilitation? Should one be rewarded for turning oneself in and coming clean. Should one be allowed a confessional with appropriate authorities to share one's disaffection and tensions before the betrayal occurs without irreparably harming one's career?

To describe common reactions, I'll share an analogy with government policy on illicit drug use and possession. If legalization led to less use, possession, and damage, many authorities might support the policy change, but they don't accept that the desired consequences would occur. The same applies to betrayals of trust—at least for the people with whom I've had discussions. In fact, many of them thought allowing confessionals and redemption would increase the problem including providing additional opportunities for double and triple agent operations run against the USG. Others vehemently believe that people who can't cut it or have betrayed the USG deserve to and must be punished; let the chips fall where they may. What do readers think?

Now it's time for readers to engage with LO 8.1 and *dec* the various constructs and theories advanced to profile espionage. The context is a film fragment from *Taxi Driver* (Phillips, Phillips, & Scorsese, 1976). A cliché of espionage is that entering its world and that of personnel security and counterintelligence is like entering a hallway of mirrors. In the film fragment the taxi driver Travis Bickle (played by Robert DeNiro) is standing in front of a mirror and having a dialogue, maybe dialogues. But with who or what? Are inner dialogues externalized only via the mirror that would not be heard by anyone else who might be in the room? Note that we seem to see and hear Bickle talking out loud in front of the mirror and then still hear his voice even louder as he seems to be no longer talking but just alternately standing and lying down. One can hear the dialogues of the streets—mostly traffic noises—from his flat, a cluttered, filthy cubicle of hell, a gaping wound into his festering mind. Are we all the summations of dialogues, and how might we access them and those in others in profiling espionage?

9 Profiling Applications
Deception

As with terrorism and espionage, *deception* has its problematics with definition. For example, an individual may intend to deceive but not successfully deceive. That individual's intent to deceive may be part of some other individual's successful deception in that the first individual's intent to deceive has been desired by the second individual because it will likely lead to some consequence desired *by* that second individual, not the first. As with the *vicarious conditioning* described in Chapter 3, observers of the first two individuals may be affected in a manner leading to *their* intents to deceive and actual deception attempts. And readers should note that all espionage and much of terrorism are but examples subsumed by whatever deception may be.

Then again, much of the epistemological complexities in seeking knowledge described in Chapter 4 may lead to self-deception even concerning one's own deceptive intent and attempts. The most significant philosophical complexities are twofold. One, often cited in this book, relates to controversies on whether an individual perceives in a manner corresponding to some objective reality or constructs it or has it constructed in a manner that has no necessary implication for objective reality even if it seems to have practical utility. (And there are many other variants besides these two options including how one considers the possibility that *one* objective reality exists as opposed to various perspectives—with all or some being so construed.) At issue are the hermeneutics of suspicion, that is, the very interpretive strategies of our minds being so compromised that deceptive intent and attempt exemplify a cardinal hubris. Ultimately, how do we know?

The second philosophical complexity bears on controversies between the constructs of free will and determinism (see Chapter 7 for prior discussion of this). One may believe and feel that one is intending and attempting to deceive—even to the point of intending and attempting to appear deceived by others—and that one is doing all of this by choice. But all of this may be causally determined, actually causally predetermined by other factors. In other words, the *event of interest* of deception is inevitable for a specific point and duration in time and space because of preceding and concurrent *events*. Another possibility for an individual believing in some types of god, spirit, or nature is that some events of interest including deception or what one desires to occur via deception are preordained in a manner that transcends causality. Here the mechanistic perspective on how the world works popularized in the writing of histories (White, 1973), such as post-dictive profiling and elements of predictive and peri-dictive profiles, becomes moot.

So profilers engaged with deception as events of interest may merely be joining what the Austrian philosopher Ludwig Wittgenstein would term a *language game* and what some psychopathologists would call a delusion, even if the social language buy-in is certified by a referral from political or legal authorities. And one might just ignore all problematics of deception so far described, much as Chapter 4 does. But if one does, what does one do with a confession of deception by a suspect or prisoner, a formal conviction overturned by the discovery of deceptive intent or attempt by a defendant or prosecutors, or some other social behavior and resolution within a deception narrative?

In any event, there are sources of information of value to profilers in understanding this thing called deception and how one might want to go about identifying it. One involves strategic political and military deception. Sources include Betts and Mahnken (2003), Daniel and Herbig (1982), Godson and Wirtz (2002), and Jervis (1976). Here the stakes may be huge involving significant world events, types of life, and life-and-death consequences for many people. The authors usually assume there is deception, that deception is the currency of the realm, and that many values may mask the quest for glory, riches, even love with power as the ultimate value. (George Orwell's *1984* is so significant because deception is transparently an everyday policy, and power is sought and maintained without the need for the opiates of other values like freedom, rights, happiness, and well-being or of other things as well.) I've published in this area and offer a reference (Bloom, 1984) that I'm now embarrassed about because it's much too mechanistic in its approach. (At the time, I was rather proud of it but now wish to warn off profilers who might take too much stock in any article in any refereed journal.) Chapter 4 captures the sorts of events that this source on deception most analyzes.

A second source embraces plays and novels from trashy to classical—and one could add entertainment films and shows as well. The trashy often involve steamy sex, violence, and blatant lying for high stakes discovered in time to titillate the reader. I won't provide references for what are guilty pleasures for many people. The classical include Shakespeare's tragedies (e.g., *Othello*'s Iago), Moliére's comedies (e.g., *Tartuffe*), Homer's epic (*Odyssey*), and Hawthorne's novel *The Scarlet Letter*. (Here I'm displaying ignorance on non-Western sources.) The point of the classical takes on deception is that deception is intrinsic to the human condition regardless of philosophical problematics.

A third source comprises what I term the world of tactical counterintelligence. At issue is tradecraft bearing on how to most securely protect and pass information, protect equipment and infrastructure, and select and manage people to attenuate deception threats. As well, there's tradecraft on using deception to achieve protection or other quite different goals. A classic example is William Johnson's *Thwarting Enemies at Home and Abroad* (2009) that, while outdated on technology issues, is contemporary and, perhaps, timeless on the human element.

Of more than passing interest as a fourth source, however, is just that: *passing*. This source comprises writings and other cultural products on *how* one attempts to look the way that one wants or thinks one wants to look, that one thinks others want one to think one wants to look or to just look. As examples, I'm about to discuss ethnicity, professional culture, and gender identity and sexual orientation but first will note that *passing* has much to do for all of us with creating a self or selves, an identity or identities, as ongoing life tasks. One decides to look a certain way and that helps one be or become that way, or at least something. One decides to be or become something and then chooses to look a certain way—even if that choice is to look different from how one wishes to be. One might desire to look capable and accomplished, but because one despairs of pulling this off, one attempts instead to look as incapable and unaccomplished as possible—in a way, to disengage from being perceived as a failure by others and by oneself by looking as if that which one would be perceived as failing is not even something that has been attempted but unachieved. (As complicated as this might read, try passing this way.) In these senses, we *are* all actors, not that we are just acting, and acting like we're not acting is still acting—still how we are, not how we feign. Or we can't feign our nature, if feigning is, indeed, our nature. Sincerely believing that we're not acting but just *are* seems more a combination of unconscious and conscious willful blindness—or deception. But, again, how can this be? So we're all passing through life with this *reducto ad absurdum*. We're all wanting to and attempting to be something we're not. And profilers are attempting to predict, post-dict, peri-dict, understand, and influence events and events of interest that are by most definitions *deception*—even as profilers pass as profilers. Because *life is passing is deception*.

I here confess my great admiration for the work of Cindy Sherman (2012), who some consider a performance artist, some a visual artist or just unique as a creator of cultural product. For over 30 years, she has created photographs—usually as the only person in each—in which she poses with different postures, cosmetics and hairstyles, clothing and accessories, facial expressions, and backdrops. Commenters on these photographs often describe each photograph as something much more than just a picture of Sherman. Instead, each may be a captured element in an ongoing stream of sociocultural life or of the inner human condition or both. Each might be viewed as real or imaginary, surreal or real or hyperreal (see Baudrillard in the preface). Her passing lets us in on the passing, passing as the march of life. And to emphasize, I note that passing is not equated with but overlaps with the many changes people go through in life, what the Irish author James Joyce in *Ulysses* (1922) wrote: "As we, or mother Dana, weave and unweave our bodies, from day to day, their molecules shuttled to and fro, so does the artist weave and unweave his image."

So with ethnicity, one may view oneself or others of some *ethnic kind* engaged in cultural practices and trying them on, performing them, if you will, in an attempt at being something—although one might be best judged to always be in a state of unbecoming or becoming that something. Whether one lives with others of one's *ethnic kind* or not, one still makes choices of attempting to be as much like others of that kind as possible or create and preserve some differences that often may be viewed by oneself as the most unique and highly valued aspects of one self (or again not, differences in the self and others of *one's kind* to be avoided at all costs). These days, performing these aspects of passing is facilitated and complicated by vast amounts of images online compared with previous eras wherein one might have access only to small numbers of people, cultural artifacts and products, and one's ineluctably constrained imagination. Contemporary passing is a challenge for profilers who claim to depend on empirical associations (or their approximations) among events and events of interest because these associations already may be outdated or superseded by newer ways of living. And so the new wave, the next wave, and the avant-garde are always insistent upon profilers' attempts to make sense.

The same is the case with passing professionally—as doctor, lawyer, tinker, tailor, soldier, spy. One chooses to try on dressing the part, acting the part, thinking the part, learning the skills of the part. One chooses the degree of consistency with which one attempts to professionally pass. Thus, an explanation for a group of employees on a business trip: Some never vary, never leave the professional role. They're always *on*. Others engage in substance abuse, various promiscuities, and the bonfire of the bizarre. Passing may take its toll and lead commentators on the human condition to posit some inner nonpassing core. The toll is explained as attempting to pass too far from the nonpassing. Of course, if the nonpassing is itself a variant of passing, one may be left only with self-implosion or a life of hypervigilance against the void. Profilers may be deceived only if they buy into passing as hiding the truth. Maybe there's an essential truth in a statement by Marilyn Monroe passing as Miss Harrington in the film *All About Eve* (see Chapter 2), who explains her familiarity with George Sanders passing as Addison DeWitt—"That's how he met me, in passing."

Given the popularity of sex crimes and violations of sexual proprieties in popular cultural products, in public and private discussions, and, presumably in the thoughts of some of us, profilers can benefit from considering the passing involved in gender identity and sexual orientation. Many people seem to take on elements of socially prescribed, proscribed, and conditioned aspects of constructs labeled as gender identities, *masculinity* and *femininity*—assuming one can identify consensually validated aspects of each. It seems to be the case that some individuals dip from both and other still evolving constructs as well. And this dipping may have elements of choice and of none at all.

Assuming that seemingly preponderant gender identities are socially constructed to the degree that they imperfectly mask aspects of yet other gender identities that could arise and often enough do, profilers in their work may be confronted with powerful inclinations within those they study permeated by passing attempts and outright deception. The same applies to sexual orientation with the huge variations in preferences and inclinations as to who does what to who or what, when, how, why, and where. Black-socked former governors of New York patronizing elite escort clubs, cigar-toting former U.S. presidents cavorting in the Oval Office, Canadian flag officers engaging in serial murders under the maple leaf, and famous televangelists passing through the low lives of seedy Baton Rouge motels are the result. The larger deception is not that people are hiding some passing behavior and trying not to get caught but that they are passing as a way of life, as the human condition.

One last example of passing that should be very significant in the profiling of social and cultural violations—especially ethical ones—as well as outright crimes involves *psychopaths*. Although there are many definitions—well written and not— of what this term may denote, I'll paraphrase aspects of psychopathy bearing on *passing* based on my reading of two giants in the field—the American psychiatrist Hervey Cleckley (1982/1941) and the Canadian psychologist Robert Hare (Hare & Neumann, 2008). Like most of us, a psychopath wishes to achieve success even if success may be sometimes very idiosyncratically defined. And like most of us, the psychopath may be psychologically characterized as if there are some intrapsychic or behavioral deficiencies or dysfunctions along for the ride to desired success.

More characteristic of the psychopath, however, is what those deficiencies or dys-functions (i.e., events) seem to be. Most significantly, they often include a lack or an inadequate degree of empathy, a shallowness of emotions even if they can experience intense spikes of feeling especially when things aren't going their way, a lack or an inadequate degree of remorse, grandiosity, various difficulties in recognizing emotions and emotional situations, and dispositions to lie and manipulate others. To be successful, all of these must carefully be masked, controlled, and employed. So deception is not just a tool of the psychopath applied in social situations, it's as importantly the essential aspect of psychopathic passing. The psychopath—success-ful or not—needs to pass as if one feels and can express empathy, remorse, and vari-ous other emotions, as if there is no significant grandiosity, no significant difficulty in recognizing emotions and emotional situations, and no undue penchant for lying and manipulating others. And this passing of the psychopath is alive and well not only in our prisons and criminal neighborhoods but also in high politics, business, academia, and anywhere people with infinite needs vie for finite resources.

So the deception of life should be vital to the development of profiling matrices and narratives in passing. It should be a common theme in profiling—not that it occurs but the who, what, where, when, why, and how. And, thus, it is most ironic that much profiling effort has been spent on identifying specific indicators that pre-sumably are associated with elements of deception—as if there are such simple pathways to the human soul in a decontextual fashion. What follows is the latest on one research tradition relating deception detection and profiling—the detecting of deception in interviewing, interrogation, speechifying, and conversation.

Although somewhat dated, the best consolidated reference for a conceptual over-view of deception related to the four behaviors just described is Aldert Vrij's (2008) *Detecting Lies and Deceit*. I base the following on this book with more current illus-trations from research studies (including some by Vrij) and from another book about which I recently published a review (Bloom, 2012).

The preponderance of research focuses on three classes of deception indica-tors. The first is verbal, namely speech and writing, expressed by an individual. These indicators may include the content of information; its logical structure; the chronology of the various events described; the richness of details; how informa-tion is contextualized and interrelated; its coherence; unexpected details or lack of expected details; degree of expressed certainty; spontaneous corrections; ratios of content expressing an introduction to an event versus that to the event itself and to consequences of the event; ratio of objective to subjective information; tenses of verbs; amount of pronouns used; and degree of content ambiguity. (That's quite a bit for deceivers and deception detectors alike to keep track of, if all were indeed contextual-less valid indicators.)

The second class is nonverbal. It contains body movements; orientations and pos-tures including facial expressions and micro-movements; vocal but nonverbal char-acteristics accompanying speech; handwriting or typing characteristics transcending direct verbal or quantitative content; and content and style of drawing and other nonverbal cultural productions. More specific examples include direct eye contact or averting one's gaze; type and frequency of bodily gestures; the orientation of one's body toward that to whom one may be speaking; eye blinking; self-stimulation (whether and how and how much one touches oneself when communicating); vocal pitch; smiling and frowning; and facial movements one might be able to detect only with a frame-by-frame analysis of a video. Again, quite a bit for deceivers and deception detectors to manage, if they need to.

The third class comprises physiological and neurophysiological phenomena. They include blood pressure, respiration, sweating, blood flow around the eyes, and various brain phenomena usually indirectly measured by technologies such as electroencephalography (EEG) and functional magnetic resonance imaging (fMRI). While much of what I've just described may be immediately understandable to readers, I'll briefly gloss on the fMRI because of its significant role in deception detection research and because most readers including profilers may not be familiar with how this and similar technologies measure brain phenomena.

So, the fMRI is an indirect measure of neural activity. A researcher applies a magnetic field to a brain region. This aligns nuclei of cells in that region. Then another magnetic field is applied that further magnetizes the nuclei and causes further movement. When this second field is removed, the nuclei slowly return to their original states, with the energy they emit measured to portray what were their initial positions. This sequence of events gives researchers an estimate of the ratio of blood oxygen level, which, in turn, allow estimates of yet other neural activity—sort of like in a *reductio ad absurdum* fashion. (However, the process is anything but absurd, and Columbia University physicist Isaac Rabi won a Nobel prize in 1944 for delineating the physics underlying what became the fMRI.)

Now, back to our three classes of deception indicators and the most common rationale on which they are based—that deception is stressful. For over 160 years, most scientific researchers have assumed that people find it more difficult to lie than to tell the truth. And there should be indicators of this presumed difficulty—actually indicators of cognitive effort, attempted behavioral control (to look as if one is not deceiving), and emotional reactions accompanying cognitive efforts, attempted behavioral control, and being in a stressful situation. Thus, the deception indicators so far described are really indicators of the *stress* of deception, not deception itself.

But for all of us who have been lied to or have lied, that deception is stressful and difficult might seem a problematic assumption. This assumption may be based on residues of Judeo-Christian and other religious dictates about the sanctity of telling the truth—in that violating the sacred commandments should be stressful. But there are other religious constructs like *taqqiya* and *kitman* from some variants of Islam that countenance outright deception and deception through omission of some truth. The assumption may be based on conflation of what ethically *should* be with what *is*—as in it should be stressful to do what's wrong. It may be based on beliefs that one is more transparent to others than one actually is so that lying may be more easily found out than one desires—even if one has some religious dispensation to lie. Again, as goes the assumption, sop may go the validity of the deception indicators I have described.

But how empirically validated are these indicators. It turns out that there are problems here as well. First, the empirical validation of these indicators usually has occurred in low-stakes events—lying about something within an experiment that has no significant bearing on one's life. Even if the empirical validation can be supported, there may be little correspondence with high-stakes events like whether one has engaged in terrorism or espionage or crimes of passion, the kinds that profilers find of most interest. Second, researchers must first have identified what is termed *ground truth*. In other words, they must know ahead of time what the truth actually is, before a deception can be identified, let alone indicators of this deception. Again, this is simple in a low-stakes experiment, as when the experimenter asks a subject to lie about a playing card that's been shown and placed back into a marked deck ensuring the experimenter knows what card it was. However, knowledge of truth and deception seems often unknowable with high-stakes events in a world where the possibilities include false confessions, false convictions, tainted evidence, speculation confronting the meaning of facts, corruption of the criminal justice and other social systems, and the like. Third, researchers have often enough come up with contradictory findings. The same indicator, that is, some event, associated with deception by one researcher may be linked to truth telling by another. For example, some researchers link gaze aversion to deception, but other researchers believe deceivers attempt to control their external behaviors according to the theories of deception assumed to be believed by whomever they are talking to. These deceivers may look into people's eyes to look truthful. This leads to a more general fourth challenge for empirical research. How valid and useful can such indicators be for profilers, if people being profiled can access empirical research, identify what their future marks, including profilers, believe about deception, and act accordingly? Wouldn't things be better if all indicators were beyond conscious control? (If they were, even intelligent psychopaths would face huge deception challenges.)

But another approach to coming up with events associated with the event of interest—indicators associated with deception—has arisen in the last 50 years. In essence, it obviates the search for indicators directly linked with some *intention* to deceive by instead attempting to identify indicators associated with whether specific pieces of information have been previously experienced and are now recognized by an individual. These indicators are usually neurophysiological in nature—the fMRI again being a common research technology—and based on the assumption that there are differential neurophysiological responses to whether we are presented with a specific face, weapon, name, or even a smell we have previously experienced and now recognize or not.

So an individual may lie or not, agree or disagree or not, or engage in various sorts of verbal and nonverbal impression management or not. It doesn't matter. Much as Freud wrote in 1905 from *Fragment of an Analysis of a Case of Hysteria*, "... He that has eyes to see and ears to hear may convince himself that no mortal can keep a secret. If his lips are silent, he chatters with his fingertips; betrayal oozes out of him at every pore...," (pp. 77–78) the betrayal is seemingly uncontrollable, the tell-tale signs are not in the heart but in the brain. As readers of Freud's *Project for a Scientific Psychology* (1950/1895) are aware, he would feel vindicated by this conclusion.

But there are problems with this approach—some of which also apply to deception indicators based on the presumed association of deception and stress. First, in developing indicators, researchers may inadvertently leak information about something that subjects otherwise wouldn't have known anything about. So now subjects have the experience, but not the experience at the right time, and may look guilty when innocent. Second, subjects in research or, better yet, individuals being investigated for real may choose to look like they know something or not based on premeditated attention strategies. For example, they may choose to create an apocryphal story with images around the image of a something they've never experienced before, as if they've experienced it. Or they may try the brick wall technique used by the hero of the film *Village of the Damned* (Kinnoch & Rilla, 1960). The hero does not allow mind-reading, murderous children into his plan to destroy them by concentrating on the image of a brick wall. Or engage in yet other idiosyncratic attention strategies. Third, subjects in research often overlearn items that they will be tested on and then are tested soon after the learning process on whether neurophysiological phenomena suggest they experienced the items. However, in high stakes applications, individuals being investigated often are not formally examined for deception indicators until well after an alleged event has occurred. Fourth, even if subjects are guilty of some allegation, it is rarely knowable what they know. That is, do they even remember what may be to them extraneous or even more significant components of the event of interest? If not, their inferred brain activity via the fMRI or some other technology will suggest that they don't recognize something that, presumably, only the guilty party would know. So they'll be falsely identified as innocent. So, in my opinion, the jury is still out on how often in high-stakes situations something that seems associated with an event of interest, like a crime, is falsely recognized via inferred brain activity by innocents or unrecognized by guilties.

In any case, in today's world, research on indicators that may be used by profilers continues. What follows are representative. The redoubtable Vrij (Vrij et al., 2012) developed what he termed an undercover interviewing technique in the context of a "crime-related reconnaissance mission" (p. 231) by subjects who actually are double-crossed by the experimenters. Sounds like life. Findings suggest that deceivers seem more verbally uncertain and less concrete about their intentions than truth tellers. They also verbalize less accurately about places they claim they're about to visit. I wonder whether these findings would occur if those with premeditated evil on their minds were properly trained or whether the truth tellers are really true believers instead of people who hone doubt as their weapon cutting toward whatever truth might be.

Cook et al. (2012) studied members of a university community who either committed or learned about some mock crime. The subjects subsequently read and responded to statements related to alleged involvement in the mock crime. Findings suggest that there are two cognitive processes involved in deception—vigilance and strategy. And both may be operationally defined by different ocular-motor measures, that is, eye movements. For example, mock criminals who attempted to deceive about their involvement had increased pupil responses even as they spent less time fixating on, reading, and rereading statements that they answered deceptively. This finding was even clearer when the mock criminals had more incentive to successfully deceive their involvement. The practical (utility) as opposed to statistical significance of the ocular-motor response approach to deception is questionable. So is any significance of these responses when coupled with the possibility that profilers employing such findings could be up against profiles aware of the research.

Since achieving the status of senior citizen in the eyes of local movie theaters and chain restaurants and as many First World populations continue to age even as the Third World gets younger, I've become more interested in deception for the older set. Slessor et al. (2012) found that older as opposed to younger subjects were less likely to associate direct gaze with honesty and averted gaze with dishonesty. (Did they learn through the school of hard knocks *or* by reading Vrij?) This was the case even as both older and younger subjects associated averted gaze with lying *when they were explicitly asked*. One might wonder what the results might be for those old and young at heart versus in age. As well, the findings might well suggest that what older participants tell you they do as opposed to what they do may be quite different— deception about deception if you will, perhaps, through that school of hard knocks.

Based on a wide overview of experimental data, I offer that the accuracy of detecting deception varies from less than chance to about 70–80% accuracy—depending on a host of experimental parameters (themselves varying as to impact on accuracy) like the inclusion of false positives and false negatives in a generic accuracy estimate, how high the stakes of the deception, stress versus recognition hypothesis, and type and degree of training of human deception detector. Even more underwhelming is the degree of practical utility of various group accuracies for individual cases. The very latest studies available as I write this book should not dissuade us from this opinion (cf. Masip et al., 2012; Peace & Sinclair, 2012; Van Swol, Malhotra, & Braun, 2012).

Now it's time for readers to engage with LO 9.1 and *dec* the various constructs and theories advanced to profile deception. The context is a film fragment from *The Women* (Stromberg & Cukor, 1939). There's a grand deception compromised when a successful businessman's mistress (played by Joan Crawford) is confronted in a dressing room of a very upscale retail store by the aggrieved wife (played by Norma Shearer). But how many micro-deceptions both verbal and nonverbal are there in the give-and-take between the two? And why near the end of the encounter are so many shoppers and staff alike listening through the door?

10 The Future of Profiling

Here's another quote from Joyce's *Ulysses* (1922): "So in the future, the sister of the past, I may see myself as I sit here now but by reflection from that which then I shall be." He's alluding to the interdependence of the past, present, and future. How our perspectives of the past are colored by the present, the present by the past, both impacting on the future that soon enough will be present and then past. So as I conclude with what might be next for profiling, I rightly should be constrained by what I have written and what I now think.

Will there still be something called profiling? That is, will most people continue to believe in it even as they differ in how to best do it? An alternative might be that profiling is more of a myth supported at best by underwhelming theory and data. And, thus, it should be jettisoned as human nature changes into something less based on magical thinking. I believe belief in it will remain and that controversy over the *how* will continue. And controversy will remain over what I'll now term the meaningful versus nonmeaningful approaches to profiling. The former refers to the essence of this book—psychological meaning of why something will be, has been, or is. The latter is a purely empirical relationship between variables with meaning coming after, and afterthought, or irrelevant. A contemporary example is profiling through *forensic linguistics* (Shuy, 2006). Here comparative quantitative analyses of spelling, grammar, and word and phrase choices related to speech and writing help profilers identify or believe that they've identified bad actors engaged in social deviance— even as the forensic linguistician may claim to be only comparing samples between and among known and unknown sources. The meaning of the linguistic indicators as opposed to their differentiating powers is either absent or beside the point.

A related issue involves the comparative importance and power of profiling people versus situations. As I suggested in Chapter 3, there are times when the situation impels events of interest regardless of an individual's psychological characteristics. Thus, much more study needs to occur in developing profiling languages of the situation, not the person. (I'm thinking of this as I read about the 2012 contract negotiations between DirecTV and Viacom bearing on how various *shows* are to be accessible on various platforms alone or purchased as parts of larger packages; Stelter, 2012.) At issue are owners of these shows trying to prevent others from watching them unless the price is right and the threat of others who wish to copy, capture, and otherwise distribute the shows without formal approval—an event of interest. The role of the situation is best captured in the following quote from the chief executive officer of a public interest group in Stelter's article: "It never ceases to amaze me how the studios never seem to make the connection between creating scarcity and piracy."

I hope that profiling converges into some interdisciplinary enterprise. Not just scientific psychology but integrating the physical and life sciences, humanities, philosophy, and the arts. Each presents a different pathway to human knowledge with strengths and weaknesses. This has implications for the undergraduate and graduate curricula for those who choose to be profilers and those who will be credentialing them. Given that the most significant issues of how we might know the validity and utility of profiling bear on the philosophy of science and a sociology of knowledge, the real doctor of profiling will not necessarily be a medical one, even if psychiatry is often enough treated as a most respected authority. An even better outcome might be leaving behind the controversies about terminal degrees that largely are about politics not knowledge.

I hope that interdisciplinarity takes another turn by methodologically borrowing from other profiling venues. For example, something called *quantitative descriptive analysis* is compared with something else called *temporal dominance of sensation* to profile the commercial viability (based on taste) of black currant squashes (Ng et al., 2012). Differential behavioral profiling of stimulant substances in the rat is being studied (Castagné et al., 2012). As opposed to studies of the police doing the profiling, research is being carried out on ethnic, racial, and gender differences in people profiling the police (Cochran & Warren, 2012). Other relevant studies over the course of 2012 include the (1) biological profiling of various medical disorders like Parkinson's disease and ischemic stroke, (2) educational profiling of student to best match with remedial curricula, and (3) political profiling of people who advocate for pro-environmental legislation and other activities. These may seem to be of less than immediate interest for the profiling of terrorism, espionage, and deception, but they may be applying epistemological tools with potential for higher validity and utility for the latter.

I hope that formal accountability becomes intrinsic to the public dialogue and adjudication of profiling claims. Just as some physicians are being assessed based on surgical outcomes, as *Angie's List* is being applied more systematically to more services, profilers should be carrying around their current and lifetime batting averages and strikeout rate. Continuing with the baseball analogy, each profiler may do better in certain parks, against certain teams, at certain parts of the game. Maybe we need a centralized information technology-based data capability for this. Such accountability may be more appropriate than handing out jail sentences to applied scientists who don't always get it right. A case-in-point are the seven Italian earthquake experts who were convicted of manslaughter and sentenced to six years in prison for failing to "… give adequate warning to the residents of a seismically active area … preceding an earthquake that killed more than 300 people" (Povoledo, 2012).

Continuing with an information technology-based data capability, this can help track the perishability of validity and utility for specific events associated with other events and events of interest. Alerts could be put out for credentialed profilers on the latest in evidence-based judgments. For example, researchers on profiling may attempt to differentiate between events as *indicators* and events as *expressions* following the work of the German philosopher Edmund Husserl (2001/1900–1901). In the former, one must make a leap of faith and associate something with something else as a bulge under one's jacket may indicate an incipient suicidal terrorist attack. In the latter, a certain type of smile may be an actual expression of happiness or anger or hatred. A fast walk toward a house might be an indicator of incipient mayhem or the expression of a very weak bladder.

The difficulty of identifying and associations events and events of interest is exemplified by the shootings allegedly by one individual killing 12 people and wounding over 50 at the Century 16 movie theater in Aurora, Colorado, on July 20, 2012. The plain truth at the moment is that profiling has not succeeded in coming up with anything that can be used in predictive, post-dictive, and peri-dictive pursuits for such mass public shootings be they at schools, theaters, or elsewhere. A joint study by the U.S. Secret Service and U.S. Department of Education on school shootings (with applicability to the theater shooting) still provides the current Word (Vossekuil et al., 2002). On one hand, such acts are rarely sudden and impulsive; often involve the foreknowledge of others and less often their help; are not accompanied by prior threats; and are perpetrated by people who seemed (1) to need some sort of *psychological help*, (2) to be struggling with personal loss or failure and were considering or had attempted suicide, (3) to have felt bullied, persecuted, or injured by others; and to have had access to and had used weapons prior to the attack. On the other hand, there is no useful profile given the huge false-positive and false-negative errors that would be involved. An extremely pessimistic perspective might be that just as we all may need some kind of help, we all may in some way have it coming—at least in terms of how we may be perceived by some others. (Another related difficulty is the competing pressures of what people want to believe about such incidents, what various mass media tell people to believe, and what applied research suggests with all three having the potential to cross-contaminate perceptions of validity and utility.)

A further cyber-issue involves global positioning system (GPS) technology and smartphone apps. It is just much easier now and will become even easier in the future to engage in surveillance of people with and without their knowledge. Knowledge will continue to explode about what people buy and have bought, where they are and where they have been, with whom we communicate, and so on. Such knowledge will facilitate data mining both for individuals, groups of people, and all people. Greater predictive validity may well occur even with the caveats described in Chapter 4—especially if there's massive cross-referencing of an individual's data with that of presumed friends, families, and associates. But there also will be greater deception and counterdeception possibilities for the more ingenious of good and bad actors.

As to the various statistical approaches supporting profiling, I have described a mixed picture of success and failure not just for crimes of high dudgeon but also for various commercial pursuits with huge amounts of money on the line (see Chapter 4). Another example of the latter is IBM claims in an advertisement placed in the *New Yorker* (July 9 & 16, 2012 issue) that the Japanese fashion retailer Start Today increased annual sales on its *Zozotown* website by 54.2%. IBM associates the success to its Netezza and Unica approaches to analyzing massive amounts of data "... letting [Start Today] create personalized messages for each of their 3.8 million customers...." Of direct relevance to profilers working on a specific case would be how such success translates into *knowability* of associations between specific events and a specific event of interest for a specific individual—whether purchasing, killing, spying, and lying.

To continue to develop evidence-based judgments, the huge capacities of information technology might be married to the metaphors of the *palimpsest* and the *mystic writing pad*. A palimpsest is a page or document from a book, scroll, or other writing medium from which the text has been scraped off and that can be used again. A mystic writing pad is most often a children's drawing or writing toy constituted by a wax tablet, a wax sheet of paper on top of this, and a celluloid sheet on top of the wax sheet. Both are examples of how what's apparent in the present actually is in some way incomplete taking the place of or covering the past. The former has been the title of at least two novels and one best-selling memoir—the last by the American author Gore Vidal—as a metaphor for the trajectory of one's life. The latter used as a metaphor by Freud for the human mind. I hope these metaphors are used to oppose the discrete and stable nature of events and events of interest in the development of profiling matrices and narratives. Instead, events and events of interest each should be living and ever-changing entities as intrapsychic, other internal, and external aspects of the human life space (see Chapter 3). In essence, profilers are working with ever-changing living materials each constituted by the past, present, and future in various situations and contexts. This is the case whether one is profiling longitudinally through time from past to present and future or in a cross sectional fashion for a specific moment in time. The profiling challenge is to develop software to best structure this way of thinking both for deciding what should be collected and how it's analyzed.

One promising statistical direction for profiling is *object-oriented programming*. This is commonly used in designing software systems through creating modules that pass data back and forth. More recently, it's been used for simulating the life span of very simple organisms like a single-cell bacterium. For example, American bioengineer Markus Covert has been building computational models of complex biological processes to identify and validate various metabolic, regulatory, and signaling networks as well as cell–cell interactions (Covert, 2012). Applying this approach to psychological, behavioral, and social dynamics would take profilers closer to the ever-changing nature of an individual, ongoing situation, and their interaction. "An illustration of this is how mathematical physicist Ralph Kenna and associates have been statistically analyzing the text of classical works like Homer's *Iliad* (cf. Lattimore, 1951) to better ascertain how personal and social life including, presumably, what constituted acceptable and unacceptable rationales for violent behavior and betrayal of trust at the time of the sack of Troy" (MacCarron & Kenna, 2012).

Another promising statistical direction is *dynamical systems*. This has been commonly used in the study of ecological and environmental systems. For example, the American biologist Martin Scheffer (2009) studied abrupt changes (i.e., tipping points) in complex systems—through quantitatively modeling for predictive, postdictive, and peri-dictive purposes critical transitions within lakes, oceans, terrestrial ecosystems, and climates through employing combinations of catastrophe, chaos, and other theories. He also applied this to changes in human societies. Profilers need to be thinking about tipping points bearing on the beginning of the inevitable event of interest—with implications for deterrence, prevention, and successful management.

As to contemporary and future changes in human nature due to various *cyberdevelopments* and profiling implications for associations between and among events and events of interest, I've already suggested that relevant research is just beginning to take off. I find it of interest that one area—the psychological effects of easy online access to so much information—was actually foreshadowed in a discussion described over 2,300 years ago by Plato in his *Phaedrus*. The discussion is between the Egyptian god Theuth and King Thamus about the psychological implications not of *online access* but of the creation of *writing*. The king believes that people will become less intelligent because they'll need to rely less on their memories and be more likely to misinterpret the written word as opposed to speech. The god (who has invented writing) believes the converse. If Plato had added a profiler working with security, intelligence, law enforcement, or judicial personnel, the *Phaedrus* might have included implications for the frequency, severity, and complexity of crime and moral transgression.

I'm hoping the three events of interest—terrorism, espionage, and deception—become further demystified by researchers, profilers, various political and social authorities, and the general public alike. The sense that they are all bad all of the time gets in the way of finding good events as well as bad ones to be associated with them. And as I've intimated throughout this book, we all engage in all three differing only in degrees of extremity.

A quick example from terrorism. I've just read an obituary of the Israeli Yitzhak Shamir (Brinkley, 2012)—among other things a foreign minister, prime minister, construction worker, intelligence officer, bookkeeper, and top commander of the Stern Gang (or Lehi). During the 1940s, the gang judged many of its violent acts as *personal terror*, and Shamir was viewed as a *terrorist* by many in the Jewish public and by members of other underground groups fighting against the British-ruled Palestine mandate—let alone the British authorities. Shamir viewed it as more humane to assassinate specific individual military and political British figures than to attack British targets like military installations that risked collateral civilian damage. So what events lead to the terrorism events of interest? His family being murdered by Poles and Nazis only for being Jewish? Shamir's quote is that "… [one] must believe only one thing: that by his act he will change the course of history.…" This takes us back to the political commentator and stand-up comedian Bill Maher's comments (Chapter 4) related to whether terrorists can be characterized only as lacking positive features and antiterrorists and counterterrorists lacking negative ones.

A third option to goodness and badness in profiling is that of *nihilism*—a belief in nothing. The construct of nihilism probably has been with us throughout human history but often is linked with its popularization by several Russian political movements in the mid- to late 19th century. As a number of commentators already have remarked about the Aurora shootings (cf. Douthat, 2012), as opposed to being for or against something the idea is just to sow death, destruction, and chaos; to break the world. There's no reason, there's *just do it*. Does the finding of an advertising poster for the 2012 *Batman* film *The Dark Knight Rises* in the alleged shooter's apartment suggest some affinity between the alleged shooter and the film's nihilistic protagonist—Bane? Or does the same apply to the alleged shooter's remark about the Joker—a protagonist from a previous *Batman* film and a recurrent part of the *Batman* history since a first appearance in a 1940 comic book? But there are so-called good, bad, and flawed people in the film and the history as well as various images of many inanimate objects and spaces between the animate and inanimate.

The future almost certainly will bring changes to the main profiling languages—those that already are significant may remain or fall away or be replaced by others.

The contemporary languages may experience significant drift in what constructs are more or less important. As but one example, evolutionary theories since Charles Darwin have long excluded most variations of the French biologist Jean-Baptiste Lamarck's *soft inheritance* or the *heritability of acquired characteristics*—for example, that people can inherit characteristics acquired by their parents and other ancestors during the latters' lifetimes. Yet recent developments in *epigenetics*—the study of heritable changes in gene expression or the physical characteristics of cells caused by mechanisms other than DNA changes—suggest that Lamarckism may be on the way back. Profilers, then, may have more versions of biologically based hypotheses to associate events and events of interest.

As I've noted throughout the book, the construct of *free will* often becomes implicated in a profiling matrix and narrative (see Chapters 5 and 7). I believe that philosophical analysis coupled with research in neuroscience will continue to support the hypothesis that free will is an illusion, that our free will experiences are associated (if not caused by) with factors of which we're not aware and do not have control over. This prediction is based on work going back at least as far as the American physiologist Benjamin Libet's discovery of brain activity associated with decisions about 300 milliseconds before people are aware of these decisions and further elaborated upon by the American psychologist Daniel Wegner (2002). As always, there are skeptics among some philosophers of science about such findings, but there are profiling implications for developing predictive, post-dictive, and peri-dictive explanations; for the defenses of alleged criminal perpetrators who can claim they are not responsible for what may have happened; and even for what may be an increase in crime once the word gets out that there may be an irrefutable defense against criminal charges of premeditation, complicity, and guilt. (Case precedents and legislation will point the way here.)

There may well be advances in modifying the social cognition preferences of both profilers and alleged criminal perpetrators. The former might lead to more accurate profiles and the latter to less crime and socially inappropriate behavior. Just one example of the latter comprises the work of American psychologists like David DeSteno and colleagues (e.g., Condon & DeSteno, 2011) who have been able to demonstrate how compassion for others can be increased across individuals through simple social manipulations. Profilers would still have to worry that this might up the frequency of compassion-induced crime and lead to reverse engineering to induce less compassion as well.

Another source of applied research that might improve the social cognitions of profilers resides in a study from the National Research Council on the behavioral and social scientific foundations of intelligence analysis (Fischhoff & Chauvin, 2011). Because generic intelligence analysis and profiling have much in common as to the incompleteness and ambiguity of information and interrelationships and as to time pressures, the study's recommendations of best practices and for future research are germane. Generalizing to profilers, these would include (1) giving profilers short-term academic assignments to deepen methodological and subject matter expertise; (2) developing cadres of personnel or consultants with specialized behavioral and social science expertise throughout the profiling community; (3) institutionalizing a *Profiling Olympiad* to test competing approaches and to foster values toward continuous improvement; (4) initiating an applied research program that reviews contemporary and historical profiling efforts again to compare alternative methods in real world conditions; (5) creating and continuously updating a profiling course for field workers based on the latest applied research—characteristics of types of perpetrators and of situations and the optimal analytic methodologies; (6) systematically providing profilers with prompt feedback on the validity and utility of their work—similar to the accountability I brought up earlier; and (7) engaging in research on the latest psychological characteristics bearing on the best profilers and then developing compatible selection, training, management, and evaluation programs.

Still I may have left close readers of this book with a sense of consternation, maybe confusion, maybe dismay. Although developing a matrix and narrative necessarily is a profiling task, the possible pathways toward their development have been much discussed, each with accompanying strengths and weaknesses. Of two very different pathways have been (1) the scientific with systematic data collection, logic, and quantitative and qualitative analysis and (2) an artful openness to nature, with the profiler being less the inscriber of truths but the vellum on which nature inscribes. In the profiling world, the first is much more highly valued than the second. Perhaps, this is how it should be. But perhaps this is how it should be because today Western and Eastern cultures have been captured by a science-based *hegemon*. What does this mean? The science that has been so successful in controlling the physical world on which political power is based continues to be forced on the nonphysical world by those with political power. So we look for terrorists, spies, and deceivers through data mining even if poetry better mines the soul. So the soul is thrown out as a sign of progress when matters of security, intelligence, and the law are paramount. Even the work I've periodically cited by Meehl (1954), Faust (2012), and Dawes (1994) must be qualified by what aspects of humans have been chosen to be known and what indicators of knowledge have been use as predictive, post-dictive, and peri-dictive criteria. I'm not sure there's been any profiling progress from ancient times to the present. Instead, I believe that different epistemologies have been more or less valued at different times. So too with different social standards of what counts as knowledge. Perhaps with such a tenuous conclusion, I can still counsel profiling efforts of some kind because it would be ethically and morally unacceptable not to work even with imperfect means to help (following the American professor of literature David Mikics's, 2009, take on Derrida) what Levinas termed *the fate of the other,* Freud *the traumatic origins of history,* Nietzsche the *coming transformational world,* and Yeats *whatever may be slouching next towards Bethlehem to be born.*

I'll now approach the close of this chapter with the Irish novelist and playwright Samuel Beckett's *Waiting for Godot* (1953). The play has been interpreted in many ways: life as absurd; life as the *waiting for* wherein *waiting* itself or the *for* added to it is the essence, as opposed to what follows the *for*; life as *nothing* or as *no meaning,* a struggle with *whether the nothing is something* or *no meaning is the something of no meaning one is only waiting for.* An implication for profilers is that as opposed to looking for events associated with events of interest, the events *are* the events of interest. Or that the same person or thing or component of one or each continuously fluctuates from event to event of interest and back again. The interdisciplinary approach may be our default mode of believing we know something of people and situations. Especially as we act in our own lives as if there is such knowledge.

Now it's time for readers to engage with LO 10.1 and *dec* the various comments about the future of profiling. The context is a film fragment from *Grand Hotel* (Thalberg & Goulding, 1932)—actually the opening of the film. Is life a hotel with people coming and going? With the opportunity to work, play, pass, and live? With different roles of passing to pick up and drop off at check-in and check-out? As Dr. Otternschlag (played by Lewis Stone) comments at the end of the film fragment, "Grand Hotel. People coming, going, nothing ever happens." There may be plenty happening if one knows how to look.

Appendix: Matching of Learning Outcomes With Film Fragments

LO P.1 To describe, exemplify, and critique why profiling is of interest to the general public: *Silence of the Lambs* (1991), http://www.youtube.com/watch?v=aEaxwyBjTwU

LO P.2 To describe, exemplify, and critique at least three areas of interdisciplinary knowledge relevant to profiling: *The Apartment* (1960), http://www.youtube.com/watch?v=_kIcHsbeobY

LO 1.1 To describe and critique definitions of profiling: *Double Indemnity* (1944), http://www.youtube.com/watch?v=r69dQZHjkmY

LO 1.2 To describe, exemplify, and critique the history of profiling: *Duck Soup* (1933), http://www.youtube.com/watch?v=e8aKKF1-f-A

LO 1.3 To describe, exemplify, and critique the politics of profiling: *Who's Afraid of Virginia Woolf* (1966), http://www.youtube.com/watch?v=nInE5TITzE8

LO 2.1 To define, describe, exemplify, and critique the validity of profiling: *The Unknown* (1927), http://www.youtube.com/watch?v=Zhl8aSl2bQQ [2:50–3:11]

LO 2.2 To describe, exemplify, critique, and employ social deviancy theories applied to profiling: *Rebel Without a Cause* (1955), http://www.youtube.com/watch?v=pz2E93p9XeM

LO 2.3 To describe, exemplify, critique, and employ literary criticism and hermeneutics applied to profiling: *All About Eve* (1950), http://www.youtube.com/watch?v=Eg-ckMup6SI

LO 3.1 To describe, exemplify, critique, and employ major languages of profiling: *The Godfather* (1972), http://www.youtube.com/watch?v=DPA9-kpPo_g

LO 3.2 To describe, exemplify, critique, and employ psychological schematics applied to profiling: *Snow White and the Seven Dwarfs* (1937), http://www.youtube.com/watch?v=vswJS-EVIh4

LO 3.3. To describe, exemplify, and critique cyberpsychological phenomena applied to profiling: *Network* (1976), http://www.youtube.com/watch?v=90ELleCQvew

LO 4.1 To describe, exemplify, critique, and employ epistemology including historiography, critical theory, philosophy of science, and cultural studies applied to profiling: *Do the Right Thing* (1989), http://www.youtube.com/watch?v=6zgzp83dL1E

LO 4.2 To describe, exemplify, and critique logical fallacies related to profiling: *Of Human Bondage* (1934), http://www.youtube.com/watch?v=ZZn1zmwrJG0

LO 4.3 To describe, exemplify, and critique logic and logical fallacies related to profiling: *Metropolis* (1927), http://www.youtube.com/watch?v=fZ97wzMOOS0

LO 4.4 To describe, exemplify, and critique social cognition-related heuristics applied to profiling: *Pride of the Yankees* (1942), http://www.youtube.com/watch?v=CgcSg2CvE8k

LO 4.5 To describe, exemplify, and critique basic statistical issues related to profiling: *The Deerhunter* (1978), http://www.youtube.com/watch?v=lqakCa-MysE [2:50 through 7:24]

LO 4.6 To describe, exemplify, and critique deception analysis applied to profiling: *Betrayal* (1983), http://www.youtube.com/watch?v=PG78hkm-hvQ

LO 4.7 To describe, exemplify, and critique interdisciplinary close reading applied to profiling: *Sunset Boulevard* (1950), http://www.youtube.com/watch?v=jMTT0LW0M_Y

LO 4.8 To describe, exemplify, and critique political phenomena affecting profilers and profiling: *Citizen Kane* (1941), http://www.youtube.com/watch?v=HyJAytr1ebc

LO 5 To describe, exemplify, critique, and employ matrix constructs applied to profiling: *Lawrence of Arabia* (1962), http://www.youtube.com/watch?v=z7TnY94x_mI

LO 6 To describe, exemplify, critique, and employ narrative constructs applied to profiling: *The Last Picture Show* (1971), http://www.youtube.com/watch?v=__T3WJVmBY8

LO 7 To develop and assess a profiling matrix and narrative applied to terrorism: *Casablanca* (1942), http://www.youtube.com/watch?v=7SQuyKlt1Ew

LO 8 To develop and assess profiles and profiling text applied to espionage: *Taxi Driver* (1976), http://www.youtube.com/watch?v=cUBfzq8ysdg

LO 9 To develop and assess profiles and profiling text applied to deception: *The Women* (1939), http://www.youtube.com/watch?v=T4XTeh6tjIs

LO 10 To describe, exemplify, critique recommendations to optimally employ profiling in the future: *Grand Hotel* (1932), http://www.youtube.com/watch?v=T5-LyF_ja4o&feature = related

References

Abrams, M. (1953). *The mirror and the lamp: Romantic theory and the critical tradition.* New York: Oxford University Press.

Adler, A. (March 7, 2001). The perverse law of child pornography. *Columbia Law Review, 101*(2). Retrieved Apirl 14, 2012, from http://papers.ssrn.com/sol3/papers.cfm?abstract_id=255990.

Ainsworth, M., Blehar, M., Waters, E., & Wall, S. (1978). *Patterns of attachment: Assessed in the strange situation and at home.* Hillsdale, NJ: Erlbaum.

Alison, L., & Rainbow, L. (Eds.). (2011). *Professionalizing offender profiling: Forensic and investigative psychology in practice.* London: Routledge.

Alison, L., Smith, M. D., Eastman, O., & Rainbow, L. (2003). Toumlin's philosophy of argument and its relevance to offender profiling. *Psychology, Crime & Law, 9,* 173–183.

Allport, G. W. (1937). *Personality: A psychological interpretation.* New York: Henry Holt and Company.

American Psychological Association. (APA). (2012). *PsycNET Gold.* Retrieved June 19, 2012, from http://my.apa.org/apa/portal/home.seam.

Anderson-Cutright-Cisneros, A., Child, R., Johnson, J., Munden, A., & Small, S. (2012). *Profiling matrix on Jim Jones.* Draft manuscript. Embry-Riddle Aeronautical University, Prescott, AZ.

Angell, M. (June 23/July 14, 2011). The epidemic of mental illness: Why?/The illusions of psychiatry. *New York Review of Books,* 20-22/20-22. [2-part multiple book reviews].

Aristotle. (1999). *Nicomachean Ethics,* 2d ed. (T. Irwin, Trans.). Indianapolis, IN: Hackett Publishing Company.

Armed Forces Health Surveillance Center. (2011). *Medical Surveillance Monthly Report, 18*(9). Retrieved April 27, 2012, from http://www.afhsc.mil/viewMSMR?file=2011/v18_n09.pdf.

Associations between repeated deployments to Iraq (OIF/OND) and Afghanistan (OEF) and post-deployment illnesses and injuries, active component, U.S. Armed Forces, 2003–2010. Part II. Mental disorders by gender, age group, military occupation, and "dwell times" prior to repeat (second through fifth) deployments. (2011). *Medical Surveillance Monthly Report, 19.* Silver Spring, MD: Armed Forced Health Surveillance Center. Retrieved October 20, 2012, from http://www.afhsc.mil/viewMSMR?file=2011/v18_no9.pdf.

Bandura, A. (2004). The role of selective moral disengagement in terrorism and counterterrorism. In F. Moghaddam & A. J. Marsella (Eds.), *Understanding terrorism: Psychosocial roots, consequences, and interventions* (pp. 121–150). Washington, DC: American Psychological Association.

Bandura, A. (1969). *Principles of behavior modification.* New York: Holt, Rinehart, & Winston.

Barnes, B. (April 21, 2012). After flops, Disney studio chief resigns. *New York Times.* Retrieved April 21, 2012, from http://www.nytimes.com.

Barthes, R. (1978). Introduction to the structural analysis of narratives. In R. Barthes, *Image music text* (pp. 79–124). (S. Heath, Trans.). New York: Hill & Wang,

Barzun, J. (1965). Meditations on the literature of spying. *American Scholar.* Retrieved March 31, 2012, from http://www.theamericanscholar.org.

Baudrillard, J. (2008). *Fatal strategies.* (P. Beitchman & W. G. J. Niesluchowski, Trans.). Semiotext(e). Los Angeles, CA: Semiotext(e).

Beckett, S. (1978). *The unammable.* New York: Grove Press.

Beckman, M. (2004). Crime, culpability, and the adolescent brain. *Science, 305,* 596–599.

Bender, L. (Producer), & Tarantino, Q. (Director). (1990). *Pulp fiction*. [Motion Picture]. Miramax.

Berlin, I. (1969/1958). Two concepts of liberty. In I. Berlin, *Four essays on liberty*. New York: Oxford University Press. Retrieved June 24, 2012, from http://www.wiso.uni-hamburg. de/fileadmin/wiso_vwl/johannes/Ankuendigungen/Berlin_twoconceptsofliberty.pdf.

Berman, P. S. (Producer), & Cromwell, J. (Director). (1934). *Of human bondage* [Motion Picture]. RKO Pictures. Retrieved August 2, 2012, from http://www.youtube.com/ watch?v=ZZn1zmwrJG0.

Bernstein, B.E., Birney, E., Dunham, I., Green, E.D., Gunter, C., & Snyder, M. (September 6, 2012). An integrated encyclopedia of DNA elements in the human genome. *Nature, 489*, 57–74.

Berryhill, W., Lauterbach, K., Olesky, M., & Pacheco, V. (2012). *Profiling narrative on Anders Behring Breivik*. Draft manuscript. Embry-Riddle Aeronautical University, Prescott, AZ.

Betts, R. K., & Mahnken, T. G. (2003). *Paradoxes of strategic intelligence: Essays in honor of Michael I. Handel*. London: Routledge.

Bickman, L. (1997). Resolving issues raised by the Fort Bragg evaluation: New directions for mental health services research. *American Psychologist, 52*(5), 562–565.

Bickman, L. (1996). A continuum of care: More is not always better. *American Psychologist, 51*, 689–701.

Bilefsky, D. (March 30, 2012). Toulouse killer's path to radicalism a bitter puzzle. *New York Times*, Retrieved March 30, 2012, from http://www.nytimes.com.

Bilefsky, D., & De La Bauame, M. (March 22, 2012). Suspect in France shootings seen as homegrown militant. *New York Times*. Retrieved March 22, 2012, from http://www. nytimes.com.

Binswanger, L. (1975). *Being-in-the-world. Selected papers*. (J. Needleman, Trans.). London: Souvenir Press.

Bjelopera, J. P. (May 15, 2012). *The domestic terrorist threat: Background and issues for Congress*. Congressional Research Service. 7-5700. R42536.

Blei, D. (2012). Topic modeling. Retrieved June 7, 2012, from http://www.cs.princeton. edu/~blei/topicmodeling.html.

Bloom, R. W. (2012). Knowledge on knowledge and deception. A review of memory detection: Theory and application of the Concealed Information Test. *PsycCRITIQUES, 57*(15). Retrieved June 29, 2012, from http://www.psyccritiques.com.

Bloom, R. W. (May 16, 2010a). Spot off: The GAO takes on the TSA's behavior detection program. *International Bulletin of Political Psychology, 15*(8). Retrieved March 31, 2012, from http://security.pr.erau.edu.

Bloom, R. W. (August 4, 2010b). The profiler's story. *International Bulletin of Political Psychology, 16*(22). Retrieved March 31, 2012, from http://security.pr.erau.edu. Bloom, R. W. (2005). Who is dying to win? Review of *Dying to win: The strategic logic of suicide terrorism*. *PsycCRITIQUES, 50*(47). Retrieved June 28, 2012, from http://www. psyccritiques.com.

Bloom, R. W. (March 14, 2003a). A profile of national leader profiles and the social construction of the self: An example of information warfare. *International Bulletin of Political Psychology, 14*(9). Retrieved June 2, 2012, from http://security.pr.erau.edu.

Bloom, R. W. (October 24, 2003b). Biometric, psychometric, and sociometric profiling. *International Bulletin of Political Psychology, 15*(8). Retrieved May 14, 2012, from http://security.pr.erau.edu.

Bloom, R. W. (June 8, 2001). Personology, profiling, and terrorism. *International Bulletin of Political Psychology, 10*(20). Retrieved June 27, 2012, from http://security.pr.erau.edu.

Bloom, R. W. (1999). Racial profiling: Should it be used for aviation security? *Leader*. Retrieved March 10, 2012, from http://www.erau.edu/er/newsmedia/leader/fall1999/ perspec.html.

Bloom, R. W. (1984). Military surprise: Why we need a scientific approach. *Air University Review, 35*, 17–21.

Bloom, H. (1973). *The anxiety of influence*. New York: Oxford University Press.

Bloom, R. W., & Dess, N. (2003). (Eds.) *Evolutionary psychology and violence: A primer for policymakers and public policy advocates*. Westport, CN & London, UK: Praeger.

Boyer, P., & Nissenbaum, S. (1974). *Salem possessed: The social origins of witchcraft*. Cambridge, MA: Harvard University Press.

Breasted, J. H. (1944). *Ancient times: A history of the ancient world*. Boston, MA: Ginn and Company.

Bregman, M. (Producer), & Lumet, S. (Director). (1975). *Dog day afternoon*. [Motion Picture]. Warner Brothers Home Video.

Brackett, C. (Producer), & Wilder, B. (Director). (1950). *Sunset boulevard*. [Motion Picture]. Paramount Pictures. Retrieved October 20, 2012, from http://www.youtube.com/watch?v=jMTT0LW0M_Y.

Brinkley, J. (July 1, 2012). Yitzhak Shamir, former Israeli Prime Minister and militia leader, dies at age 96. *New York Times*. Retrieved July 1, 2012, from http://www.nytimes.com.

Brown, D., & Zanuk, R. D. (Producers), & Lumet, S. (Director). (1982). *The verdict*. [Motion Picture]. Twentieth Century Fox.

Brussel, J. (March 23, 1982). Dr. James A. Brussel, criminologist is dead. *New York Times*. Retrieved March 13, 2012, from http://www.nytimes.com.

Brussel, J. (1968). *Casebook of a crime psychiatrist*. New York: Bernard Geis Associates.

Bumiller, E., & Cushman, J. H., Jr. (March 18, 2012). Suspect's multiple tours call attention to war strain. *New York Times*. Retrieved March 18, 2012, from http://www.nytimes.com.

Butcher, J. N., Perry, J. N., & Atlis, M. M. (2000). Validity and utility of computer-based test interpretation. *Psychological Assessment, 12*, 6–18.

Butterfield, H. (1981). *The origins of history*. New York: Basic Books.

Campana, A., & Lapointe, L. (2012). The structural "root" causes of non-suicidal terrorism: A systematic scoping review. *Terrorism and Political Violence, 24*, 79–104.

Camus, A. (2008). *Notebooks: 1951–1959*. (R. Bloom, Trans.). Lanham, MD: Ivan R. Dee.

Canter, D. (2011). Resolving the offender "profiling equations" and the emergence of an investigative psychology. *Current Directions in Psychological Science, 20*, 5–10.

Canter, D., & Youngs, D. (2009). *Investigative psychology: Offender profiling and the analysis of criminal action*. Chichester, UK: Wiley.

Caruso, F., & Gottfried, H. (Producers), & Lumet, S. (Director). (1976). *Network*. [Motion Picture]. Metro-Goldwyn-Mayer & United Artists. Retrieved August 2, 2012, from http://www.youtube.com/watch?v=90ELleCQvew.

Castagné, V., Wolinsky, T., Quinn, L., & Virley, D. (2012). Differential behavioral profiling of stimulant substances in the rat using the LABORAS™ system. *Pharmacology, Biochemistry and Behavior, 101*(4), 553–563.

CERT. (2012). The CERT insider threat center. Retrieved April 1, 2012, from http://www.cert.org/insider_threat.

Chapman, L. J., & Chapman, J. P. (1975). The basis of illusory correlation. *Journal of Abnormal Psychology, 84*(5), 574–575.

Charney, D. (2010). True psychology of the insider spy. *Intelligencer: Journal of U.S. Intelligence Studies,* Fall–Winter, 47–54.

Chicago Project on Security and Terrorism. (2012). Suicide attack database. Retrieved June 28, 2012, from http://cpost.uchicago.edu.

Chivers, C. J. (June 14, 2012). Syrian liberators, bearing toy guns. *New York Times*. Retrieved June 16, 2012, from http://www.nytimes.com.

Choe Hang-Sun. (April 27, 2012). New North Korean missile is called into question. *New York Times*. Retrieved April 30, 2012, from http://www.nytimes.com.

Cicero. (1927). *Tusculan disputations*. (J. E. King, Trans.). Loeb Classical Library.

Cleckley, H. (1982/1941). *The mask of sanity*, rev. ed. Mosby Medical Library.

Cochran, J. C., & Warren, P. Y. (2012). Racial, ethnic, and gender differences in perceptions of the police: The salience of officer race within the context of racial profiling. *Journal of Contemporary Criminal Justice, 28*(2), 206–227.

Coll, S. (2012). *Private empire: ExxonMobil and American power*. New York: Penguin.

Condon, P., & DeSteno, D. (2011). Compassion for one reduces punishment for another. *Journal of Experimental Social Psychology, 47*(3), 698–701.

Conn, S. R., & Rieke, M. L. (1994). *The 16PF fifth edition technical manual*. Champaign, IL: Institute for Personality and Ability Testing, Inc.

Cook, A. E., Hacker, D. J., Webb, A. K., Osher, D., Kristjansson, S. D., Woltz, D. J., & Kircher, J. C. (2012). Lyin' eyes: Ocular–motor measures of reading reveal deception. *Journal of Experimental Psychology: Applied*, 18(3), 301–313.

Cottee, S., & Hayward, K. (2011). Terrorist (e)motives: The existential attractions of terrorism. *Studies in Conflict & Terrorism, 34*, 963–986.

Covert, M. (2012). *Covert Systems Biology Lab*. Retrieved July 21, 2012, from http://covertlab.stanford.edu/subpages/research.php.

Cowell, A. (June 14, 2012). Churches challenge British government over same-sex marriage. *New York Times*. Retrieved June 14, 2012, from http://www.nytimes.com.

CQ Homeland Security News. (2012). Retrieved March 20, 2012, from http://homeland.cq.com/hs/news.do.

Crawford, L. (1984). Viktor Shklovskij: Différance in defamiliarization. *Comparative Literature*, 36, 209–219.

Cronbach, L., & Meehl, P. (1955). Construct validity in psychological tests. Psychological Bulletin, 52(4), 281–302.

Culturomics. (2012). Retrieved June 7, 2012, from http://www.culturomics.org/cultural-observatory-at-harvard.

Daniel, D. C., & Herbig, K. L. (1982). *Strategic military deception*. Oxford, UK: Pergamon.

Dawes, R. (1994). *House of cards: Psychology and psychotherapy built on myth*. New York: Free Press.

Defense Personnel Security Research Center. (2012). Selected reports. Retrieved from http://www.dhra.mil/perserec/index.html.

Defense Science Board. (August, 2012). *Task force report: Predicting violent behavior*. Office of the Under Secretary of Defense for Acquisition, Technology, and Logistics. Washington, DC.

Delafuente, C. (September 10, 2004). Terror in the age of Eisenhower: The mad bomber, whose rampage shook New York. *New York Times*. Retrieved March 13, 2012, from http://www.nytimes.com.

Department of Defense. (May 4, 2012). Countering espionage, international terrorism, and the counterintelligence insider threat. Department of Defense Instruction 5240.26.

Director of Central Intelligence. (2012). *DCI Directive 6/4 Personnel Security Standards and Procedures Governing Eligibility for Access to Sensitive Compartmented Information (SCI). Annex C*. Retrieved April 4, 2012, from http://www.fas.org/irp/offdocs/dcid6-4/dcid6-4.pdf.

Director of Central Intelligence/Intelligence Community Staff. (1990). *Project SLAMMER Interim Report (U)*. Retrieved May 24, 2012, from http://antipolygraph.org/documents/slammer-12-04-1990.shtml.

DeSilva, B. (Producer), & Wilder, B. (Director). (1944). *Double indemnity*. [Motion Picture]. Universal Studios. Retrieved August 2, 2012, from http://www.youtube.com/watch?v=r69dQZHjkmY.

Disney, W. (Producer), & Hand, D. (Director). (1937). *Snow White and the seven dwarfs*. [Motion Picture]. RKO Radio Pictures. Retrieved August 2, 2012, from http://www.youtube.com/watch?v=vswJS-EVIh4.

Dollard, J., & Miller, N. E. (1950). *Personality and psychotherapy: Analysis in terms of learning, thinking, and culture.* New York: McGraw-Hill.

Dollard, J., Miller, N. E., Doob, L. W., Mowrer, O. H., & Sears, R. R. (1939). *Frustration and aggression.* New Haven, CT: Yale University Press.

Douthat, R. (July 21, 2012). The way we fear now. *The New York Times.* Retrieved from http://www.nytimes.com.

Doyle, A. C. (1995). *The memoirs of Sherlock Holmes.* New York: Oxford University Press.

Drury, S., Hutchens, S. A., Shuttlesworth, D. E., & White, C. (2012). Philip G. Zimbardo on his career and the Stanford Prison Experiment's 40th anniversary. *History of Psychology, 15,* 161–170.

DuBois, W. E. B. (2012). *The souls of black folks.* Retrieved April 13, 2012, from http://xroads.virginia.edu/~HYPER/DUBOIS/toc.html.

Duhigg, C. (February 16, 2012). How companies learn your secrets. *New York Times.* Retrieved March 10, 2012, from http://www.nytimes.com.

Dutter, L. (2012). Why don't dogs bark (or bomb) in the night? Explaining the non-development of political violence of terrorism: The case of Quebec separation. *Studies in Conflict & Terrorism, 35*(1), 59–75.

Duyvendak, J. J. L. (Trans.). (1928). *Kung-san Yang: The book of Lord Shang.* Chicago: University of Chicago Press.

Dwyer, J. (March 16, 2012). For detained whistle-blower, a hospital bill, not an apology. *New York Times.* Retrieved March 16, 2012, from http://www.nytimes.com.

Eastwood, C. (Producer & Director). (1992). *Unforgiven* .[Motion Picture]. Warner Brothers.

Edwards, S. (1977). *The Vidocq dossier: The story of the world's first detective.* Boston, MA: Houghton Mifflin.

Erikson, E. (1993/1950). *Childhood and society.* W.W. Norton & Company.

Ewing, C. P., & McCann, J. T. (2006). *Minds on trial: Great cases in law and psychology.* New York: Oxford University Press.

Fahim, K., & El Sheikh, M. (May 3, 2012). Egypt's military rulers deny role in fatal clashes. *The New York Times.* Retrieved October 19, 2012, from http://nytimes.com.

Fanon, F. (1967). *Black skin, white masks.* (C. L. Markmann, Trans.). Grove Press.

Fabrigar, L. R., Petty, R. E., Smith, S. M., & Crites Jr., S. L. (2006). Understanding knowledge effects on attitude-behavior consistency: The role of relevance, complexity, and amount of knowledge. *Journal of Personality and Social Psychology, 90,* 556–577.

Fackler, M. (June 8, 2012). Japan relives gas attack after suspect is arrested. *New York Times.* Retrieved June 8, 2012, from http://www.nytimes.com.

Faust, D. (Ed.). (2012). *Coping with psychiatric and psychological testimony: Based on the original work by Jay Ziskin,* 6th ed. New York: Oxford University Press.

Feder, J. (April 16, 2012). Racial profiling: Legal and constitutional issues. *Congressional Research Service* 7-5700, RL31130.

Federal Bureau of Investigation. (2012a). *Behavioral Sciences Unit.* Retrieved March 12, 2012, from http://www.fbi.gov/about-us/training/bsu.

Federal Bureau of Investigation. (2012b). *Counterintelligence cases past and present.* Retrieved April 1, 2012, from http://www.fbi.gov/about-us/investigate/counterintelligence/cases.

Federal Bureau of Investigation (FBI). (2012c). *The Year of the Spy.* Federal Bureau of Investigation. Retrieved March 10, 2012, from http://www.fbi.gov/about-us/history/famous-cases/the-year-of-the-spy.

Feldman, C. K. (Producer), & Kazan, E. (Director). (1951). *A streetcar named desire.* [Motion Picture]. Warner Brothers.

Fenichel, M. (2012). *Cyberpsychology: Psychology in the 21st century.* Retrieved April 18, 2012, from http://www.cyberpsychology.com.

Fiedler, L. (1952). Archetype and signature: A study of the relationship between biography and poetry. *Sewanee Review, 60,* 253–273.

Finney, J. *The body snatchers*. New York: Dell.

Fischhoff, B., & Chauvin, C. (2011). *Intelligence analysis: Behavioral and social scientific foundations*. National Academies Press.

Foster, J., Rice, B., & the Big Bopper. (1958). Chantilly Lace. Chicago, IL: Mercury Records. Retrieved April 16, 2012, from http://www.youtube.com/watch?v=mj6haLBe8s4.

Foucault, M. (1990). *The history of sexuality: Volume I: An introduction*. (R. Hurley, Trans.). New York: Vintage.

Foucault, M. (1977). *Discipline and punish*. (A. Sheridan, Trans.). New York: Vintage.

Fraser, R. (1988). *1968: A student generation in revolt*. New York: Pantheon.

Freud, S. (1925). A note upon the 'Mystic Writing-Pad.' *The Standard Edition of the Complete Psychological Works of Sigmund Freud*, 19, 225–232. (J. Strachey, Trans.). London: Hogarth.

Freud, S. (1986/1886–1939). *The standard edition of the complete psychological works of Sigmund Freud*. (J. Strachey, Trans.). London: Hogarth, pp. 77–78.

Friedman, S. J. (Producer), & Bogdonovich, P. (Director). (1971). *The last picture show*. [Motion Picture]. Columbia Pictures. Retrieved August 2, 2012, from http://www.youtube.com/watch?v=__T3WJVmBY8.

Frye, N. (1957). *Anatomy of criticism: Four essays*. Princeton, NJ: Princeton University Press.

Gay, P. (1961). Rhetoric and politics in the French Revolution. *American Historical Review*, 66, 664–676.

Gibson, M. (Producer & Director). (1995). *Braveheart*. [Motion Picture]. Paramount Pictures. Foreign: Twentieth Century Fox.

Godson, R., & Wirtz, J. (Eds.). (2002). *Denial and deception: The twenty-first century challenge*. Piscataway, NJ: Transaction Publishers.

Goldman, A. (1999). *Knowledge in a social world*. New York: Oxford University Press.

Goldwater, B. (1964). Quote. Retrieved April 2, 2012, from http://www.youtube.com/watch?v=RVNoClu0h9M.

Goldwyn, S. (Producer), & Wood, S. (Director). (1942). *Pride of the Yankees*. [Motion Picture]. RKO Radio Pictures. Retrieved August 2, 2012, from http://www.youtube.com/watch?v=CgcSg2CvE8k.

Gould, S. J. (September 25, 1986). Cardboard Darwinism. *New York Review of Books*. Retrieved June 8, 2012, from http://www.nybooks.com.

Greimas, A. J. (1987). *On meaning: Selected writings in semiotic theory*. Minneapolis, MN: University of Minneapolis.

Groscup, J. (2011). Statistical principles in forensic research. In B. Rosenfeld & S. D. Penrod (Eds.), *Research methods in forensic psychology*. New York: John Wiley & Sons, Inc.

Gross, H. G. (1911). *Criminal psychology*. Boston, MA: Little, Brown & Company.

Grosskurth, P. (1991). *The secret ring: Freud's inner circle and the politics of psychoanalysis*. Boston, MA: Addison-Wesley.

Hacking, I. (1982). Language, truth, and reason. In M. Hollis & S. Lukes (Eds.), *Rationality and relativism*. Oxford: Blackwell, 48–66.

Hamilton, N. (2008). *How to do biography: A primer*. Cambridge, MA: Harvard University Press.

Harcourt, B. E. (2007). *Against prediction: Profiling, policing, and punishing in an actuarial age*. Chicago: University of Chicago Press.

Hare, R. D., & Neumann, C. S. (2008). Psychopathy as a clinical and empirical construct. *Annual Review of Clinical Psychology*, 4, 217–246.

Hegel, G. W. F. (1953/1837). *Reason in history*. (R. Hartman, Trans.). Arlington, TX: Liberal Arts Press.

Heidegger, M. (2010). *Being and time*. (J. Stambaugh, Trans.). (D. J. Schmidt, Rev.). Albany, NY: State University of New York Press.

Herbig, K. L. (March 2008). *Changes in espionage by American citizens 1947-2007.* DOD TR 08-05, Defense Personnel Security Research Center.

Herbig, K. L., & Wiskoff, M. (July, 2005). *Espionage against the United States by American citizens 1947-2001.* DOD TR 02-05. Defense Personnel Security Research Center.

Heuer, R. J., & Pherson, R. H. (2011). *Structured analytic techniques for intelligence analysis.* Washington, DC: CQ Press.

Hicks, S. J., & Sales, B. D. (2006). *Criminal profiling: Developing an effective science and practice.* Washington, DC: American Psychological Association.

Holmes, R. M., & Holmes, S. T. (2009). *Profiling violent crimes: An investigative tool*, 4th ed. Thousand Oaks, CA: SAGE.

Horgan, J., O'Sullivan, D., & Hammond, S. (2003). Offender profiling: A critical perspective. *Irish Journal of Psychology, 24*(1–2), 1–21.

Hsu, H. Y. (2012). Unstoppable? A closer look at terrorism displacement. *Dissertations Abstracts International Section A: Humanities and Social Sciences, 72*(7-A), 2582.

Hume, D. (2003). *A treatise of human nature.* New York: Dover.

Husserl, E. (2001/1900–1901). *Logical investigations.* (N. Findlay, Trans.). Routledge.

International Bulletin of Political Psychology. (2012). Retrieved June 24, 2012, from http://security.pr.erau.edu.

Investigative Report by the Committee of the Judiciary. (May 25, 2006). *Plane clothes: Lack of anonymity at the federal air marshal service compromises aviation and national security.* 109th Congress, 2nd Session.

Jacobs, A. (March 23, 2012). Tibetan self-immolations rise as China tightens grip. *New York Times.* Retrieved March 23, 2012, from http://www.nytimes.com.

Jacobs, A., & Bullock, P. (March 16, 2012). A U.S. tie to push on surveillance in Chinese cities. *New York Times.* Retrieved from http://www.nytimes.com.

Jacques, K., & Taylor, P. J. (April 30, 2012). Myths and realities of female-perpetrated terrorism. *Law and Human Behavior* [volume and number not yet specified]. Retrieved October 20, 2012, from http://psycnet.apa.org/psycarticles/2012-10788-001.pdf.

JASON Program Office. (October 2009). *Rare events.* The MITRE Corporation. Washington, DC: Office of the Secretary of Defense. JSR-09-108.

Jervis, R. (1976). *Perception and misperception international politics.* Princeton, NJ: Princeton University Press.

Johnson, W. R., & Hood, W. (2009). *Thwarting enemies at home and abroad: How to be a counterintelligence officer.* Washington, DC: Georgetown University Press.

Joint Mental Health Advisory Team 7. (February 22, 2011). *Joint Mental Health Advisory Team 7 (J-MHAT 7) Operation Enduring Freedom 2010 Afghanistan report.* Retrieved April 27, 2012, from http://www.armymedicine.army.mil/reports/mhat/mhat_vii/J_MHAT_7.pdf.

Joyce, J. (1922). *Ulysses.* Paris: Sylvia Beach. Retrieved from the Literature Network on October 20, 2012, from http://www.online-literature.com/james_joyce/ulysses/9.

Jung, C. (1924). *Psychological types.* (H. G. Baynes, Trans.). London: Kegan Paul, Trench, Trubner & Co., Ltd.

Kahneman, D. (2011). *Thinking fast and slow.* New York: Farrar, Straus, and Giroux.

Kahneman, D., Slovic, P., & Tversky, A. (1982). *Judgment under uncertainty: Heuristics and biases.* Cambridge, UK: Cambridge University Press.

Kant, I. (1963/1784). Idea for a universal history from a cosmopolitan point of view. (L. W. Beck, Trans.). In I. Kant, *On history.* Indianapolis, IN: Bobbs-Merrill Co.

Kaplan, A. (2012). *Dreaming in French: The Paris years of Jacqueline Bouvier Kennedy, Susan Sontag, and Angela Davis.* Chicago: University of Chicago Press.

Kassim, S. M. (2012). Why confessions trump innocence. *American Psychologist, 67*(6), 431–445.

Kates, G. (April 20, 2012). A spate of teenage suicides alarms Russians. *New York Times.* Retrieved April 20, 2012, from http://www.nytimes.com.

Keats, J. (2012). *When I have fears that I may cease to be.* Retrieved March 14, 2012, from http://www.poetryfoundation.org/poem/173753.

Kelly, H. H. (1967). Attribution theory in social psychology. *Nebraska Symposium on Motivation,* 15, 192–238.

Kernberg, O. (1970). Factors in the psychoanalytic treatment of narcissistic personalities. *Journal of the American Psychoanalytic Association,* 18, 51–85.

Khan, G., & Johar, K. (Producers), & Johar, K. (Director). (2010). *My name is Khan.* [Motion Picture]. Dharma Productions, Fox Star Studios & Red Chillies Entertainment.

Khurana, A., Romer, D., Betancourt, L., Brodsky, N., Giannetta, J. M., & Hurt, H. (February 27, 2012). Early adolescent sexual debut: The mediating role of working memory ability, sensation seeking, and impulsivity. *Developmental Psychology.* Retrieved April 9, 2012, from http://www.apa.org.

Kinnoch, R., (Producer), & Rilla, W. (Director). (1960). *Village of the damned.* [Motion Picture]. Metro-Goldwyn-Mayer.

Klein, M. (1987). *The selected Melanie Klein.* Ed. J. Mitchell. New York: Free Press.

Kocsis, R. N. (2010). Criminal profiling works and everyone agrees. *Journal of Forensic Psychology Practice, 10*(3), 224–237.

Kocsis, R. N. (2009). Criminal profiling: Facts, fictions, and courtroom admissibility. In J. L. Skeem, K. S. Douglas, & S. O. Lilienfeld, *Psychological science in the courtroom: Consensus and controversy* (pp. 245–262). New York: Guilford Press.

Kocsis, R. N. (2006). *Criminal profiling: Principles and practice.* Totowa, NJ: Humana Press.

Kocsis, R. N. (2003). Criminal psychological profiling: Validities and abilities. *International Journal of Offender Therapy and Comparative Criminology, 47*(2), 126–144.

Kohlberg, L. (1984). *The psychology of moral development: The nature and validity of moral stages.* San Francisco: Harper and Row.

Krauss, D. A., McCabe, J. G., & Lieberman, J. D. (2011). Dangerously misunderstood: Representatives jurors' reactions to expert testimony on future dangerousness in a sexually violent predator trial. *Psychology, Public Policy, and Law, 18,* 18–49.

Kroner, D., Mills, J., & Reddon, J. (2005). A coffee can, factor analysis, and prediction of antisocial behavior: The structure of criminal risk. *International Journal of Law & Psychiatry, 28,* 360–374.

Kubrick, S. (Producer & Director). (1971). *A clockwork orange.* [Motion Picture]. Warner Brothers.

Kuhn, T. S. (1962). *The structure of scientific revolutions.* Chicago: University of Chicago Press.

Kydd, A. H. (2011). Terrorism and profiling. *Terrorism and Political Violence, 23*(3), 458–473.

Lacan, J. (2006/1953–1981). *Ecrits: The first complete edition in English.* (B. Fink, H. Fink, & R. Grigg, Trans.). W.W. Norton & Co.

Lamiell, J. T. (1991). Explanation in a reconceived psychology of personality. *Journal of Theoretical and Philosophical Psychology, 11,* 1–23.

Lamiell, J. T. (1981). Towards an idiothetic psychology of personality. *American Psychologist, 36,* 276–289.

Langer, E. J. (1975). The illusion of control. *Journal of Personality and Social Psychology, 32,* 311–328.

Lattimore, R. (Trans.). (1951). *The Iliad of Homer.* Chicago: University of Chicago Press.

Law and Order. (2012). Created by Dick Wolf. Retrieved March 14, 2012, from http://www.imdb.com/title/tt0098844.

Lee, S., Kilik, J., Ross, M. (Producers), & Lee, S. (Director). (1989). *Do the right thing.* [Motion Picture]. Universal Pictures. Retrieved August 2, 2012, from http://www.youtube.com/watch?v=6zgzp83dL1E.

Lee, T. T. C., Graham, J. R., Sellbom, M., & Gervais, R. O. (February 6, 2012). Examining the potential for gender bias in the prediction of symptom validity test failure by MMPI-2 symptom validity scale scores. *Psychological Assessment*. Retrieved May 17, 2012, from http://www.apa.org.

Legendary *Cosmo* editor funds media institute. (Spring 2012). *Columbia Magazine*. 53.

Lehman, E. (Producer), & Nichols, M. (Director). (1966). *Who's afraid of Virginia Woolf?* [Motion Picture]. Warner Brothers. Retrieved August 2, 2012, from http://www.youtube. com/watch?v=nInE5TITzE8.

Lester, P. (2012). Retrieved June 15, 2012, from http://commfaculty.fullerton.edu/lester/ writings/letters.html.

Levinson, H. (1972). *Organizational diagnosis*. Cambridge, MA: Harvard University Press.

Levinas, E. (1987). *Time and the Other and additional essays*. (R. Cohen, Trans). Pittsburgh: Duquesne University Press.

Lewin, K. (1936). *Principles of topological psychology*. New York: McGraw-Hill.

Lewis, M. (April 24, 2012). Norwegian who killed 77 says he shared in loss. *New York Times*. Retrieved May 14, 2012, from http://www.nytimes.com.

Lewis, M., & Jolly, D. (April 19, 2012). Prosecutors press Norwegian on extremist affiliations. *New York Times*. Retrieved April 19, 2012, from http://www.nytimes.com.

LexisNexis. (2012). Retrieved March 30, 2012, from http://www.lexisnexis.com.

Ley, S. (1997). *The analects of Confucius*. New York: Norton.

Liptak, A. (April 4, 2012). Supreme Court ruling allows strip searches for any arrest. *New York Times*. Retrieved April 5, 2012, from http://www.nytimes.com.

Lohr, S. (March 26, 2012). Seeking an edge in data analysis. *New York Times*. Retrieved June 7, 2012, from http://www.nytimes.com.

Lyons, R. D. (April 22, 1968). Ultimate Speck appeal may cite a genetic defect. *New York Times*. Retrieved April 6, 2012, from http://www.nytimes.com.

Lyotard, F. (1984). *The postmodern condition: A report on knowledge and meta-narratives*. (G. Bennington & B. Massumi, Trans.). Minneapolis: University of Minnesota Press.

MacCarron, P., & Kenna, R. (September 9, 2012). If Achilles used Facebook. *The New York Times*, 4SR.

Maher, B. (December 11, 2002). The *Salon* interview: Bill Maher. Interviewer J. Tapper. *Salon*. Retrieved March 14, 2012, from http://www.salon.com.

Mankiewicz, H. J. (Producer), & McCarey, L. (Director). (1933). *Duck soup* [Motion Picture]. Paramount Pictures. Retrieved August 2, 2012, from http://www.youtube.com/ watch?v=e8aKKF1-f-A.

Manzi, J. (2012). Uncontrolled: *The surprising payoff of trial-and-error for business, politics, and society*. New York: Basic Books.

Marston, W. M. (1938). *The lie detector test*. New York: Smith.

Martin, S. D., Martin, E., Rai, S. S., Richardson, M. A., & Royall, R. (2001). Brain blood flow changes in depressed patients treated with interpersonal psychotherapy or venlafaxine-hydrochloride: Preliminary findings. *Archives of General Psychiatry, 58*(7), 641–648.

Marx, K. (1932). *Economic and philosophical manuscripts of 1844*. Retrieved March 12, 2012, from http://www.marxists.org/archive/marx/works/download/pdf/Economic-Philosophic-Manuscripts-1844.pdf.

Masip, J., Bethencourt, M., Lucas, G., Sánchez–San Segundo, M., & Herrero, C. (2012). Deception detection from written accounts. *Scandinavian Journal of Psychology, 53*(2), 103–111.

Maslow, A. H. (1943). A theory of human motivation. *Psychological Review 50*(4), 370–396.

Matarazzo, J. D. (1986). Computerized clinical psychological interpretations: Unvalidated plus all mean and no sigma. *American Psychologist, 41*, 14–24.

Matt, S. J. (2011). *Homesickness: An American history*. New York: Oxford University Press.

McAdams, D. P. (1988). *Power, intimacy and the life story: Personological inquiries into identity*. New York: Guilford Press.

McCrae, R. R., & Costa, P. T., Jr. (1997). Personality trait structures as a human universal. *American Psychologist, 52*, 509–516.

Meehl, P. (1954). *Clinical vs. statistical prediction: A theoretical analysis and a review of the evidence*. Minneapolis: University of Minnesota Press.

Meichenbaum, D. (1980). A cognitive-behavioral perspective on intelligence. *Intelligence, 4*, 271–283.

Melville, H. (2011). *Benito Cereno*. London: Penguin Classics. Retrieved from http://www.readaclassic.com.

Melville, H. (2011/1855). Benito Cereno. In *Billy Budd & other stories*. London: Penguin.

Mikics, D. (2009). *Who was Jacques Derrida? An intellectual biography*. New Haven, CT: Yale University Press.

Milgram, S. (1963). Behavioral study of obedience. *Journal of Abnormal and Social Psychology, 67*, 371–378.

Miller, N. E., & Dollard, J. (1941). *Social learning and imitation*. New Haven, CT: Yale University Press.

Millon, T. (2011). Classifying personality disorders: An evolution-based alternative to an evidence-based approach. *Journal of Personality Disorders, 25*(3), 279–304.

Mischel, W., & Shoda, Y. (1995). A cognitive-affective system of personality: Reconceptualizing situations, dispositions, dynamics, and invariance in personality structure. *Psychological Review, 102*, 246–268.

MIT. (2012). *MIT Initiative on Technology and Self*. Retrieved April 20, 2012, from http://web.mit.edu/sturkle/techself.

Moghaddam, F. (2005). The staircase to terrorism: A psychological explanation. *American Psychologist, 60*, 161–169.

Monahan, J. (2012). The individual risk assessment of terrorism. *Psychology, Public Policy, and Law, 18*, 167–205.

Moos, R. H. (2012). *An introduction to the nine climate scales*. Retrieved from http://www.mindgarden.com/products/scsug.htm#ms.

Moos, R. H. (1973). Conceptualization of human environments. *American Psychologist, 28*, 652–665.

Morton, J. (2011). *The first detective: The life and revolutionary times of Vidocq: Criminal, spy and private eye*. London: Penguin.

Narasimhan, C. V. (1965). *The Mahabharata*. New York: Columbia University.

National Security Archive. (2012). *Digital National Security Archive*. Retrieved March 30, 2012, from http://www.gwu.edu/~nsarchiv.

Neale, B. M., Kou, Y., Liu, L., Ma'ayan, A., Samocha, K. E., Sabo, A. et al. (2012). Patterns and rates of exonic *de novo* mutations in autism spectrum disorders. *Nature* 485: 242–245.

Newell, A., & Simon, H. (1972). *Human problem solving*. Prentice Hall.

Ng, M., Lawlor, J. B., Chandra, S., Chaya, C., Hewson, L., & Hort, J. (2012). Using quantitative descriptive analysis and temporal dominance of sensations analysis as complementary methods for profiling commercial black currant squashes. *Food Quality and Preference, 25*(2), 121–134.

Nietzsche, F. (1980/1874). *On the advantage and disadvantage of history for life*. (P. Preuss, Trans.). Hackett Publishing Company.

Nietzsche, F. (1966). *Beyond good and evil*. (W. Kaufmann, Trans.). Random House.

Nocera, J. (May 7, 2012). The story isn't over yet. *New York Times*. Retrieved May 9, 2012, from http://www.nytimes.com.

Nordgren, L. F., McDonnell, M.-H. M., & Loewenstein, G. (2011). What constitutes torture?: Psychological impediments to an objective evaluation of enhanced interrogation tactics. *Psychological Science, 22*(5), 689–694.

Office of the National Counterintelligence Executive. (2012). Retrieved April 1, 2012, from http://www.ncix.gov.

Oxford English Dictionary (OED). (2012). Retrieved March 12, 2012, from http://www.oed.com.

Paglia, C. (2012). Lady Gaga and the death of sex. *Sunday Times.* Retrieved June 16, 2012, from http://www.thesundaytimes.co.uk.

Palermo, G. B., & Kocsis, R. N. (2005). *Offender profiling: An introduction to the sociopsychological analysis of violent crime.* Charles C. Thomas.

Pape, R. (2005). *Dying to win: The strategic logic of suicide terrorism.* Chicago: University of Chicago Press.

PBS. (2012). Jonestown: The life and death of Peoples Temple. *American Experience.* Retrieved May 8, 2012, from http://www.pbs.org/wgbh/americanexperience/features/transcript/jonestown-transcript.

Peace, K. A., & Sinclair, S. M. (2012). Cold-blooded lie catchers? An investigation of psychopathy, emotional processing, and deception detection. *Legal and Criminological Psychology, 17*(1), 177–191.

Petherick, W. (Ed.). (2009). *Serial crime.* Elsevier Academic Press.

Pew Research Center. (2012). Retrieved June 15, 2012, from http://pewresearch.org.

Phillips, J., Phillips, M. (Producers), & Scorsese, M. (Director). (1976). *Taxi driver.* [Motion Picture]. Columbia Pictures. Retrieved August 2, 2012, from http://www.youtube.com/watch?v=cUBfzq8ysdg.

Phillips, S. (2012). *Epistemology in classical India: The knowledge sources of the Nyāya School.* New York: Routledge.

Piekkola, B. (2011). Traits across culture: A neo-Allportian perspective. *Journal of Theoretical and Philosophical Psychology, 31,* 2–24.

Pike, A. W. G., Hoffmann, D. L., Garcia-Diez, M., Pettit, P. B., Alcolea, J., De Balbin, R., Gonzalez-Sainz, C., de las Heras, C., Lasheras, J. A., Monetras, R., & Zilhao, J. (2012). U-series dating of Paleolithic art in 11 caves in Spain. *Science, 336,* 1409–1413.

Pinizzotto, A. J., & Finkel, N. J. (1990). Criminal personality profiling: An outcome and process study. *Law and Human Behavior, 14*(3), 215–233.

Pinker, S. (2011). *The better angels of our nature: Why violence has declined.* New York: Viking.

Plato. (2008/380 BCE). *The Republic.* (R. Waterfield, Trans.). New York: Oxford University Press.

Polkinghorne, D. (1984). *Methodology for the human sciences: Systems of inquiry.* State University of New York Press.

Pollack, H. (1977). Epidemiological data on American personnel in the Moscow Embassy. *Bulletin of the New York Academy of Medicine.* Retrieved June 14, 2012, from http://www.scribd.com/doc/13616226/The-Moscow-Embassy-incident.

Pommer, E. (Producer), & Lang, F. (Director). (1927). *Metropolis.* [Motion Picture]. UFA. Retrieved August 2012, from http://www.youtube.com/watch?v=fZ97wzMOOS0.

Post, J. (1990). Terrorist psycho-logic: Terrorist behavior as a product of psychological forces. In W. Reich (Ed.), *Origins of terrorism: Psychologies, ideologies, theologies, states of mind* (25–42). Washington, DC: Woodrow Wilson Center Press.

Povoledo, E. (October 23, 2012). Italy orders jail terms for 7 who didn't warn of deadly earthquake. *The New York Times.* Retrieved on October 27, 2012, from http://www.nytimes.com.

Press, W. H. (2009). Strong profiling is not mathematically optimal for discovering rare malfeasors. *PNAS Proceedings of the National Academy of Sciences of the United States of America, 106*(6), 176–1719.

ProQuest. (2012). Retrieved March 30, 2012, from http://www.proquest.com.

Protess, B., Sorkin, A. R., Scott, M., & Popper, N. (May 12, 2012). Bet by a bank: Its confidence yields to loss. *New York Times*. Retrieved May 12, 2012, from http://www.nytimes.com.

Psychoanalytic Electronic Publishing. (2012). Retrieved March 17, 2012, from http://www.pep-web.org.

Psychosis. (2012). *PubMed Health*. Retrieved May 14, 2012, from http://www.ncbi.nlm.nih.gov/pubmedhealth/PMH0002520.

Pyszczynski, T., Greenberg, J., & Solomon, S. (1999). A dual-process model of defense against conscious and unconscious death-related thoughts: An extension of terror management theory. *Psychological Review, 106*, 835–845.

Pyszczynski, T., Greenberg, J., & Solomon, S. (1997). *Psychological Inquiry, 8*(1), 1–20.

Ragavan, V. (November 10, 2003). A spy who changed history. *U. S. News & World Report*. Retrieved April 1, 2012, from http://www.usnews.com.

Rentfrow, P. J., Gosling, S. D., & Potter, J. (2008). A theory of the emergence, persistence, and expression of geographic variation in psychological characteristics. *Perspectives on Psychological Science, 3*(5), 339–369.

Ricoeur, P. (1981). *Hermeneutics and the human sciences*. (J. Thompson, Trans. & Ed.). Cambridge, UK: Cambridge University Press.

Ricoeur, P. (1970). *Freud and philosophy: An essay on interpretation* New Haven, CT: Yale University Press.

Rogers, J. H., & Widiger, T. (1989). Comparing idiothetic, ipsative, and normative indices of consistency. *Journal of Personality, 57*(4), 847–869.

Rosen, G. M. (1975). Effects of source prestige on subjects' acceptance of the Barnum effect: Psychologist versus astrologer. *Journal of Consulting and Clinical Psychology, 43*, 95.

Rosenhan, D. (1973). On being sane in insane places. *Science 179*, 250–258.

Rosenthal, R., & Rubin, D.B. (1982). A simple general purpose display of magnitude of experimental effect. *Journal of Educational Psychology, 74*, 166–169.

Ross, L. (1977). The intuitive psychologist and his shortcomings: Distortions in the attribution process. In L. Berkowitz (Ed.), *Advances in experimental social psychology* (pp. 173–220). Volume 10. New York: Academic Press,

Rossmo, K. (2000). *Geographic profiling*. Boca Raton, FL: CRC Press.

Rotter, J. (1954). *Social learning theory and clinical psychology*. Upper Saddle River, NJ: Prentice-Hall.

Rowland, I. (2008). *The full facts book of cold reading*. 4th ed. London: Ian Rowland Limited.

Ruddy, A. S. (Producer), & Coppola, F. F. (Director). (1972). *The godfather.* [Motion Picture]. Paramount Pictures. Retrieved August 2, 2012, from http://www.youtube.com/watch?v=DPA9-kpPo_g.

Ruesch, J., & Bateson, G. (1987). *Communication: The social matrix of psychiatry*. New York: W.W. Norton & Company.

Said, E. (1978). *Orientalism: Western conceptions of the Orient*. New York: Random House.

Saks, M. J., & Koehler, J.J. (August 5, 2005). The coming paradigm shift in forensic identification science. *Science, 309*, 892–895.

Salfati, C. G. (2011). Criminal profiling. In B. Rosenfeld & S. D. Penrod (Eds.), *Research methods in forensic psychology* (122–135). New York: John Wiley & Sons, Inc.

Sante, L. (February 5, 2012). After "lunch": William Burroughs's letters from the years of his literary success. *New York Times Book Review*, 21.

Sarris, A. (1996/1968). *The American Cinema: Directors and directions, 1929–1968*. Da Capo Press.

Sartre, J.-P. (1958). *Being and nothingness: An essay on phenomenological ontology*. (H. E. Barnes, Trans.). London: Methuen.

Savage, C. (June 8, 2012a). Holder directs U.S. attorney to track down paths of leaks. *New York Times*. Retrieved June 27, 2012, from http://www.nytimes.com.

Savage, C. (March 23, 2012b). U.S. relaxes limits on use of data in terror analysis. *New York Times*. Retrieved March 23, 2012, from http://www.nytimes.com.

Savage, C. (March 26, 2011). F.B.I. casts wide net under relaxed rules for terror inquiries, data show. *New York Times*. Retrieved March 10, 2012, from http://www.nytimes.com.

Saxon, E., Bozman, R., & Utt, K. (Producers), & Demme, J. (Director). (1991). *The silence of the lambs*. [Motion Picture]. Orion Pictures. Retrieved August 2, 2012, from http://www.youtube.com/watch?v=aEaxwyBjTwU.

Sayare, S. (March 26, 2012). French authorities file charges against brother of gunman in Toulouse killings. *New York Times*. Retrieved March 26, 2012, from http://www.nytimes.com.

Sayare, S., Erlanager, S., & Berry, R. (March 22, 2012). French slaying suspect dead after police raid hideout. *New York Times*. Retrieved March 22, 2012, from http://www.ntyimes.com.

Scheffer, M. (2009). *Critical transitions in nature and society*. Princeton: Princeton University Press.

Schmidt, M. S. (April 16, 2012). President speaks out on guard investigation. *New York Times*. Retrieved April 16, 2012, from http://www.nytimes.com.

Schmitt, E., & Austen, I. (March 31, 2012). Canadian gave intelligence to Russia, U.S. officials say. *New York Times*. Retrieved from April 2, 2012, from http://www.nytimes.com.

Secrecy News. (2012). Retrieved March 30, 2012, from http://www.fas.org/blog/secrecy.

Seifert. J. W. (June 5, 2007). Data mining and homeland security: An overview. *CRS Report for Congress*, RL31798.

Seligman, M. E. P., Steen, T. A., Park, N., & Peterson, C. (2005). Positive psychology progress: Empirical validation of interventions. *American Psychologist, 60*(5), 410–421.

Sengupta, S. (February 26, 2012). WikiLeaks to publish emails. *New York Times*. Retrieved June 24, 2012, from http://www.nytimes.com.

Shamasastry, R. (Trans.). (1909). *Kautilya's Arthasastra*. Mysore: Wesleyan Mission Press.

Shane, S. (June 12, 2012a). Groups to help online activist in authoritarian countries. *New York Times*. Retrieved June 15, 2012, from http://www.nytimes.com.

Shane, S. (March 13, 2012b). U.S. supporters of M.E.K. face scrutiny. *New York Times*. Retrieved March 25, 2012, from http://www.nytimes.com.

Shane, S. (August 11, 2009). 2 U.S. architects of harsh tactics in 9/11's wake. *New York Times*. Retrieved March 13, 2012, from http://www.nytimes.com.

Sharp, G. (2010). *From dictatorship to democracy: A conceptual framework for liberation*. East Boston, MA: Albert Einstein Institution.

Shaw, E. D., Ruby, K. G., & Post, J. M. (1998). The insider threat to information systems. *Security Awareness Bulletin, 2*(98), 27–47.

Sherif, M., Harvey, O. J., White, B. J., Hood, W. R., & Carolyn W. Sherif, C. W. (1954/1961). *Intergroup conflict and cooperation: The robbers cave experiment*. Retrieved June 1, 2012, from http://psychclassics.yorku.ca/Sherif/.

Sherman, C. (2012). Exhibition at the Museum of Modern Art. (February 26–June 11). E. Respini with J. Burton and J. Waters. *Catalog of the exhibition*. New York.

Shipstead, Z., Redick, T. S., & Engle, R. W. (March 12, 2012). Is working memory training effective? *Psychological Bulletin*. Retrieved May 6, 2012, from http://www.apa.org.

Shuy, R. W. (2006). *Linguistics in the courtroom: A practical guide*. New York: Oxford University Press.

Skinner, B. F. (1936). Conditioning and extinction and their relation to drive. *Journal of General Psychology, 14*, 296–317.

SITE Institute. (2012). Retrieved March 30, 2012, from http://www.siteintelgroup.com.

Slessor, G., Phillips, L. H., Bull, R., Venturini, C., Bonny, E. J., & Rokaszewicz, A. (2012). Investigating the "deceiver stereotype": Do older adults associate averted gaze with deception? *Journals of Gerontology: Series B: Psychological Sciences and Social Sciences, 67*(B)(2), 178–183.

Smith, M. B. (1968). A map for the analysis of personality and politics. *Journal of Social Issues, 24*(3), 15–28.

Snook, B., Eastwood, J., Gendreau, P., Goggin, C., & Cullen, R. M. (2007). Taking stock of criminal profiling: A narrative review and meta-analysis. *Criminal Justice and Behavior, 34*(4), 437–453.

Solo, R. H. (Producer). & Ferrara, A. (Director). (1993). [Motion Picture]. *Body snatchers.* Warner Brothers.

Solo, R. H. (Producer). & Kaufman, P. (Director). (1978). [Motion Picture]. *Invasion of the body snatchers.* United Artists.

Sontag, S. (2012). *As consciousness is harnessed to flesh: Journals and notebooks, 1964–1980.* (D. Rieff, Ed.). New York: Farrar, Straus, and Giroux.

Spiegel, S. (Producer), & Jones, D. (Director). (1983). *Betrayal.* [Motion Picture]. Twentieth Century Fox. Retrieved August 2, 2012, from http://www.youtube.com/watch?v=PG78hkm-hvQ.

Spiegel, S. (Producer), & Lean, D. (Director). (1962) *Lawrence of Arabia.* [Motion Picture]. Columbia Pictures. Retrieved August 2, 2012, from http://www.youtube.com/watch?v=z7TnY94x_mI.

Spikings, B., Deeley, M., Cimino, M., & Peverall, J. (Producers), & Cimino, M. (Director). (1978). *The deerhunter.* [Motion Picture]. Universal Pictures. Retrieved August 2, 2012, from http://www.youtube.com/watch?v=lqakCa-MysE [2:50 through 7:24].

Staats, A., Staats, C. K., & Heard, W. G. (1961). Denotative meaning established by classical conditioning. *Journal of Experimental Psychology, 61*, 300–303.

Stanford, P. K. (2006). *Exceeding our grasp: Science, history, and the problem of unconceived alternatives.* New York: Oxford University Press.

START. (2012). *National Consortium for the Study of Terrorism and Responses to Terrorism.* Retrieved March 25, 2012, from http://www.start.umd.edu/start/data_collections.

Stelter, B. (July 20, 2012). DirecTV and Viacom settle dispute over fees. *The New York Times.* Retrieved on October 27, 2012, from http://www.nytimes.com.

Stratfor. (2012). Retrieved March 30, 2012, from http://www.stratfor.com.

Strindberg, A. (1913/1886). *The son of a servant.* (C. Field, Trans.). Strindberg, A: G.P. Putnam's Sons.

Stromberg, H. (Producer), & Cukor, G. (Director). (1939). *The women.* [Motion Picture]. Metro-Goldwyn-Mayer. Retrieved August 2, 2012, from http://www.youtube.com/watch?v=T4XTeh6tjIs.

Suedfeld, P. (December, 2007). Torture, interrogation security and psychology: Absolutistic versus complex thinking. *Analyses of Social Issues and Public Policy (ASAP), 7*(1), 55–63.

Sugarman, J. (2009). Historical ontology and psychological description. *Journal of Theoretical and Philosophical Psychology, 29*, 5–15.

Sullivan, P. (2005). Vivian Psachos: Helped catch spy at CIA. Retrieved April 1, 2012, from http://www.arlingtoncemetery.net/vepsachos.htm.

Tabak, J. A., & Zayas V. (2012). The roles of featural and configural face processing in snap judgments of sexual orientation. *PLoS ONE, 7*(5). Retrieved June 3, 2012, from http://www.plosone.org/article/info%3Adoi%2F10.1371%2Fjournal. pone.0036671.

Tennessen, J. A., Bigham, A. W., O'Connor, T. D., Fu, W., Kenny, E. E., Gravel, S. et al. (2012). Evolution and functional impact of rare coding variation from deep sequencing of human exomes. *Science, 337*, 64–69.

Thalberg, I. (Producer), & Browning, T. (Director). (1927). *The unknown.* [Motion Picture]. Metro-Goldwyn-Mayer.

Thalberg, I. (Producer), & Goulding, E. (Director). (1932). *Grand hotel.* [Motion Picture]. Metro-Goldwyn-Mayer. Retrieved August 2, 2012, from http://www.youtube.com/watch?v=T5-LyF_ja4o&feature=related.

That makes it. (1966). Retrieved April 16, 2012, from http://www.youtube.com/watch?v=0CRj_MIT_EM.

Tiedens, L. Z., Unzueta, M. M., & Young, M. J. (2007). An unconscious desire for hierarchy? The motivated perception of dominance complementarity in task partners. *Journal of Personality and Social Psychology, 93*(3), 402–414.

Transportation Security Administration. (2012). *Behavior detection officers.* Retrieved March 10, 2012, from http://www.tsa.gov/what_we_do/layers/bdo/index.shtm.

Turvey, B. E. (2011). *Criminal profiling: An introduction to behavioral evidence analysis,* 4th ed. New York: Academic Press.

Ult, K. (Producer), & Demme, J. (Director). (1991). *Silence of the lambs.* Orion Pictures. Retrieved March 10, 2012, from http://www.imdb.com/find?q=slience+of+the+lambs&s=all.

U.S. Department of State. (2012). *Country reports on terrorism.* Retrieved March 25, 2012, from http://www.state.gov/j/ct/rls/crt/index.htm.

US-CERT. (2012). Retrieved April 1, 2012, from http://www.us-cert.gov/security-publications.

Van Swol, L. M., Malhotra, D., & Braun, M. T. (2012). Deception and its detection: Effects of monetary incentives and personal relationship history. *Communication Research, 39*(2), 217–238.

Verschuere, B., Ben-Shakhar, G., & Meijer, E. (Eds.). (2011). *Memory detection: Theory and application of the concealed information test.* Cambridge, UK: Cambridge University Press.

Villejoubert, G., Almond, L., & Alison, L. (2011). Interpreting claims in offender profiling. The role of probability phrases, base rates, and perceived dangerousness. In L. Alison & L. Rainbow (Eds.), *Professionalizing offender profiling: Forensic and investigative psychology in practice* (206–227). New York: Routledge.

Vossekuil, B., Fein, R. A., Reddy, M., Borum, R., & Modzeleski, W. (2002). *The final report and findings of the safe school initiative: Implications for the prevention of school attacks in the United States.* United States Secret Service and the United States Department of Education. Retrieved July 22, 2012, from http://www.secretservice.gov/ntac/ssi_final_report.pdf.

Vrij, A. (2008). *Detecting lies and deceit: Pitfalls and opportunities,* 2d ed. New York: Wiley.

Vrij, A., Mann, S., Judi, S., Hope, L., & Leal, S. (2012). Can I take your picture? Undercover interviewing to detect deception. *Psychology, Public Policy, and Law, 18*(2), 231–244.

Wallis, H. B. (Producer), & Curtiz, M. (Director). (1942). *Casablanca.* [Motion Picture]. Warner Brothers. Retrieved August 2, 2012, from http://www.youtube.com/watch?v=7SQuyKlt1Ew.

Wanger, W. (Producer). & Siegel, D. (Director). (1956). [Motion Picture]. *Invasion of the body snatchers.* Allied Artists Pictures Corporation.

Watson, J. B. (1930). *Behaviorism,* rev. ed. Chicago: University of Chicago Press.

Wegner, D. (2002). *Illusion of conscious will.* Cambridge, MA: MIT Press.

Weisbart, D. (Producer), & Ray, N. (Director). (1955). *Rebel without a cause.* [Motion Picture]. Warner Brothers. Retrieved August 2, 2012, from http://www.youtube.com/watch?v=pz2E93p9XeM.

Weiss, T. (2010). *Post-traumatic growth and culturally competent practice.* New York: Wiley.

Welles, O. (Producer & Director). (1941). *Citizen Kane.* [Motion Picture]. Warner Brothers. Retrieved August 2, 2012, from http://www.youtube.com/watch?v=HyJAytr1ebc.

White, H. (1973). *Metahistory: The historical imagination in nineteenth-century Europe.* Baltimore, MD: Johns Hopkins University Press.

White, J. H. (2011). Serial murder: Developmental affect control theory. *American Journal of Forensic Psychology, 29,* 5–21.

Wickens, T. (2011). *Elementary signal detection theory.* New York: Oxford University Press.

Wilder, B. (Producer & Director). (1960). *The apartment.* [Motion Picture] United Artists. Retrieved March 12, 2012, from http://www.youtube.com/watch?v=_kIcHsbeobY.

Wilson, E. O. (2012). *The social conquest of earth.* New York: Liveright.

Wilson, E. O. (1975). *Sociobiology: The new synthesis.* Cambridge, MA: Harvard University Press.

Wittgenstein, L. (2009). *Philosophical investigations,* 4th ed. (G. E. M. Anscombe, P. M. S. Hacker, & J. Schulte, Trans.). Malden, MA: Blackwell.

Wood, J. M., Lilienfeld, S. O., Nezworski, M. T., Garb, H. N., Allen, K. H., & Wildermuth, J. L. (2010). Validity of Rorschach inkblot scores for discriminating psychopaths from nonpsychopaths in forensic populations: A meta-analysis. *Psychological Assessment, 22*(2), 336–349.

Woodhams, J., & Toye, K. (2007). An empirical test of the assumptions of case linkage and offender profiling with serial commercial robberies. *Psychology, Public Policy and Law, 13*(1), 59–85.

World Values Survey. (2012). World Values Survey—Organization. Retrieved June 1, 2012, from http://www.worldvaluessurvey.org/index_organization.

Youth: The Hippies. (July 7, 1967). *Time.* Retrieved June 24, 2012, from http://www.time.com/time/magazine.

Zimbardo, P. G., Haney, C., Banks, W. C., & Jaffe, D. (1974). The psychology of imprisonment: Privation, power and pathology. In Z. Rubin (Ed.), *Doing unto others: Explorations in social behavior* (61–73). Upper Saddle River, NJ: Prentice-Hall.

Zanuck, D. F. (Producer), & Mankiewicz, J. (Director). (1950). *All about Eve.* [Motion Picture]. Twentieth Century Fox. Retrieved August 2, 2012, from http://www.youtube.com/watch?v=Eg-ckMup6SI.

Zuckerman, E. (Spring 2012). A small world after all? *Wilson Quarterly.* Retrieved June 1, 2012, from http://www.wilsonquarterly.com.

Zuckerman, M. (2009). Sensation seeking. In M. R. Leary & R. H. Hoyle (Eds.), *Handbook of individual differences in social behavior.* Washington, DC: American Psychological Association. (pp. 455-465).

Index

For Product Safety Concerns and Information please contact our EU
representative GPSR@taylorandfrancis.com
Taylor & Francis Verlag GmbH, Kaufingerstraße 24, 80331 München, Germany

* 9 7 8 0 3 6 7 8 6 7 7 7 5 *